The Contemporary
Post-Apocalyptic Novel

New Horizons in Contemporary Writing

In the wake of unprecedented technological and social change, contemporary literature has evolved a dazzling array of new forms that traditional modes and terms of literary criticism have struggled to keep up with. *New Horizons in Contemporary Writing* presents cutting-edge research scholarship that provides new insights into this unique period of creative and critical transformation.

Series Editors:
Martin Eve and Bryan Cheyette

Editorial Board: Siân Adiseshiah (University of Lincoln, UK), Sara Blair (University of Michigan, USA), Peter Boxall (University of Sussex, UK), Robert Eaglestone (Royal Holloway, University of London, UK), Rita Felski (University of Virginia, USA), Rachael Gilmour (Queen Mary, University of London, UK), Caroline Levine (University of Wisconsin–Madison, USA), Roger Luckhurst (Birkbeck, University of London, UK), Adam Kelly (York University, UK), Antony Rowland (Manchester Metropolitan University, UK), John Schad (Lancester University, UK), Pamela Thurschwell (University of Sussex, UK), Ted Underwood (University of Illinois at Urbana-Champaign, USA).

Volumes in the series:
David Mitchell's Post-Secular World, Rose Harris-Birtill
Life Lines: Writing Transcultural Adoption, John McLeod
New Media and the Transformation of Postmodern American Literature, Casey Michael Henry
The Politics of Jewishness in Contemporary World Literature, Isabelle Hesse
South African Literature's Russian Soul, Jeanne-Marie Jackson
Transatlantic Fictions of 9/11 and the War on Terror, Susana Araújo
Wanderwords: Language Migration in American Literature, Maria Lauret
Writing After Postcolonialism: Francophone North African Literature in Transition, Jane Hiddleston
Postcolonialism After World Literature, Lorna Burns
Jonathan Lethem and the Galaxy of Writing, Joseph Brooker

Forthcoming volumes:
Contemporary Posthumanism, Grace Halden
Northern Irish Writing After the Troubles, Caroline Magennis
David Foster Wallace's Toxic Sexuality, Edward Jackson

The Contemporary Post-Apocalyptic Novel

Critical Temporalities and the End Times

Diletta De Cristofaro

BLOOMSBURY ACADEMIC
LONDON • NEW YORK • OXFORD • NEW DELHI • SYDNEY

BLOOMSBURY ACADEMIC
Bloomsbury Publishing Plc
50 Bedford Square, London, WC1B 3DP, UK
1385 Broadway, New York, NY 10018, USA
29 Earlsfort Terrace, Dublin 2, Ireland

BLOOMSBURY, BLOOMSBURY ACADEMIC and the Diana logo are
trademarks of Bloomsbury Publishing Plc

First published in Great Britain 2020
This paperback edition published in 2021

Copyright © Diletta De Cristofaro, 2020

Diletta De Cristofaro has asserted her right under the Copyright, Designs and
Patents Act, 1988, to be identified as Author of this work.

For legal purposes the Acknowledgements on p. viii constitute
an extension of this copyright page.

Cover design: Eleanor Rose
Cover illustration © Alice Marwick

All rights reserved. No part of this publication may be reproduced
or transmitted in any form or by any means, electronic or mechanical,
including photocopying, recording, or any information storage or retrieval
system, without prior permission in writing from the publishers.

Bloomsbury Publishing Plc does not have any control over, or responsibility for,
any third-party websites referred to or in this book. All internet addresses given
in this book were correct at the time of going to press. The author and publisher regret
any inconvenience caused if addresses have changed or sites have ceased
to exist, but can accept no responsibility for any such changes.

A catalogue record for this book is available from the British Library.

A catalog record for this book is available from the Library of Congress.

ISBN: HB: 978-1-3500-8577-0
        PB: 978-1-3502-3593-9
        ePDF: 978-1-3500-8578-7
        eBook: 978-1-3500-8579-4

Series: New Horizons in Contemporary Writing

Typeset by Integra Software Services Pvt. Ltd.

To find out more about our authors and books visit www.bloomsbury.com
and sign up for our newsletters.

To Ileana and Luigi

Contents

Acknowledgements	viii
List of Abbreviations	x
Introduction: Apocalypse Now – Critical Temporalities	1
1 Biblical Parodies	27
2 Apocalypse America	57
3 The New Worlds of the Anthropocene	95
4 After the Neoliberal Future	131
Conclusion: The Post-Apocalyptic Archive	163
Bibliography	172
Index	188

Acknowledgements

This book has its origins in my doctoral research at the University of Nottingham. Thus, I owe a deep and lasting debt of gratitude to my PhD supervisors, Judie Newman and Graham Thompson, whose generous and helpful guidance continues today. Many thanks also to my PhD examiners, Ruth Maxey and Andrew Tate, for their supportive engagement with my work, then and now. David Avital, Bryan Cheyette and Martin Eve have given this manuscript a welcoming home at Bloomsbury's New Horizons in Contemporary Writing series; thank you for making this book possible. Martin was particularly encouraging of the project from the very beginning and, together with Bryan, suggested that I expand the scope of the book, for which I am grateful. Dan Cordle offered precious comments on the book proposal, while Rachele Dini, Arin Keeble and Rachel Sykes did the same for chapters of the manuscript – thank you, all.

The Contemporary Post-Apocalyptic Novel was written while working in those precarious roles that form the core of academia today, an experience that has shaped my discussion of the neoliberal no future in Chapter 4. In this predicament, which entailed plenty of teaching but little or no research time, I was fortunate enough to be awarded a Harry Ransom Center Fellowship – more on this later – which provided some much-needed space to think. It is in my sunny office in the Center that I started work on the manuscript. My thanks to those that offered concrete support to alleviate this precarity: Rona Cran, Rachel Sykes and especially Dorothy Butchard, who covered some of my teaching at crucial stages of the project. My solidarity with those whose dreams, ambitions and futures are slowly killed by neoliberal academia.

Many friends – but in particular Riccardo Briganti, Federico Cittadini, Chiara Dellerba, Chiara Destri, Saria Digregorio, Arin Keeble and Rachel Sykes – offered welcome distractions from writing. Special thanks to Rossella Pulvirenti, indefatigable supporter, wise listener and GIF sender extraordinaire. And to Jason Nesbitt, who never tires of asking the right questions, even when they are uncomfortable, and who makes me excited about life.

This book is dedicated to my parents: Ileana Romano and Luigi De Cristofaro. Thank you for encouraging me to think critically, always, and for showing me what true passion and determination mean. Without your love, support and example this book would not exist.

* * *

Initial research on the contemporary post-apocalyptic novel was funded through a VC EU-Excellence PhD Scholarship at the University of Nottingham. The archival research for my analysis of Jim Crace's *The Pesthouse* in Chapter 2 was generously supported by a Harry Ransom Center Research Fellowship in the Humanities (Alfred A. and Blanche W. Knopf Fellowship). My thanks to the sponsors, and to the helpful and friendly staff of the HRC, in particular, Bridget Gayle Ground, Kathryn Millan and Rick Watson, for giving me access to the invaluable resource of the Jim Crace Papers. Many thanks also to Jim Crace for granting me permission to quote from his papers and for his kind and supportive engagement with my work. Excerpts from my analysis of *The Pesthouse* were published as '"False Patterns out of Chaos": Writing beyond the Sense of an Ending in *Being Dead* and *The Pesthouse*' in *Jim Crace: Into the Wilderness*, edited by Katy Shaw and Kate Aughterson (Palgrave Macmillan 2018), 65–79, and as 'The Representational Impasse of Post-Apocalyptic Fiction: *The Pesthouse* by Jim Crace' in *Altre Modernità* 9 (2013): 66–80. An early version of my analysis of David Mitchell's *Cloud Atlas* in Chapter 3 was published as '"Time, No Arrow, No Boomerang, but a Concertina": *Cloud Atlas* and the Anti-Apocalyptic Critical Temporalities of the Contemporary Post-Apocalyptic Novel' in *Critique: Studies in Contemporary Fiction* 59 (2) (2018): 243–257. Excerpts from my analysis of Emily St. John Mandel's *Station Eleven* in Chapter 1 and Chapter 4 were published as 'Critical Temporalities: *Station Eleven* and the Contemporary Post-Apocalyptic Novel' in *Open Library of Humanities* 4 (2) (2018).

List of Abbreviations

AoM	*The Age of Miracles*
AW	*American War*
BoD	*The Book of Dave*
BoJ	*The Book of Joan*
CA	*Cloud Atlas*
FHLG	*Future Home of the Living God*
GiaC	*Girlfriend in a Coma*
IEW	*The Island at the End of the World*
J	*Jamestown*
OAT	*Odds Against Tomorrow*
O&C	*Oryx and Crake*
PO	*Player One*
SE	*Station Eleven*
TF	*The Flood*
TL	*The Leftovers*
TP	*The Pesthouse*
TR	*The Road*
TSG	*The Stone Gods*
YoF	*The Year of the Flood*
ZO	*Zone One*

Introduction: Apocalypse Now – Critical Temporalities

Climate breakdown, floods, pandemics, nuclear holocausts, impact events, zombies, genetic experimentations gone awry, artificial intelligence overpowering humankind, alien invasions, oil exhaustion – these are some of the most typical apocalypses that populate twenty-first-century culture. But the catastrophe that befalls the world of Karen Thompson Walker's *The Age of Miracles* (2012) is different: Earth's rotation slows down and the days grow longer and longer, with disastrous consequences for human lives. The novelty of this apocalypse is metafictionally emphasized within *The Age of Miracles* itself. As the eleven-year-old narrator Julia explains, people 'had worried over the wrong things: the hole in the ozone layer, the melting of the ice caps, West Nile and swine flu and killer bees' (Walker 2012: 29); they had worried, thus, over what the contemporary apocalyptic imagination and the news had prepared them to expect.[1] While Walker's apocalypse may well be one of the most atypical, it is also most revealing, a word I am using hardly by chance, as it is the etymological meaning of the term 'apocalypse' itself. The 'slowing' signals the imbrication of apocalyptic discourse with time and it is to this imbrication that *The Contemporary Post-Apocalyptic Novel: Critical Temporalities and the End Times* turns. This book traces the shift from the temporality of the traditional apocalyptic paradigm to that of the contemporary apocalyptic imagination by taking up as its case study a major trend in twenty-first-century writings: the flourishing of British and North American post-apocalyptic novels beyond the domain of science fiction (SF). I introduce the notion of critical temporality – a construction of time that debunks the entrenched understandings of time and history contributing to the novels' catastrophes – to offer a new critical model for the contemporary obsession with the end.

---

[1] All further references to Walker's *The Age of Miracles* as *AoM*.

That ours is a culture pervaded by apocalyptic anxieties has become almost a truism. 'Everybody wants to own the end of the world' – so begins Don DeLillo's 2016 novel *Zero K* (3), a novel concerned with the 'terminal visions' (Wagar 1982) of aging, death and cryopreservation but not with an apocalypse per se, an element that perfectly encapsulates the prevalence of end-times imagery in twenty-first-century culture, even beyond the genre of (post-)apocalyptic narratives.[2] The commercial success of post-apocalyptic franchises like *Mad Max* (1979–2015), *The Hunger Games* (novels: 2008–2010; movies: 2012–2015) and *Divergent* (novels: 2011–2013; movies: 2014–2016) indicates just how profitable a business 'owning the end of the world' is. And if apocalyptic tropes abound in narratives across media – not only novels, as considered in this book, but also movies and TV series, like *A Quiet Place* (2018), *Birdbox* (2018), *2012* (2009), *The Rain* (2018–) and *The Walking Dead* (2010–); comics and video games, like *Sweet Tooth* (2009–2013), *ATOM RPG* (2018) and *Fallout* (1997–); as well as podcasts, like *Our Fair City* (2011–) – the news, too, liberally use the term 'apocalypse' to refer to catastrophes of various kind, from the looming next giant financial crash (Mason 2015) to the closing of a large number of retail stores in North America (Thompson 2017).[3] In twenty-first-century literary culture, apocalypse and its end-of-the-world scenarios are no longer the sole province of SF but have increasingly attracted non-SF writers, whose novels constitute the case study through which my book theorizes the contemporary apocalyptic imagination.[4] Apocalypse, as summed up by Lee Konstantinou's satiric take on the genre of apocalyptic narratives, is now 'the hottest mediasphere frenzy … and a truly global brand' (2009: 221).

What is at stake, then, in the contemporary apocalyptic imagination and its thriving dystopian visions? What are the implications for agency of a culture obsessed with the thought of its own approaching end? The answer to these questions, I argue through my analysis of the contemporary post-apocalyptic novel, is intertwined with the answer to another question: what is at stake in the shift from narratives that uphold a teleological conception of history to narratives in which this utopian end is removed? And in turn, how is this shift, in which the end is no longer the privileged site of meaning, reflected in narrative

---

[2] On this, see Andrew Tate, who identifies a 'certain kind of *pre*-apocalyptic anxiety' in much twenty-first-century fiction (2017: 7; emphasis in original).

[3] Cf. also, for instance, the 12 September 2001 cover of the *Daily Mail* that featured the word 'apocalypse' to describe 9/11, a 2013 *RollingStone* reportage on a desolate town in 'Apocalypse, New Jersey' (Taibbi), and a 2018 piece on the 'jellyfish apocalypse' published in *The Atlantic* (Giggs).

[4] For the sake of simplicity, 'the contemporary post-apocalyptic novel' and 'contemporary post-apocalyptic fiction' henceforth refer to the subject of this study: twenty-first-century novels written by non-SF authors.

form? For, while in the disparate apocalyptic scenarios that the contemporary produces 'apocalypse' denotes a catastrophe of overwhelming proportions and dystopian consequences that leads to the end of the world as we know it, in the traditional apocalyptic paradigm 'apocalypse' is essentially about a 'revelation' of a sense-making utopian teleology.[5]

In limiting the scope of my corpus of texts to British and North American fictions produced by non-SF writers, I treat SF mainly as a marketing category, noting, as many critics do, that although 'Any bookstore will have a section devoted to SF', 'The term "science fiction" resists easy definition' (Roberts 2006: 1), for 'It encompasses an extraordinarily wide range of different sub-genres, styles, emphases, tropes and motifs' (Baker 2014: 2). In very broad terms, however, SF is typically conceived as a 'future-oriented genre' (Hollinger 2013: 242), which is why narratives of a future in ruins are generally subsumed under the umbrella term of SF. Yet, Veronica Hollinger argues:

> These days science fiction is everywhere, as a discourse of choice through which to describe a present, which perceives itself as both technological and apocalyptic. In fact, this is a present which perceives itself as already existing into the future. The implication here is that, when faced with the immediacy of millennial/apocalyptic events, science fiction's future orientation becomes blocked and science fiction becomes a *present*-tense kind of literature. That is, it begins to function in the popular imagination more and more as a metaphorical discourse though which to describe/construct the present, rather than as an extrapolative exercise through which to imagine the future. (2000: 217–218).

I shall return to this collapse of the future into the present in Chapter 4, where I consider the extended neoliberal present and fictions set in a near future or even an alternate catastrophic present/near past, but for now the significance of Hollinger's argument lies in framing just how pervasive a catastrophic apocalyptic imagination is in the contemporary, even beyond the domain of SF.

The novels analysed in *The Contemporary Post-Apocalyptic Novel*, indeed, are often empathically marketed as non-SF. For instance, when discussing her *Station Eleven* (2014), ironically a winner of the 2015 Arthur C. Clarke Award for SF, Emily St. John Mandel muses: 'I don't think of *Station Eleven* as speculative fiction ... I set out to write a literary novel that takes place partly

---

[5] To maintain the sense of the dual meaning of 'apocalypse', while gesturing to what I argue is the contemporary post-apocalyptic novel's critique of the traditional apocalyptic paradigm, 'apocalypse' and the related terms 'post-apocalyptic' and 'pre-apocalyptic' will henceforth denote catastrophic events and the times before and after these events, while 'apocalyptic' and 'apocalypticism', unless otherwise qualified through terms like 'contemporary', 'dystopian' and 'catastrophic', will refer to the traditional paradigm.

in the future. But, well, it turns out if you set your novel partly in the future, you've written speculative fiction' (McCarry 2014).[6] The dichotomy Mandel traces here between SF and literary fiction – a dichotomy whose implicit hierarchy is reinforced by reviews of the novel, which dismiss *Station Eleven*'s generic elements as accidental while praising its literariness (Cameron 2014) – speaks volumes about how SF is to some extent still struggling with that 'crisis of legitimation' born from its origins in pulp magazines (Baker 2014: 1), despite the definition of literary fiction being just as elusive as that of SF itself.[7] As Michael Chabon sharply puts it in his review of Cormac McCarthy's *The Road* (2006):

> The anti-science fiction prejudice among some readers and writers is so strong that in reviewing a work of science fiction by a mainstream author a charitable critic will often turn to words such as "parable" or "fable" to warm the author's bathwater a little, and it is an established fact that a preponderance of religious imagery or an avowed religious intent can go a long way toward mitigating the science-fictional taint. (2007)

But if the marketing decision, by writers and/or publishers and/or reviewers, to avoid identifying the texts I discuss in what follows as straightforwardly SF betrays the fear of the 'literary ghetto' (Le Guin 2009), I wish to stress that in choosing to focus on post-apocalyptic novels by non-SF authors, I am not trying to reinforce ill-founded hierarchical distinctions between genre and literary fiction but I merely seek to trace a major trend in twenty-first-century literature.[8] If anything, by tracing this trend of non-SF writers engaging with SF imagery, I too, like Hollinger, argue for SF, and specifically imagery of wrecked post-apocalyptic worlds, as a pervasive discourse though which to deconstruct the present.

As I contend by developing my notion of critical temporalities, the catastrophic apocalyptic imagination of the contemporary post-apocalyptic novel serves to

---

[6] SF and speculative fiction are cognate labels. As Brian Baker explains, the term speculative fiction was proposed by Judith Merril in the 1960s to encompass those emerging New Wave texts that were more formally experimental than previous SF and that moved away from the genre's emphasis on science and technology to focus on sociological and psychological aspects (2014: 18). More recently, 'speculative fiction' 'has become particularly used for writers in the literary mainstream who deploy SF tropes or ideas' (Baker 2014: 18), which explains Mandel's choice of the term and further conveys her attempts to distance herself from SF.

[7] Mandel's own conception of literary fiction is incredibly vague: 'I don't know how to define literary fiction. I'm not sure anyone does. It might be one of those "I know it when I see it" things, like pornography' (McCarry 2014). At the time of finalizing this introduction for publication, it is Ian McEwan who is rehashing these tired debates by distancing himself from 'conventional science fiction' upon the publication of his novel *Machines Like Me* (2019) (Adams 2019).

[8] SF writer Ursula K. Le Guin is here taking issue with another Arthur C. Clarke Award winner, Margaret Atwood, who refuses the label of SF for works like *The Handmaid's Tale* (1985) and the *MaddAddam* trilogy (2003–2013).

expose and subvert the apocalyptic conception of history that underlies today's risks and power structures. The post-apocalyptic trend among non-SF writers began well before the twenty-first century – consider, for instance, texts like E. M. Forster's 'The Machine Stops' (1909), Paul Auster's *In the Country of Last Things* (1987), P. D. James's *The Children of Men* (1992), José Saramago's *Blindness* (1995), John Updike's *Toward the End of Time* (1997) and Michel Houellebecq's *Atomized* (1998). Yet it is in the twenty-first century that this trend has reached important dimensions, so much so that Heather J. Hicks speaks of an 'unprecedented outpouring of fully developed post-apocalyptic narratives by major, critically acclaimed anglophone writers' (2016: 5–6). Some of these writers, like McCarthy with *The Road* and Jim Crace with *The Pesthouse* (2007), make only one foray into the realm of post-apocalyptic fiction, others, like Atwood with the *MaddAddam* trilogy and David Mitchell with *Cloud Atlas* (2004) and *The Bone Clocks* (2014), return more frequently to the theme of a wrecked world. More broadly, dystopian apocalyptic novels are, of course, not an exclusively twenty-first-century phenomenon. The second half of the twentieth century has seen the flourishing of a rich SF dystopian apocalyptic tradition fuelled by historical events that have allowed us to 'see in a strange perspective what the end would actually look like: it would look like a Nazi death camp, or an atomic explosion, or an ecological or urban wasteland' (Berger 1999: xiii).[9] The contemporary post-apocalyptic novels considered in this book often build on this previous tradition and its concerns – I am thinking, for instance, of how both Will Self's *The Book of Dave* (2006) and Mitchell's *Cloud Atlas* have Hoban's *Riddley Walker* as an explicit inspiration, or how global warming, which is a major preoccupation for contemporary narratives, was already explored in a text like Ballard's *The Drowned World*. Yet, the contemporary post-apocalyptic novel is distinctive in that it engages with the concerns that give origins to today's dystopian apocalyptic visions in such a way that the roots of these concerns in traditional apocalyptic logic are exposed. For instance, as we shall see in Chapter 3, the fictions of environmental breakdown I discuss bring to the fore a pernicious imbrication of apocalyptic understandings of time and history, colonialism and climate change. Thus, while all dystopian post-apocalyptic narratives implicitly question the utopian revelations of the traditional apocalyptic paradigm, the contemporary post-apocalyptic novel's

---

[9] Examples of this tradition include, for instance, George R. Stewart's *Earth Abides* (1949), John Wyndham's *The Day of the Triffids* (1951), Richard Matheson's *I Am Legend* (1954), John Cristopher's *The Death of Grass* (1956), Nevil Shute's *On the Beach* (1957), Pat Frank's *Alas, Babylon* (1959), Walter M. Miller Jr.'s *A Canticle for Leibowitz* (1959), J. G. Ballard's *The Drowned World* (1962) and Russell Hoban's *Riddley Walker* (1980).

interrogation of the apocalyptic temporality that underwrites today's power structures and risks makes it the ideal body of writings to frame the shift in the apocalyptic imagination from apocalypse as utopian revelation to apocalypse as dystopian catastrophe as a shift that challenges traditional apocalyptic logic. Qua case study, indeed, the contemporary post-apocalyptic novel allows me to develop the notion of critical temporality as an innovative critical model for the apocalyptic imagination of catastrophe at large.

The reason for the popularity of end-of-the-world scenarios in contemporary culture may appear rather obvious. Apocalyptic writings, ever since their religious origins, flourish at times of crisis and the last few decades have been increasingly qualified as times of unprecedented crisis and risk, as encapsulated by the Doomsday Clock.[10] Created in 1947 as a design for the *Bulletin of the Atomic Scientists* aimed at conveying the urgency of nuclear dangers, the hands of the Clock move closer to or away from midnight – the apocalypse – based upon events.[11] The sense of a dystopian, rather than utopian, teleology, embodied by the Clock's timeline – 'it is X minutes to midnight' – reflects the growingly catastrophic apocalyptic imagination of the second half of the twentieth century and of the twenty-first century. If the Clock started at seven minutes to midnight straight after WWII, it reached its furthest setting away from midnight – seventeen minutes – in 1991, at the close of the Cold War. Yet, ever since then, the Clock has been moving steadily closer to the apocalypse, which is in many ways hardly surprising, as turns of the millennia, and even of the centuries, have been periods rife with apocalyptic terrors and expectations (Focillon 1969; Schwartz 1990). 'Expectations' is however the key word here, for as we shall see further shortly, in the traditional apocalyptic paradigm fear of the end times is accompanied by the hope for a utopian renewal, which is precisely what is missing from the cultural atmosphere of crisis and risk embodied by the Clock and what my study accounts for through the notion of critical temporality. Since 2018, the Clock has been set at two minutes from midnight, the closest it has ever been to the apocalypse.

Theoretical accounts of this growing sense of crisis and risk speak of late twentieth and twenty-first-century society as a 'risk society' in the sense that it is increasingly occupied with debating, preventing and managing risks that

---

[10] To take the example of the Book of Revelation, 'th[is] archetypal apocalypse in literary history ... [was w]ritten some time during the reign of Roman Emperor Domitian (81–96 C.E.), who had persecuted Christians and confined the author of the book to a labor camp on the island of Patmos, so that the Apocalypse of John bears the marks of its provenance in crisis and suffering' (Hamerton-Kelly 2007: 12).

[11] For a history of the Doomsday Clock, including its timeline since inception, see its informative website: https://thebulletin.org/doomsday-clock/.

it itself has produced' (Beck 2006: 332), from reactor meltdowns and nuclear proliferation, to pandemics and unchecked genetic experimentations, economic crisis and terrorism. Importantly, theorists of the risk society frame these escalating risks as a by-product of modernity itself (Beck 1992; Giddens 1990), which compounds my own theorization of the contemporary post-apocalyptic novel as a critique of the apocalyptic roots of modernity's dangerous legacies in today's world. Risks associated with anthropogenic climate breakdown have become particularly pressing and more widely acknowledged in recent years. The term 'Anthropocene', to which we shall return in Chapter 3, was itself popularized in 2000 by Paul J. Crutzen and Eugene F. Stoermer to denote the current geological epoch, in which human activities are having such an impact on Earth's ecology that they are leaving an enduring imprint on the geological strata. Reflecting the twenty-first century's increasing sense of environmental risks, since 2007 the Doomsday Clock has taken into account, alongside dangers associated with nuclear weapons, those posed by climate change. It seems only logical, then, that a society dominated by the Clock's countdown would produce more and more fictional scenarios in which its risks play out with catastrophic consequences. Environmental dangers, for instance, are consistently reflected in contemporary post-apocalyptic fictions: from the 'deadlands' of Mitchell's *Cloud Atlas* and the end of the Holocene caused by climate change in his later novel *The Bone Clocks*, to the various 'Great Dead Zones' of the world depicted in Atwood's *MaddAddam* trilogy and the geographies of Self's *The Book of Dave* and Omar El Akkad's *American War* (2017a), significantly altered by rising sea water levels.

Yet the problem with reading the popularity of post-apocalyptic scenarios in twenty-first-century culture exclusively through the conjuncture in which they are produced is that this critical strategy tends to sidestep the history of apocalyptic discourse.[12] This history is a history of temporality, and while my book does engage with twenty-first-century events and contexts that inform the selected novels – 9/11 (Chapter 2), the rising awareness of the Anthropocene and climate change (Chapter 3), and neoliberalism and the financial crisis of 2007/2008 (Chapter 4) – it does so through the lens of temporality. It is the pervasive influence of the apocalyptic construction of time on Western modernity, the present conjuncture and its risks that my study of the contemporary post-apocalyptic novel uncovers. In this sense, if twenty-first-century novels and

[12] For readings of the (post-)apocalyptic imagination informed by the framework of risk theory, see, for instance, Kearney (2012), Mizruchi (2010), Curtis (2010); within the context of anthropogenic climate change, Skrimshire (2010), Trexler (2015); in relation to historical traumas and trauma theory, Berger (1999), Mousoutzanis (2014).

contexts constitute the main subject of my study, *The Contemporary Post-Apocalyptic Novel* traces a broad transhistorical trajectory in that it explores how apocalyptic beliefs, in particular apocalyptic temporality, have relentlessly shaped the modern world and theorizes the texts in question as a critique of these beliefs.

The revelations of the traditional apocalyptic paradigm are intertwined with time and history. Traditional apocalyptic narratives, epitomized by the Book of Revelation in the New Testament, are written during periods of crisis for they are aimed at making sense of troubled times through the projection of utopia in the future. These writings are 'fictions of historical order' (Zamora 1989: 4) in that they seek to order time and make it intelligible, by revealing that the whole course of human history is tending towards a final resolution, a telos, which will make sense of everything that happened before. Apocalypticism, as Frank Kermode puts it, relies upon the end to 'confer organization and form on the temporal structure' ([1966] 2000: 45). The end of traditional apocalyptic history is, however, of a peculiar kind, for it paves the way for a radical utopian renewal. As Peter Freese remarks, there is a 'constitutive doubleness' to the traditional understanding of apocalypse, since this is 'both an end and a beginning' (1997: 27). The biblical Revelation does disclose the future catastrophic end of the material world but, more fundamentally, after announcing the Last Judgment which will separate the damned from the elect, the Book reveals the advent of a transcendent utopian world for the righteous: the New Jerusalem. It is because the telos of traditional apocalyptic history consists in the goal of a utopian new beginning, and not merely in a cataclysmic end, that apocalyptic discourse is able to make sense of a time of crisis as part of a larger design and, hence, to comfort people.

The British and North American novels considered in this book, instead, self-reflexively emphasize that they are part of a vast array of dystopian, rather than utopian, end-of-the-world narratives. To the suicidal mother of McCarthy's *The Road*, the survivors are 'the walking dead in a horror film' ([2006] 2007: 55); in Mitchell's *Cloud Atlas*, the allusion to the 1973 film *Soylent Green* (2004: 179) indicates how Sonmi-451's narrative appropriates elements of this dystopian SF movie; in Mandel's *Station Eleven*, the post-pandemic world reminds Jeevan of the descent into barbarism of disaster movies ([2014] 2015: 256), a cultural form that is also evoked in Colson Whitehead's *Zone One* ([2011] 2012: 136).[13] All these references foreground how the understanding of apocalypse is now informed by

---

[13] All further references to McCarthy's *The Road* as *TR*; to Mandel's *Station Eleven* as *SE*; to Whitehead's *Zone One* as *ZO*; to Mitchell's *Cloud Atlas* (UK edition) as *CA* – I specify UK edition following Martin Paul Eve's article (2016), which has pointed out textual variants between the UK and the US editions, especially in the section 'An Orison of Sonmi-451'.

the SF, horror and disaster narratives that have been increasingly popular since the twentieth century, rather than by the utopian revelations of the Bible, so much so that the dystopian imagery of the former appears to be the only way the characters can actually grasp and convey their post-apocalyptic experiences. In other words, these references signal that the contemporary apocalyptic paradigm profoundly differs from the traditional one, for the former conceives the end as a catastrophe leaving little or no hope for the utopian renewal which is so central to the latter. As the father of the protagonist of *Zone One* pithily puts it, in the twenty-first-century imagination 'apocalypse' means that 'in the future, things will be even worse than they are now' (ZO 120). Thus, in some of the novels discussed in this book, such as *The Road* or *Zone One* itself, human survival appears to be highly unlikely in the long run; in others, such as Crace's *The Pesthouse* and Mandel's *Station Eleven*, the tone is more optimistic, but the apocalypse has made civilization revert to a more primitive state – a critical temporality I term temporal inversion – and the result is hardly a pastoral utopia.

The Contemporary Post-Apocalyptic Novel is the first study to fully theorize the implications of this shift in the apocalyptic imagination from apocalypse as utopian revelation to apocalypse as dystopian catastrophe. While many scholars of apocalyptic narratives have noticed the shift (see, for instance, Tate (2017), Hicks (2016), Heffernan (2008), Rosen (2008), Berger (1999), Wojcik (1997), Zamora (1989)), a thoroughgoing theorization of it beyond the typical observation that 'a story which was once grounded in hope about the future has become instead a reflection of fears and disillusionment about the present' (Rosen 2008: xiv) is still lacking. Teresa Heffernan comes closest in an important study that deploys the 'term post-apocalypse to suggest that we live in a time after the apocalypse, after the faith in a radically new world, of revelation, of unveiling' (2008: 6). Yet Heffernan's study does not deal with post-apocalyptic fiction and the post-apocalyptic imagination in the strict sense but, more broadly, with twentieth-century novels that exhibit a form of disenchantment with historical or narrative teleology, so that the term 'post-apocalyptic' risks losing its specificity and heuristic significance. Instead, taking as its case study the expanding body of twenty-first-century novels of the end times by British and North American authors, my book turns to the core of apocalyptic logic – its conception of time – to argue, through the notion of critical temporality, that contemporary apocalyptic discourse is a subversion of the traditional apocalyptic paradigm.

The shift in meaning of the term 'apocalypse' from 'revelation' to 'catastrophe' signifies the core structure of what I identify as the critical temporalities of the contemporary post-apocalyptic novel: the reversal of the utopian teleology of traditional apocalyptic history into the dystopian teleology of the contemporary imagination in order to uncover the legacies of apocalyptic logic on the present and their catastrophic consequences. I trace an intellectual history of apocalyptic discourse to show how the apocalyptic conception of history as a homogeneous and teleological continuum underlies the ideological constructions of Western modernity, from progress and capitalism to American exceptionalism and colonialism, which have significant import in the risks of the contemporary moment. And, through readings of the contemporary post-apocalyptic novel that focus on fictions by Will Self, Sam Taylor, Cormac McCarthy, Jim Crace, David Mitchell, Jeanette Winterson, Emily St. John Mandel, Douglas Coupland and Lidia Yuknavitch, I theorize the notion of critical temporalities, constructions of time that debunk entrenched apocalyptic temporal regimes. Drawing on postmodern theories of historiography, I argue that the critical temporalities of the contemporary post-apocalyptic novel expose the hegemonic apocalyptic temporality at the core of Western modernity as a narrative enmeshed with power structures, thus framing the contemporary apocalyptic imagination as a critique of the ideological foundations of Western modernity.[14] In foregrounding the nexus between the apocalyptic construction of history and oppressive power structures, the contemporary post-apocalyptic novel seeks to foster the readers' agency to shape a future beyond this nexus. Therefore, these fictions also deconstruct the apocalyptic model of narrative, which, with its emphasis on closure, is inherently deterministic and which, when transposed to history, makes for an equally deterministic understanding of time. Through formal features that critique the epistemic primacy of the end, that is, its sense-making function, the contemporary post-apocalyptic novel makes space for unwritten, non-teleological futures, inviting us to conceive of history beyond the apocalyptic 'sense of an ending' (Kermode [1966] 2000).

It may be tempting to qualify the shift from utopian revelation to dystopian catastrophe merely as a shift from a religious to a secular understanding of apocalypse. After all, as my opening catalogue of apocalypses indicates, the catastrophes of recent post-apocalyptic narratives are generally man-made, rather than the result of god's will.[15] John R. May, for instance, distinguishes

---

[14] Therefore, my study discusses these fictions' engagement with the episteme of modernity like Hick's recent study of the post-apocalyptic novel in the twenty-first century (2016). Unlike Hicks, however, I focus specifically on the temporal aspects of the modern episteme, uncovering how it is informed by apocalyptic logic, and arguing that the contemporary post-apocalyptic novel works to deconstruct, rather than to 'salvage' (Hicks 2016), modernity.

[15] Exceptions are texts like Tim LaHaye and Jerry B. Jenkins's *Left Behind* series (1995–2007), which are a fictional take on premillennialist dispensational theology. I will return to this more orthodox kind of contemporary apocalyptic literature in Chapter 1, alongside works that parodically deconstruct the biblical urtext.

between 'the Judaeo-Christian apocalypses[, which] result in something new [and] are basically optimistic in that they yield new life, a new creation', and the literature of the 'apocalypse of despair', which belongs to a secular imagination (1972: 39). Hicks similarly points out that 'dystopian content is symptomatic of the distinction between the Christian apocalyptic tradition, which culminates in the utopian New Jerusalem, and the secular post-apocalyptic genre, which without fail, imagines the destruction of modernity as leading to a state of at least provisional suffering and oppression' (2016: 7). Warren W. Wagar also argues for a 'secularization of eschatology' taking place between 'the middle of the seventeenth century and the middle of the nineteenth', when 'The ideas of "progress" and "utopia" [emerge] to supplant the sacred myths of heaven and the millennium', and 'Visions of the end', 'as expressions of cultural despair and fatigue', slowly begin to appear (1982: 60–61). Yet, when it comes to traditional apocalyptic logic, the boundary between the religious and the secular is blurred and, hence, the shift from the former to the latter cannot account for the contemporary sense of apocalypse.

Scholars agree that apocalyptic logic, in its attempt to make sense of time, is the *'fons et origo* of the concept of history and historiography' (Hamerton-Kelly 2007: 14–15).[16] The apocalyptic understanding of time marks a decisive break from the ancient one. In ancient societies, 'History as an extended chronological sequence of events did not exist', since all events were subsumed into the timeless order of myth through archetypes that kept repeating themselves (Hall 2009: 16–17). History, as a homogeneous, neutral and teleological temporal continuum, is instead the enduring legacy of apocalypticism, as expressed in particular by the Book of Revelation. While secularization theories assume that in modernity a rationalistic historicism replaces the supernatural fictions of salvation history, the apocalyptic myth continues to underlie the Western notion of history and the defining ideological constructions of the modern era.

With their progressive stages, the totalizing systems of modern historical thought – from Comte's, to Hegel's and Marx's, to name just a few examples – are imbued with a secular version of apocalyptic teleology (Löwith 1949), as

---

[16] Cf., for instance, 'Apocalypse and History [are] connected at birth' (Hall 2009: 17); '[the apocalyptic] vision of history gives rise to "history" as a theoretical production' (Keller 1996: 89); 'the prototype of the Western concept that history has an intelligible and end-determined order, whether fideistic or naturalistic, is the scheme of the course of earthly affairs from genesis to apocalypse which is underwritten by a sacred text' (Abrams 1984: 344); the Western 'historical consciousness is, indeed, determined by an eschatological motivation, from Isaiah to Marx, from Augustine to Hegel, and from Joachim to Schelling. The significance of this vision of an ultimate end, as both *finis* and *telos*, is that it provides a scheme of progressive order and meaning' (Löwith 1949: 18).

are the great revolutions of modernity, from the American, to the French, to the Russian. For the faith in the advent of a new and better world after the violent cleansing of the revolution is intrinsically apocalyptic (Abrams 1984; Gray 2007). Secular modern metanarratives in general continue to 'rely on that positive understanding of the end and apocalypse as culmination and resolution' (Heffernan 2008: 5). Indeed, apocalyptic logic, in its totalizing explanation of time through utopian teleology, can be considered a model for all metanarratives, with progress, the modern metanarrative *par excellence*, 'represent[ing] the main example of the secularization of apocalypse' and of its utopian telos (Keller [1996] 2005: 6).[17] Similarly, modernity's 'rationalizing of time and space – by which national, international, and, in time, a global market emerged' can be traced back, Catherine Keller argues, to the 'universal chronology of the apocalyptic vision' ([1996] 2005: 18, 20). As John Gray powerfully puts it, 'If a simple definition of western civilization could be formulated it would have to be framed in terms of the central role of millenarian thinking' (2007: 6), the expectation of a perfect new world to come on earth.

But while Revelation, because of this projection of utopia in the future, is often interpreted as resistance literature against the oppressions perpetrated by the Roman Empire, and has indeed inspired the Western revolutionary tradition, the text, as Keller underlines in her critique of apocalyptic logic, 'was canonized by the very sort of imperial Roman establishment for whose overthrow [John] provided the symbolic *locus classicus*' ([1996] 2005: 18). This canonization is the beginning of Revelation's 'strange doubleness' (Keller [1996] 2005: 18), namely, of the modern use of apocalyptic logic to defuse resistance and enforce exploitations, rather than to oppose them. The moral dualism of good versus evil underlying apocalyptic teleology too easily translates into oppressive power dynamics: the elect versus the rest, us versus the other, insiders versus outsiders. D. H. Lawrence gestures towards this aspect of apocalyptic logic when commenting upon the modern incarnations of the Antichrist as simply 'the fellow who is different from me' ([1980] 2002: 89). A teleological understanding of history is necessarily predicated upon the erasure of those who are different and do not fit its grand telic scheme. Colonialism is itself profoundly apocalyptic, an element which I shall further explore in Chapter 3. The colonial trope of the New World is the 'objectification of the apocalyptic millennial future' (Keller [1996] 2005: 141), an objectification which fuels the violent and

---

[17] On the relationship between apocalyptic logic and progress cf. also Gray: 'In that they view history as a movement, not necessarily inevitable but in the direction of a universal goal, theories of progress also rely on a teleological [and hence apocalyptic] view' (2007: 6–7).

genocidal European expansion in the modern era and is particularly important in the birth of the American nation, as we shall see in Chapter 2. The apocalyptic metanarrative, Lee Quinby sums up, is a 'quintessential technology of power/knowledge', since its 'tenet of preordained history disavows questionings of received truth, discredits skepticism, and disarms challengers of the status quo' (1994: xiii). In religious terms, the very idea of a utopian teleology facilitated by divine, rather than human, agency is hardly conducive to resistance and politics of liberation. And even with a more secular application of apocalyptic logic, because of the emphasis on a predetermined end, the apocalyptic model of history compromises the possibility of choices and ethics and risks legitimizing power's oppressions as part of a necessary pattern tending towards betterment.

The modern and apocalyptic conception of history may appear increasingly untenable in the present conjuncture of a world 'without predictability or teleology, but with proliferating instability' (Buell 2013: 15). Yet it is precisely because of this instability that apocalyptic logic, with its promise of a sense-making order, continues to perform its seduction. In a study that focusses on the profound connection between apocalyptic logic and the United States, Matthew Avery Sutton cites a 2010 Pew Poll that evidences that '41 percent of all Americans (well over one hundred million people) and 58 percent of white evangelicals believed that Jesus is "definitely" or "probably" going to return by 2050', concluding that, as we shall see in Chapter 1, 'We now live in a world shaped by evangelicals' apocalyptic hopes, dreams, and nightmare' (2014: 372). More broadly, Gray foregrounds the 'unmistakably apocalyptic tone' (2007: 33) of neoliberalism and post-9/11 politics.

As we shall further discuss in Chapter 4, neoliberalism is characterized by the teleological belief that 'the world is converging on a single type of government and economic system – universal democracy, or a global free market' (Gray 2007: 1).[18] There is no alternative, to put it with Margaret Thatcher's infamous words, or, we are at the end of history, as argued by Francis Fukuyama (1992). September 11, as we shall see in Chapter 2, is cast in the reassuring apocalyptic terms of moral dualism – the good elect versus the evil other – and as an attack against the neoliberal teleological convergence, 'trigger[ing] an attempt to accelerate this process throughout the Middle East' through War (Gray 2007: 74). Neoliberalism's underlying apocalypticism precipitates the violence of the War on Terror, for those who posit a telos to history also conceive of themselves

---

[18] Throughout the book, I use the terms neoliberalism, global capitalism and late capitalism interchangeably as they are all characterized by this apocalyptically informed teleological belief.

as the rightful agents of this telos, and justifies profound global inequality – itself a legacy of colonial apocalypticism – as a necessary phase in a historical pattern tending towards betterment. The same logic conceals that the 'fantasy of plenitude, regeneration, and persistence lying behind [the late capitalist] structures of accumulation' (E. C. Williams 2011: 2) is complicit in, and deeply threatened by, anthropogenic climate breakdown. Indeed, despite being called into question by environmental threats, 'the perspective of growth, identified with progress [itself an apocalyptic metanarrative, as discussed] … continues to impose itself as the only conceivable horizon' (Stengers 2015: 20). The deconstruction of traditional apocalyptic logic is therefore an urgent task which, I argue in this study, is taken up by the contemporary post-apocalyptic novel. These fictions' critical temporalities target the nexus between apocalypticism and American ideologies, (neo-)colonialism, the Anthropocene, and neoliberalism, exposing the modern apocalyptic conception of history as a pervasive and dangerous narrative. In doing so, the contemporary post-apocalyptic novel reflects the postmodern distrust of totalizing explanations.

The equation of the post-apocalyptic with the postmodern is often acknowledged. Jessica Hurley, for instance, points out that the opening of Fredric Jameson's *Postmodernism, or, the Cultural Logic of Late Capitalism*, with its reference to an 'inverted millenarianism in which premonitions of the future, catastrophic or redemptive, have been replaced by senses of the end of this or that' (Jameson 1991: 1), frames how postmodernism is characterized by the 'sense that an ending has already occurred, and that we have somehow outlived it' (Hurley 2013: 61). Similarly, noticing how theories by 'Lyotard, Baudrillard, and Jameson all take as their starting point some cataclysmic and irrevocable shattering or flattening or decentering', James Berger writes that the 'rhetorical gambit of much postmodern theory is that the "end," or some end, has, in fact, already taken place, perhaps without our knowledge' and that, therefore, 'postmodernity is a condition somehow "after the end"' (1999: 31, 35, 36). This view that the 'conclusive catastrophe has already occurred' in postmodernity and that the 'ceaseless activity of our time – the news with its procession of almost indistinguishable disasters – is only a complex form of stasis' (Berger 1999: xiii) leads some scholars to critique the boom of (post-)apocalyptic narratives as 'confirmation of the utter exhaustion of our ability to imagine the future as difference, an inability that signals the full subsumption of culture under neoliberal logics' (Nilges 2015: 369). By the same token, Frederick Buell maintains that the popularity of post-apocalyptic narratives is part of disaster capitalism and that these scenarios are 'uncommitted to social movement and change' (2013: 21). As I argue in Chapter 4, though, the sense of a static present devoid of genuine futurity represents the underside of neoliberal proclamations about a utopian end of history, proclamations whose roots in apocalyptic logic and its foreclosed possibilities are deconstructed by the critical temporalities of the contemporary post-apocalyptic novel.

In positing a connection between the contemporary post-apocalyptic novel and the postmodern, indeed, I am not suggesting that these fictions reflect the postmodern condition as being 'after the end' and characterized by depleted agency. As the following analyses demonstrate, the contemporary post-apocalyptic novel repeatedly insists on the power of agency, even in the midst of precarious situations that leave little room for manoeuvre, and on the power of narrative itself to inspire action, from Adam in Mitchell's *Cloud Atlas*, who urges for action although it is 'one drop in a limitless ocean' (*CA* 529), to Mandel's Travelling Symphony, who performs Shakespeare's plays in a depopulated post-pandemic world because 'survival is insufficient' (*SE* 58), to Lidia Yuknavitch's *The Book of Joan* (2017), which reminds us that 'Stories save lives. They give shape to action' (Yuknavitch [2017] 2018: 163).[19] Rather, my study outlines the connection between the contemporary post-apocalyptic novel's critical temporalities and the critique of apocalyptic logic articulated by postmodern theories, in particular by the narrative turn in historiography, with its emphasis on the narrative nature of history and the openness to multiple histories as antidote to power's totalizing visions.

Heffernan maintains that 'if one line of thinking from modernism to postmodernism is that the world has ended, another line suggests a discontentment and impatience with the very investment in the idea of the end' (2008: 11). Hollinger equally underlines how postmodern theory 'argued strongly against the perceived seductions of apocalyptic logic and rhetoric' (2002: 161). Her examples include 'Jean-François Lyotard's by-now classic definition of postmodernism as "incredulity toward metanarratives," suggesting as it does an intellectual refusal of the logic of apocalypse, which is nothing if not the logic of a totalizing master narrative' as well as 'Jacques Derrida's deconstructive (anti)philosophy, which challenges deep-seated anxieties about, and desires for, originary moments and revelatory closures in human history' (2002: 161). Indeed, Derrida's 'Of an Apocalyptic Tone Newly Adopted in Philosophy', in the face of the various ends of postmodern theory – from the 'end of history' to the 'death of philosophy' from the 'end of the subject [and] of man' to the 'end of

---

[19] All further references to Yuknavitch's *The Book of Joan* as *BoJ*.

the West' (1992: 48) – and in typical deconstructive fashion that recognizes the pervasiveness of, and our implication in, what needs to be deconstructed, calls for an 'apocalypse without apocalypse, an apocalypse without vision, without truth, without revelation', a 'closure without end, an end without closure' (1992: 66–67). Michel Foucault's genealogy is equally critical of apocalyptic logic, in particular of its emphasis on linear development and a single line of causality, calling instead for the necessity to 'record the singularity of events outside of any monotonous finality' (1977: 139) and draw attention to unrealized possibilities. Thus, if 'postmodernity is a condition somehow "after the end"' (Berger 1999: 36), it is because postmodern theory debunks the end as the privileged site of meaning, as the site of totalizing explanations. The critical temporalities of the contemporary post-apocalyptic novel, I argue, respond to the postmodern call for the subversion of history with a capital H, that is, history as constructed in Western modernity by apocalyptic logic.

Lyotard's definition of the postmodern condition as 'incredulity towards metanarratives' (1984: xxiv) points to the basic tenet of the narrative turn: the critique of a transparent correspondence between language and reality, namely, the critique of the notion that language can capture the truth about the world. Rather, language, as organized in narratives, constructs reality, for the former is our only way of apprehending the latter, an understanding that is particularly central to my argument in Chapter 1 and the Conclusion. If modernity is about the belief in the epistemic neutrality and objectivity of our representations, postmodernity is ultimately about foregrounding the constructedness of our representations and of neutrality itself (Ermarth 1992). As Keith Jenkins underlines, when applied to history the narrative turn entails that 'the world/the past comes to us always already as stories and that we cannot get out of these stories (narratives) to check if they correspond to the real world/past, because these "always already" narratives constitute "reality"' ([1991] 2003: 11). There is no history, but only histories, which is to say that both narrativity, with its role in our conceptualization of time, and the power dynamics informing these histories come to the fore (White 1987). As Jenkins maintains, 'for the past to link up with and support the ongoing present and its expectant future, then one could not and cannot – just cannot – allow the past to be read "any way you like" by just anybody' (2003: 17–18). Power demands the past to be closed to interpretations alternative to its own, it sustains itself by positing a historical 'truth' which legitimizes the present status quo as part of a necessary and univocal historical development. But, as Jenkins's reference to the 'expectant future' suggests, power's view of the future also informs its understandings of the past, an element that takes us back to apocalyptic logic. To return to DeLillo's words, from which we started – 'Everybody wants to own the end of the world' (2016: 3) – 'owning' the end, determining what shapes it takes, is a matter of power, for those who posit a telos to history use it to legitimize their often oppressive deeds.

Gesturing to the connection between the narrative turn and apocalypticism, theorists like Foucault (1977), Jean Baudrillard (1994a) and Michael André Bernstein (1994) foreground how the fiction of a future historical closure and the retrospective judgment this closure allows always underlie modern historicism. To Foucault, the perspective of 'history in the traditional sense ... on all that precedes it implies the end of time, a completed development. The historian's history finds its support outside of time and pretends to base its judgments on an apocalyptic objectivity' (1977: 152). Baudrillard speaks instead of the 'illusion of the end', a 'simulation' which is nevertheless essential to the time of history, 'that linear time which is at once the time of an ending and of the unlimited suspending of the end' (1994a: 7). The operative words are 'pretends' and 'illusion', since a perspective from after the end of time is manifestly impossible in human terms: it is an aporia, as I discuss in Chapters 1 and 2. The end of time and the understanding of history it sustains are narrative constructs. But to expose them as such is not enough since, as Bernstein remarks, this apocalyptic conception of history 'is being determined not so much by principles of historiography but by a prior and naive grasp of what constitutes a story *tout court*' (1994: 28). Thus, if postmodern theories underline the importance of narrativity in our conceptualization of time, the issue becomes which understanding of narrative is implied by these arguments.

As Paul Ricoeur argues, 'Time becomes human time to the extent that it is organized after the manner of a narrative' (1984: 3), which in turn signals the importance of narratives, like the contemporary post-apocalyptic novel, in understanding the temporal structures of our present. To some theorists, this sense-making function of narrativity depends on the epistemic primacy of the end, an element which is inherently apocalyptic. Peter Brooks talks of the 'anticipation of retrospection' as the foundation of plots, since 'we are able to read present moments – in literature and, by extension, in life – as endowed with narrative meaning only because we read them in anticipation of the structuring power of those endings that will retrospectively give them the order and significance of plot' (1984: 94). This structuring power is what Kermode ([1966] 2000) terms the sense of an ending in a study which analyses the correspondence between fictional plots and apocalyptic history. To Kermode, apocalypse, as a narrative about the end of history, is a model for fictions in general, in that it satisfies the human need for temporal concordance, a need which originates from the fact that man lives in the midst of time. By inventing the apocalyptic end, human beings make sense of time and humanize it: from *chronos*, mere successiveness, time becomes *kairos*, 'a significant season … poised between beginning and end' (Kermode [1966] 2000: 46). The same concordance is, to Kermode, typical of narratives, where the sense of an ending affords meaning and cohesion to the plot, as readers expect the conclusion to reveal the consonance between beginning, middle and end, and tie up all loose strands. Yet Brooks's and Kermode's identification of readers' expectations only tell us that the sense of an ending is a predominant narrative convention. Readers' expectations are not sufficient grounds to contend that narrativity is inherently defined by the epistemic primacy of the end and, therefore, that time can only be made sense of teleologically.[20] It is this understanding of narrative that the critical temporalities of the contemporary post-apocalyptic novel complicate. For while the sense-making function of the end may be innocuous in fiction, to construct histories as teleological is to follow apocalyptic logic and, hence, to be complicit with the ideologies and power dynamics embedded in the very notion of end.

Insofar as it depends on the sense of an ending, narrative structure 'reduces the plurality of wills and purposes to a single pattern; it makes everything fit … and it closes down time by conferring a spurious sense of inevitability on the sequence actually realized. The very possibility of possibility is ultimately eliminated' (Morson 1994: 38–39). Thus, teleological historical analyses subsume events under a single line of development whose inevitability 'removes any significance from imagining alternative paths' (Bernstein 1994: 28). Thomas Mullen's *The Revisionists* (2011) critically engages with these aspects of apocalyptic temporality. In the novel, people from a post-apocalyptic, and allegedly perfect, future travel back to various moments of history. These missions are officially aimed at preserving the 'Perfect Present' from the 'hags' who want to change it by altering the course of history. As it turns out, however, the post-apocalyptic future is a dystopian totalitarian society which uses the technology of time travel to revision history to ensure that the Perfect Present is the necessary result of historical processes, apocalypse included, creating the 'spurious sense of inevitability' Gary Saul Morson discusses above. Zed, the protagonist, learns that

---

[20] For an argument against narratives being essentially defined by the sense of an ending, see, for instance, D. A. Miller: 'the narratable inherently lacks finality. It may be suspended by a moral or ideological expediency, but it can never be properly brought to term. The tendency of a narrative would therefore be to keep going, and narrative closure would be, in Mallarmé's phrase, a "faire semblant"' (1981: x).

> We aren't preserving the integrity of history, we're *rewriting* history, remaking the world in the regime's image. There was no Great Conflagration, not originally. But they've sent so many of us back, and they've tinkered, they've eliminated the people who opposed them and eliminated the Events that went against their worldview. (Mullen [2011] 2012: 259; emphasis in original)

Apocalyptic history, *The Revisionists* points out, is a deterministic and totalitarian construction of time, which erases elements that do not conform to its grand teleology as well as contingency and the openness of the future, impairing agency and freedom.

Indeed, as the following analyses demonstrate by considering the nexus between apocalypticism and patriarchal power (Chapter 1), American ideologies (Chapter 2), (neo-)colonialism (Chapter 3) and neoliberalism (Chapter 4), the apocalyptic conception of time deploys the deceptive promise of a future utopia to legitimize oppressions and the status quo as part of a necessary teleological pattern tending towards betterment. In Jenkins's words, we therefore need to 'open time(s)' and oppose closure:

> First, because at the level of the historical text it just happens to be the case that interminable openness is logically unavoidable: there is no way that any historical closure can ever be achieved – that is certain. And second, because such unavoidable openness allows for new, disrespectful, contentious, radical readings and rereadings, writings and rewritings (2003: 3).

The critical temporalities of the contemporary post-apocalyptic novel advance agency and freedom first by deconstructing the apocalyptic foundations of today's world and power structures, second, by foregrounding the constructedness of apocalyptic history, and, third, by undercutting the deterministic and teleological narrative structure that supports this model of history. These fictions invite us to reconceive our understanding of narrative and history beyond the apocalyptic sense of an ending, opening up alternative possibilities, and thus unwritten, non-teleological futures, beyond the foreclosed possibilities of apocalyptic logic.

Where the 'apocalyptic narrative makes the conjunction of meaning and ending its theme, both in its expressed understanding of history and in its own narrative procedures' (Zamora 1989: 14), this conjunction is subverted by the critical temporalities of the contemporary post-apocalyptic novel. On the one hand, although they are set in that supposedly epistemically privileged position of after the end, these post-apocalyptic dystopian scenarios do not provide any revelation of a utopian renewal or of a plenitude of meaning. Indeed, it is in their afterness that this study locates their critical potential. Following the anticipation of retrospection, which works by anticipating the present as memory of the future (Currie [2007] 2010), in the contemporary post-apocalyptic novel our present is imagined as the post-apocalyptic future's past. Yet the narratives analysed in what follows undercut the structuring and sense-making power of this dynamic. As indicated by Self's *The Book of Dave*, our present can be thoroughly and comically misunderstood by the post-apocalyptic future. Or as epitomized by Crace's *The Pesthouse*, where the catastrophe itself is not once hinted at, the apocalypse is often a gap in the plots, thus undercutting the power of the end to make sense of history. On the other hand, in the twenty-first-century post-apocalyptic novel, the postmodern critique of metanarratives and totalizing explanations corresponds with postmodernist formal features that question an apocalyptic narrative model dominated by the end, variously defying chronology, linearity, continuity, foreshadowing, cause and effect and the sense of an ending itself. Examples of these features include narrative fragmentation and the movement between pre- and post-apocalypse, as in Mitchell's *Cloud Atlas*, Mandel's *Station Eleven*, Self's *The Book of Dave* and Atwood's *MaddAddam* trilogy; the exploration of disparate historical epochs and repetitive patterns that warp linearity, as in *Cloud Atlas*, *The Bone Clocks*, Jeanette Winterson's *The Stone Gods* (2007) and Michael Cunningham's *Specimen Days* (2005); the emphasis on the constructedness of the sense of an ending and of the apocalyptic history it sustains, as in the post-human narrative of Douglas Coupland's *Player One* (2010) and the imagined apocalypse of Sam Taylor's *The Island at the End of the World* (2009); and, more broadly, narrative endings which resist closure, reflecting the openness of time as lived.

These complications of a linear and teleological narrative time are typical of numerous postmodernist texts which 'brea[k] down the convention of historical time, ... reveal[ing] the arbitrariness of its historical "neutrality"' (Ermarth 1992: 41), from Julio Cortázar's *Hopscotch* (1966), where the author invites readers to 'hopscotch' through the text, to John Fowles's *The French Lieutenant's Woman* (1969), with its footnotes and multiple endings, and Salman Rushdie's looping narrative in *Midnight Children* (1981). Indeed, Linda Hutcheon's influential notion of 'historiographic metafiction' (1988) identifies postmodernist novels concerned with the narrative nature of history and the debunking of this neutrality.[21] Yet, what distinguishes contemporary post-

---

[21] Examples of historiographic metafictions, in addition to the already mentioned *The French Lieutenant Woman* and *Midnight Children*, are Robert Coover's *The Public Burning* (1977), D. M. Thomas's *The White Hotel* (1981) and Graham Swift's *Waterland* (1983).

apocalyptic fictions from historiographic metafiction and other postmodernist temporal experimentations is that the apocalyptic subject of the former allows them to critique the modern conception of history more fully. Since the structure of modern temporality is apocalyptic, the contemporary post-apocalyptic novel deconstructs this structure by targeting its very core: apocalyptic logic. In these fictions, the post-apocalyptic collapse of the nexus between end and meaning that underlies the modern understanding of history, combined with non-teleological narrative structures, effectively deconstructs the epistemic primacy of the end in history and narrative.[22]

The Contemporary Post-Apocalyptic Novel is a comprehensive analysis of twenty-first-century fictions of the end times written by British and North American non-SF authors. In its four chapters, the book parallels widely discussed and often award-winning novels – Self's *The Book of Dave*, McCarthy's *The Road*, Mitchell's *Cloud Atlas* and Mandel's *Station Eleven* – with fictions that have received less scholarly attention – Taylor's *The Island at the End of the World*, Crace's *The Pesthouse*, Winterson's *The Stone Gods* and Coupland's *Player One* – and closes by considering a very recent novel, Yuknavitch's *The Book of Joan*. While I concentrate on these nine novels, each chapter opens by outlining how its key focus – the relationship between apocalypticism and, respectively, biblical sources, American ideologies, (neo-)colonialism and the Anthropocene, and neoliberalism – can be applied to other twenty-first-century texts. In probing the novels' critical temporalities, there are four main areas of enquiry running throughout the book: history, narrative, power and agency.

Chapter 1, 'Biblical Parodies', provides the background to the following chapters by examining the relationship between the contemporary apocalyptic imagination and the biblical source. I argue that the contemporary post-apocalyptic novel parodically draws on biblical apocalyptic discourse to subvert it from within, emphasizing its violence and imbrication with power structures. The chapter opens by contrasting LaHaye and Jenkins's evangelical series, *Left Behind*, which follows an apocalyptic model of history and points to the continuing appeal of religious apocalypticism in the contemporary, with the critical distance deployed in Tom Perrotta's *The Leftovers* (2011) towards the apocalyptic tradition of the Rapture and the parodic use of prophetic figures

---

[22] Hardly by chance, some writers of contemporary post-apocalyptic fiction have interrogated the nature of history in other texts – for instance, Mitchell's *The Thousands Autumns of Jacob de Zoet* (2010), McCarthy's *Blood Meridian* (1985), Atwood's *The Blind Assassin* (2000) and Winterson's *Sexing the Cherry* (1989) – but arguably, given the imbrication of the western conception of history with apocalypticism, it is in their post-apocalyptic novels that history, as a narrative, is deconstructed more fully.

in fictions like Mandel's *Station Eleven*, Coupland's *Player One*, Atwood's *MaddAddam* trilogy and Maggie Gee's *The Flood* (2004). I then focus on two parodic takes on Revelation and Genesis respectively – Self's *The Book of Dave* and Taylor's *The Island at the End of the World* – whose critical temporalities expose apocalyptic history as a self-referential narrative construct, congenial for deranged minds, which is always instrumental to the moment in which it is produced. Dave's Revelation, the product of his post-divorce nervous breakdown, is adopted by the post-apocalyptic hierarchy of Ing as a sacred text, originating a society that mirrors the cab driver's worldview in minute details, including his wild misogynist fantasies, while the apocalyptic flood Ben concocts in *The Island at the End of the World* serves to raise his children far from what he sees as a corrupt society.

Chapter 2, 'Apocalypse America', turns to the most recurrent setting for twenty-first-century post-apocalyptic narratives, the United States, an element often read by critics as a response to our post-9/11 context. I argue, instead, that contemporary post-apocalyptic fictions set in America respond to a much longer history, critiquing the apocalyptic ideological foundations of the nation. From the colonial myth of a New World to the Puritan image of a 'city upon a hill', from Manifest Destiny to American exceptionalism and the good versus evil rhetoric of the War on Terror, the chapter opens by showing how America's conception of its own history is intrinsically apocalyptic. It then considers a survey of texts whose critical temporalities deconstruct the nexus Apocalypse America: El Akkad's *American War*, with its critique of America's messianic innocence; Louise Erdrich's *Future Home of the Living God* (2017), with its subversion of the exceptionalist image of America as the culmination of history; and Whitehead's *Zone One*, with its parody of the nation's endless renewal. The chapter focusses on McCarthy's *The Road* and Crace's *The Pesthouse*, tales of post-apocalyptic journeys that challenge Manifest Destiny and American exceptionalism. McCarthy's uncompromisingly dystopian wasteland leaves no hope for the renewal at the core of apocalyptic history and the exceptionalist trope of the New World, while the image of the road also challenges the teleology of apocalyptic logic and Manifest Destiny, for it does not take the man and the son to a better place. *The Pesthouse*, which I discuss by drawing on the Jim Crace Papers held at the Harry Ransom Center (University of Texas at Austin), represents the future as a return to a past which combines the American pioneer era and the European Middle Ages. This temporal inversion – a typical critical temporality of contemporary post-apocalyptic fiction that challenges the teleology of traditional apocalyptic logic and progress – parallels the novel's reversal of Manifest Destiny, for Crace's pioneers travel east to flee America.

The following two chapters turn to the capitalist world-system and its apocalyptic structures, foregrounding the dangerous legacies of apocalyptic modernity in our Anthropocene age and in the sense of no future and no alternatives that characterizes our neoliberal present. Chapter 3, 'The New Worlds of the Anthropocene', follows from the previous chapter by considering more directly the colonial undertones of apocalyptic logic. It opens by tracing the legacy of the apocalyptic trope of the colonial new world on the capitalist 'world-ecology' (Moore 2014) at the heart of the Anthropocene. I argue that Matthew Sharpe's *Jamestown* (2007), Marcel Theroux's *Far North* (2009), Yuknavitch's *The Book of Joan*, as well as the two texts which constitute the focus of the chapter, Mitchell's *Cloud Atlas* and Winterson's *The Stone Gods*, foreground the colonial roots of their environmentally devastated futures, thus challenging accounts of the geological epoch that date it back to the Industrial Revolution or the mid-twentieth century. Through patterns of repetition that trouble apocalyptic teleology, these novels' critical temporalities uncover the nexus between the apocalyptic justifications of colonialism, the modern capitalist economy that begins to emerge from the exploitation of the New World's resources and a damaging instrumentalist approach to nature. In my discussion of *Cloud Atlas* and *The Stone Gods* I focus on the texts' transhistorical narrative structures, which take up the challenge of representing the massive temporal scale of the 'hyperobject' (Morton 2013) of the Anthropocene. What I identify as *Cloud Atlas*'s concertina-like structure resists the linearity and deterministic closure of apocalyptic logic, emphasizing the power of individual agency to inform an open future, and links the various recurrences of the will to power in the novel, foregrounding the dystopian implications of apocalypticism, from colonialism to the future neo-colonial biopower of corporations and anthropogenic environmental breakdown. These implications are also explored in *The Stone Gods*, whose cyclical critical temporality warps apocalyptic teleology by subverting its central dichotomy: the new world versus the present world. Similarly to Mitchell's novel, Winterson's is structured through parallels and echoes, which turn out to be the cyclical repetition of the same environmental mistakes, with humankind colonizing and destroying 'new' worlds after 'new' worlds across the ages and, indeed, planets.

Chapter 4, 'After the Neoliberal Future', turns to the hegemonic temporality of our neoliberal present by considering post-apocalyptic novels set in the near future or even an alternate present/recent past. I open by discussing the apocalyptic echoes of neoliberalism in the notion of the end of history, which constructs the future as more of the same by deploying apocalyptic determinism to manage the contingency of the future and ensure the reproduction of the current system of accumulation. I then show how the critical temporalities of Nathaniel Rich's *Odds Against Tomorrow* (2013), Walker's *The Age of Miracles* and Whitehead's *Zone One* subvert the neoliberal utopian end of history as the site of an extended hopeless present, an ongoing slow apocalypse and no future. The chapter focusses on Mandel's *Station Eleven* and Coupland's *Player One*, two post-apocalyptic novels which convey the collapse of global capital through their end-times airports, symbols of the end of globalization and late capitalism's hyper-connectivity. I read Mandel's and Coupland's catastrophic alternate histories – *Station Eleven*'s pandemic hits soon after the financial crisis of 2007/2008, while Coupland's peak oil takes place in 2010 – as rupturing the neoliberal construction of the future as more of the same. However, *Station Eleven*'s elegiac celebration of the bygone world risks reinforcing the image of neoliberalism as the apocalyptic culmination of history, whereas *Player One*'s critique of neoliberal temporality is more effective thanks to the emphasis on 'denarration', a process where 'one's life stops feeling like a story' (*PO* 222), which reflects the sense of a stalled present devoid of futurity under neoliberal capital. I parallel *Player One* with Coupland's earlier *Girlfriend in a Coma* (1998), whose recourse to traditional apocalyptic logic as a solution to denarration *Player One* parodies, deconstructing the apocalyptic structures underlying the neoliberal end of history and its crisis of futurity.

The conclusion of *The Contemporary Post-Apocalyptic Novel*, 'The Post-Apocalyptic Archive' turns to the image of the archive to draw together the main threads of the book: history, narrative, power and agency. With their selective preservation of texts, records and memories, post-apocalyptic archives encapsulate the nexus between narrative, history and power deconstructed by the contemporary post-apocalyptic novel's critical temporalities. From a library's charred ruins in *The Road* to the erasure of records and events in Mullen's *The Revisionists*, from Sonmi's orison in *Cloud Atlas* to *The Stone Gods*' *mise en abyme* manuscript, twenty-first-century post-apocalyptic fictions repeatedly return to anxieties over the survival and manipulations of archives after the catastrophe but equally celebrate the transformative power of narrative. I focus on Yuknavitch's *The Book of Joan*, where the archive is the human body thanks to the future form of storytelling that is skin grafting, an element conveying the importance of narratives to human agency through a literal embodiment of the stories that drive our actions. Drawing on Derrida's notion of 'archive fever' (1995), I identify an anti-apocalyptic archive fever in the contemporary post-apocalyptic novel, that is, the desire to counter apocalyptic logic through the fostering of narratives that do not consume the planet and others in their self-righteous teleology and hunger for power.

1

Biblical Parodies

In the first chapter of Douglas Coupland's *Player One* (2010), one of the novel's protagonists finds herself thinking about a TV miniseries – *The Langoliers* (1995), based on a novella by Stephen King – in which the passengers of a flight abruptly vanish, leaving their clothes behind. Karen, herself on a plane, starts musing about what it means for someone to vanish: what constitutes that someone? What does not? What would be left behind? After a vertiginous catalogue of everything that is inessential to our identity and would therefore be left behind if we were to vanish – not only clothes, but pacemakers, dental veneers, hair extensions, the various bacteria and viruses that inhabit us, even the water that constitutes so much of our bodies – Karen comes to the realization that 'only her DNA is actually *her*' (Coupland [2010] 2011: 4; emphasis in original).[1] Coupland elaborates on this realization further in the 'Rapture Goo' entry of the glossary that closes *Player One*: 'The stuff that gets left behind .... Jesus gets your DNA. That's all he gets, roughly 7.6 milligrams of you' (*PO* 240). As Karen concludes, 'somebody had better tell those fundamentalist Christians waiting for the Rapture to leave out some buckets and mops' to clean up the Rapture goo (*PO* 4). Karen's quip frames the background of her considerations: the rise of Christian fundamentalism and its apocalyptic beliefs in the United States, as well as the prominence in American popular culture of images of the Rapture. Karen's irony, however, also indicates, as this chapter argues contrasting the orthodox apocalypticism of Tim LaHaye and Jerry B. Jenkins's *Left Behind* series (1995–2007) with the parodic tone of texts like Will Self's *The Book of Dave* (2006) and Sam Taylor's *The Island at the End of the World* (2009), that the contemporary post-apocalyptic novel deploys biblical tropes parodically, to subvert traditional apocalyptic discourse and its temporality from within.

Parody 'is most readily invited by doctrinal utterances that seek to present themselves as absolute' (Bernstein 1994: 80) and is, therefore, a particularly appropriate strategy for the deconstruction of the apocalyptic metanarrative

---

[1] All further references to Coupland's *Player One* as *PO*.

and its totalizing conception of history. In this chapter, I draw on Hutcheon's canonical definition of parody as what 'paradoxically both incorporates and challenges that which it parodies', with irony establishing a 'critical distance' between the parodied and the parodic texts that signals 'difference at the very heart of similarity' (1988: 11, 26). For as Hutcheon underlines drawing on the etymology of 'parody', from the Greek *'para'* (against and beside) and *'odos'* (ode), the term does not necessarily entail the ridiculing and mocking imitation with which it is commonly associated. Rather, coherently with postmodernism, which often uses parodic strategies, parody 'does not pretend to operate outside the system, for it knows it cannot; it therefore overtly acknowledges its complicity, only to work covertly to subvert the system's values from within' (Hutcheon 1988: 223), as the narratives analysed in this chapter do by drawing on apocalyptic tropes to critique them from within. After considering the phenomenon of *Left Behind* and its adherence to the traditional apocalyptic construction of history in the context of the continuing appeal of religious apocalypticism, I turn to the critical temporalities articulated by the contemporary post-apocalyptic novel through the appropriation of biblical and religious apocalyptic tropes. A text like Tom Perrotta's *The Leftovers* (2011) features a Rapture event but undermines central elements of dispensationalist history; prophets appear in fictions like Emily St. John Mandel's *Station Eleven* (2014), Maggie Gee's *The Flood* (2004), Margaret Atwood's *MaddAddam* trilogy (2003–2013) and Coupland's *Player One* but only to expose the violence of apocalyptic discourse; finally, Self's *The Book of Dave* and Taylor's *The Island at the End of the World*, the focus of this chapter, parody the biblical apocalyptic narratives of Revelation and Genesis to foreground the constructedness of apocalyptic history and its complicity with oppressive power structures.

With close to 70 million copies sold and a successful franchise of movies, video games, children's books, graphic novels and podcasts, LaHaye and Jenkins's sixteen *Left Behind* novels are the most popular example of contemporary narratives of the Rapture.[2] Adhering to premillennialist dispensationalism, the novels recount seven years of chaotic events – the Tribulation – replete with plagues, earthquakes, droughts and even an invasion by killer horsemen coming from the sky, following god's removal of the true believers from Earth – the

---

[2] Hal Lindsey's bestseller *The Late Great Planet Earth* (1970) is the predecessor to the recent slew of Rapture narratives – and Christian fundamentalist narratives more broadly – that include, in addition to the *Left Behind* franchise, Pat Robertson's *The End of the Age* (1995), James BeauSeigneur's *Christ Clone* trilogy (1997–1998), Robert Van Kampen's *The Fourth Reich* (1997), Gilbert, Lynn, and Alan Morris's *The Omega* series (1999–2000) and Jenkins's *The Underground Zealot* trilogy (2003–2005). For a discussion of these and other narratives in the genre, see Gribben (2009), Chapter 7.

Rapture – which is also represented through passengers disappearing from a transatlantic flight, leaving behind, unrealistically Karen would say, nothing more than their clothes. While a politician, who is in fact the Antichrist, rises to power, a group of people who have been left behind realize the error of their ways, convert to evangelical dispensationalism, and form a Tribulation Force devoted to resist the Antichrist and interpret the Bible to understand what the future holds, for 'Bible prophecy is history written in advance' (LaHaye and Jenkins 1995: 214). As Jennie Chapman explains in her study of the series, *Left Behind* has an 'overtly pedagogical objective: to instruct its readers in the way of dispensational hermeneutics so that they too can discern the prophetic "truth" contained in the Bible and hence avoid the terrible fate of being "left behind"' (2013: 5).[3] With this pedagogical objective, the series foregrounds the revelatory aspect and historical sense-making function central to dispensationalism and apocalyptic logic more broadly.

Dispensationalism is an apocalyptic theory of history that understands time as a series of eras, known as dispensations, which culminate in the present Church Age. This is the age that ends with the events of the *Left Behind*: the Rapture, the Tribulation, the Antichrist, the second coming of Christ and the millennium.[4] Dispensationalism has its origins in the preaching of John Nelson Darby in the nineteenth century. It is to Darby that we owe the belief in the Rapture, which he based on 1 Thessalonians 4:16-4:17 (Frykholm 2004: 15–17). As Amy Johnson Frykholm maintains, in its origins in the 'turmoil over the rapid changes in cultural life that were the result of capitalist expansion, new technologies, scientific discoveries, and large-scale immigration', the narrative of the Rapture, through the distinction between the saved and the unsaved, provided the means to react to a perceived 'loss of cultural control' and 'reject a disorienting new social terrain' (2004: 19).[5] For dispensationalism, the world grows more and more evil as the Church Age comes to an end, so that any event can be read through the prophetic framework of the Bible as a manifestation

---

[3] Chapman (2013) focusses on the hermeneutics and politics of reading the *Left Behind*. For an analysis of the series in terms of its links with the Christian Right in America, see McAlister (2003) and Swirski (2014).

[4] This is the order of events for premillennialist dispensationalism. For postmillennialists, the second coming occurs after the millennium. Both currents of dispensationalism adhere, however, to the heart of apocalyptic logic: its sense-making temporal ordering through utopian teleology. See Frykholm (2004) and Shuck (2004) for a history of dispensationalism and its influence over American evangelicalism.

[5] Cf. the same rejection of a social terrain perceived as new and disorienting in LaHaye's *The Bible's Influence on American History*, which encapsulates *Left Behind*'s politics: 'Government induced socialism in the guise of liberalism is raping the American free enterprise system, human initiative is being sapped by welfarism, the morals of our nation have dropped to an all time low, crime threatens our personal safety, and the liberal media is seeking to control the thinking of our people' (1976: 73).

of sin signifying that the end times are nigh. As ever, apocalyptic logic is a way of imposing an order on a time of disorder and crisis, as well as a way of providing a vengeful escapism from a world that is deemed to be corrupt. To those confronted with the chaos of historical contingency and social change, apocalypticism affords a revelation of the true nature of the temporal flow, a strong sense of purpose through a triumphant vision of the future for the elect and the punishment of the sinners, and a clear worldview that explains one's place in history, allowing the firm differentiation between good and evil.

It is this apocalyptic 'tone of *certainty* … against the growth toward pluralism, ambiguity, indeterminacy' (Keller 2005: 12; emphasis in original) that makes religious apocalypticism still so appealing in the twenty-first century. According to the 2014 *Bible in American Life* report, 'of the 50 percent of all Americans who have read any of the Bible in the previous year, over one-third claimed that they did so "to learn about the future"', an element that 'reveals how widespread Christian apocalyptic ideas are and how thoroughly evangelical premillennialism has saturated American culture' (Sutton 2014: 372). Indeed, in texts like the *Left Behind* series, the plotting of history in accordance to dispensationalism affords, especially in a post-9/11 context that is read by fundamentalists as proof of the imminence of the end, a 'certainty about the future, and a promise that the good guys win in the end' (McAlister 2003: 792).[6] To put it with the words of one of the followers of the 'One Way Brotherhood', the fundamentalist apocalyptic sect in Gee's *The Flood* whose name encapsulates the deterministic linearity of apocalyptic history, 'He'd never been able to imagine his future, which was why the Last Days provided the answer' ([2004] 2005: 126).[7] It is important to underline that fiction like the *Left Behind* 'never strays far from politics *tout court*', for 'many tenets of evangelical Christianity, such as the absolutist view of the scriptures, the belief in divine agency, or the desegregation of state and religion are mirrored in its political platform [the Christian Right] – such as an apocalyptic view of history, the displacement of democracy by charismatic leadership, and the advocacy of behavioral control' (Swirski 2014: 12). As we shall see in Chapter 2, after 9/11, apocalyptic views of history came to the forefront of politics, informing America's response to the attacks. Through their North American settings, texts like *The Leftovers*, *Station Eleven*, *Player One*, the *MaddAddam* trilogy and *The Island at the End of the World* engage, more or less explicitly, with

---

[6] According to a 2002 Time/CNN poll, a quarter of Americans believe that the events of 9/11 were predicted in the Bible (Gray 2007: 168).
[7] All further references to Gee's *The Flood* as *TF*.

the rise of Christian fundamentalism in the United States, while fictions set outside of North America, like *The Book of Dave*, speak to a wider persistence of spiritual and religious constructions of reality in what John A. McClure identifies as the 'post-secular' aspects of postmodernity (1995).[8] It is against the apocalyptic revelation of totalizing historical plots that close off possibility and alternative explanations, and their import on politics and power, that the critical temporalities of the novels discussed in this chapter are positioned.

A case in point is *The Leftovers*. The novel revolves around a Rapture event, the 'Sudden Departure', but immediately signals its critical distance from Rapture narratives, and *Left Behind* specifically, by opening with a sceptical character, Laurie, who defines premillennial dispensationalism as 'mumbo jumbo', 'religious kitsch', and 'feel[s] a twinge of pity, and even a little bit of tenderness, for the poor sucker who had nothing better to read' than LaHaye and Jenkins's series (Perrotta [2011] 2012: 2).[9] Although Laurie, following the Sudden Departure, goes on to join the apocalyptic sect of the Guilty Remnant (GR), and thus the ranks of the believers in the Rapture, *The Leftovers* continues to affirm its parodic distance from traditional Rapture narratives. The cause of the Sudden Departure remains unclear. Christians actually oppose the identification of the Sudden Departure with the Rapture, since 'The whole point was to separate the wheat from the chaff, to reward the true believers and put the rest of the world on notice. An indiscriminate Rapture was no Rapture at all' (*TL* 3). Perrotta's certainly is an indiscriminate Rapture, in that it sees the Pope disappearing alongside Vladimir Putin and an unspecified 'Latin American tyrant' (*TL* 51), as well as, to the dismay of fundamentalist Christians, 'Hindus and Buddhists and Muslims and Jews and atheists and animists and homosexuals and Eskimos and Mormons and Zoroastrians, whatever the heck they were' (*TL* 3). The Sudden Departure does not fulfil the apocalyptic requirements of a clear separation between good and evil and thus fails to impose an order on the temporal sequence.

Furthermore, *The Leftovers* presents the readers with two apocalyptic sects, convinced that the Sudden Departure indicates that the end times are nigh, which both serve to undermine apocalyptic discourse through parodic distance. The GR's theology is fuzzy even to its believers but includes smoking incessantly – cancer is not a worry, given the approaching end – as a form of

---

[8] McClure stresses the openness of spiritual constructions of reality and religious questionings in postmodern fiction and, indeed, it is precisely dogmatic apocalyptic closure that the contemporary post-apocalyptic novel deconstructs. On the post-secular imagination, see also Carruthers and Tate (2010).
[9] All further references to Perrotta's *The Leftovers* as *TL*.

sacrament that reminds anybody being stalked by GR members that god is keeping track of every action. The GR is later revealed to be a brainwashing death cult that demands the ultimate sacrifice of its members. Similarly, the followers of Holy Wayne, a man believed to have the power of absorbing the immense grief of people whose family and friends have suddenly disappeared, are later exposed to much more unpalatable revelations about this apocalyptic prophet: he is a rapist and a paedophile. As Tate observes, *The Leftovers* is an 'acknowledgement of American fascination with "end-times" prophecies [and] an exploration of the seductive rhetoric of fanaticism as a response to loss and a sense of powerlessness' (2017: 60) – it is, in other words, a parodic take, in Hutcheon's terms of 'difference at the very heart of similarity' (1988), on Rapture narratives like *Left Behind* and the sense-making function of the apocalyptic paradigm more broadly.

Perrotta's Holy Wayne is paralleled by other parodic prophetic figures in the contemporary post-apocalyptic novel. In its essence, the apocalyptic narrative is prophetic, in that it offers the revelation of a utopian teleology to history. Thus, John opens the Book of Revelation by presenting it as 'The revelation from Jesus Christ, which God gave him to show his servants what must soon take place' and as prophecy: 'Blessed is the one who reads aloud the words of this prophecy, and blessed are those who hear it and take to heart what is written in it, because the time is near' (Rev. 1:1, 1:3) – sentences in which the temporal nature of apocalyptic discourse clearly emerges in its deterministic nature. As Elizabeth K. Rosen underlines, the difference between apocalyptic prophecy and prophecy more broadly 'lies primarily in their visions of history and mankind's role in it':

> The future which a prophet predicts is a possible future, one which may occur if mankind does not act according to God's wishes. But that predicted future is also one which can be avoided by returning to God's word....... An apocalypticist, on the other hand, sees God's behavior as fixed. God *will* intervene and bring human history to an end. Apocalypticists warn of an unalterable end. Their aim is to comfort and prepare those who are already 'saved'. (2008: 66; emphasis in original)

Indeed, in addition to the determinism of apocalyptic history, the core of the 'apocalypse pattern', to put it with Keller, is the inclination of the apocalyptic prophet and believers to think in terms of clear-cut polarities of good versus evil, and their identification with the good that purges the evil from the old world and is worthy of the imminent utopian renewal of the new world ([1996] 2005: 11). These are all elements that the prophets of the contemporary post-apocalyptic novel exhibit, with the texts' critical temporalities underlining through parodic distance how the deterministic teleological plotting of the apocalypse pattern serves to push violent ideological agendas.

Station Eleven's prophet, Tyler, is only a child when the pandemic that is at the heart of this post-apocalyptic narrative hits the world, but grows up to be the charismatic leader of a violent doomsday cult. Echoing Holy Wayne's deterministic pronouncement after his arrest that 'Whatsoever happens to me ... do not despair. It happens for a reason' (*TL* 47), Tyler believes that 'everything that has ever happened on this earth has happened for a reason' (*SE* 59), including the novel's apocalypse. Faced with the chaos of historical contingency – chaos which is even more evident and dreadful at times of crisis, such as that of the novel's devastating Georgia Flu, with its 99 per cent mortality rate – Tyler resorts to the order afforded by apocalyptic determinism and the Book of Revelation, which he heavily annotates.[10] In an echo of Revelation 15-16, he sees the pandemic as an 'avenging angel' (*SE* 60, 286) and as punishment for the ways of the corrupt old world, which he compares to Revelation's Babylon (*SE* 259), a symbol of the sinful Roman Empire that John gleefully describes as a 'great whore ... corrupt[ing] the earth with her fornication' and receiving her comeuppance in the end times through plagues (Rev. 19:2; 18:8). This violent misogyny is something I return to throughout this chapter, and that is reflected in the 'hegemonic masculinity that is central to the conservative evangelical worldview' embodied by *Left Behind*, with its 'acts of violent retribution meted out against transgressive females' (Chapman 2013: 137, 138). Similarly to Holy Wayne in *The Leftovers*, indeed, Mandel presents her readers with a prophet that embodies the patriarchal logic of apocalyptic discourse: Tyler has several wives, including very young girls, and it is the refusal of the Travelling Symphony – a Shakespearean troupe around which the post-apocalyptic chapters revolve – to sell him another wife that provokes the confrontation between the prophet's cult and the Symphony. As opposed to those who died in the Georgia Flu, to Tyler, the survivors are the elect whose 'names are recorded in the book of life' (*SE* 286) – a reference to Revelation 20:11-15 – and who were saved because they represent the light of purity (*SE* 60). However, as Kirsten, one of the members of the Travelling Symphony, muses, 'If you are the light, if your enemies are darkness, then there's nothing that you cannot justify' (*SE* 139). *Station Eleven* signals that the apocalyptic distinction between the elect and the non-elect fuels the ruthless actions of the prophet and

---

[10] The Bible, or other religious texts, surviving the destruction of the archive of written texts brought about by the apocalypse is a trope that recurs in many of the texts explored in this chapter, signalling the contemporary post-apocalyptic novel's concern over which narratives shape our worldviews, an element I further explore in the Conclusion.

his followers – from killing to raping and enslaving – which they commit 'All the time smiling, so peaceful, like they've done nothing wrong' (*SE* 273), because they see themselves as the only rightful interpreters and agents of the apocalyptic goal of history, the utopian renewal of the post-pandemic world.

Similarly, Bruno in *The Flood*, the prophet leader of the One Way Brotherhood, 'knows that the end is coming' and reads the world around him through the Bible, looking for the 'signs and wonders' that prefigure 'the last days' (*TF* 17, 18).[11] An ex-convict who was charged with attempted murder, Bruno's apocalyptic prophecies are filled with violence and hatred. He believes that the apocalypse will 'wash [the world] clean' of those people whose sins are 'sores upon the face of the earth', first and foremost women – 'old women, who he hated the most; painted women; weak women; adulterers' (*TF* 17) – an element that again foregrounds the inherent misogyny of apocalyptic discourse. Bruno's followers also revel in vengeful, and indeed racist, apocalyptic visions: 'Dirk loved the idea of a lake, burning, black with his enemies', enemies that are qualified as 'the immigrants, the coloureds' (*TF* 126), recalling D. H. Lawrence's critique of the apocalyptic plot as what functions to demonize 'the fellow who is different from me' ([1980] 2002: 89). However, when the apocalypse (the flood) finally comes in Gee's world, there is no distinction between the elect and the non-elect, just like in *The Leftovers*, so that the sense-making function of apocalyptic logic is denied.

In Atwood's *MaddAddam* trilogy, Adam One, the leader of the environmentalist sect of the 'God's Gardeners', shares the biblical prophets' faith in god's apocalyptic renewing intervention. Adam One theorizes humankind as subject to an ongoing Fall responsible for the world's environmental problems:

> The ancestral primates fell out of the trees; then they fell from vegetarianism into meat-eating. Then they fell from instinct into reason, and thus into technology; from simple signals into complex grammars, and thus into humanity; from firelessness into fire, and thence into weaponry; and from seasonal mating into incessant sexual twitching. (Atwood [2009] 2010: 224)[12]

The sect is thus waiting for god's 'waterless flood', which will cleanse the world, finally granting the surviving human beings a utopian coexistence with nature. While the Gardeners are a peaceful sect, committed to the care of the planet while expecting the flood, their apocalypticism serves as a source of inspiration for a violent apocalyptic project, Crake's.

---

[11] Intertextual references to Revelation, as well as Genesis, given the theme of the flood, abound in Gee's text. For an analysis of these references and, more broadly, of the motif of the flood in contemporary apocalyptic narratives, see Tate (2017: 23–41).

[12] All further references to Atwood's *The Year of the Flood* as *YoF*.

An unabashedly atheist scientist, Crake is not waiting for god's renewing intervention. Rather, bringing Tyler's violent approach to its extreme consequences, he takes the matter of the creation of the perfect new world in his own hands. In a plan that closely mirrors an apocalyptic trajectory from the destruction of the corrupt old world to the utopian renewal of the new world, Crake engineers a virus to annihilate humankind, a species he deems irrational as it is damaging to Earth and hence to itself, and builds its replacement, the Crakers. Having genetically altered the human 'ancient primate brain' in the Crakers to eliminate 'its destructive features, the features responsible for the world's current illnesses', Crake foresees a new world free from racism, hierarchy, territoriality and even waste, as the Crakers recycle their own faeces (Atwood [2003] 2009: 358).[13] In order to bring this plan to fruition, Crake manipulates the public into believing that the pill that contains the deadly virus is sexually enhancing and youth prolonging – a new world on earth for everybody, as indicated by the pill's name, 'BlyssPluss', 'a whispering, seductive sound' that exploits human apocalyptic 'desire for more and better' (O&C 349, 348).

To underscore the dangerous pervasiveness of apocalyptic logic and the dystopian implications of its absolute truth claims and self-righteous moral dualism, Atwood explicitly parallels Crake's totalitarian scientific project with the peaceful religious apocalypticism of the God's Gardeners. The second book of the trilogy, *The Year of the Flood*, reveals that, as a boy, Crake hacked information for the group. As Tate notices, 'the prelapsarian identity that Adam One evokes is the condition that Crake, an avowed disbeliever, aspires to for his new creation' (2017: 73), whose genetically engineered features, from vegetarianism to periodic mating habits, are aimed at putting a stop to the Fall as theorized by Adam One. Indeed, the name of Crake's project, 'Paradice', encapsulates its religious undertones, with the scientist effectively taking up the role of god in bringing about the new creation and separating the saved from the damned. 'Paradice' harks back to the biblical episode of the Fall from the Garden of Eden already evoked by Adam One's name and his theology – notice, in this sense, how the first thing Jimmy observes about the Crakers in the Paradice dome is that they are naked but are not self-conscious about it (O&C 355), which parallels the situation of Adam and Eve before the Fall. Yet, the 'dice' of 'Paradice' also signals the element of chance, as Crake's project, against apocalyptic determinism, does not turn out as he had planned. For one thing, humankind does not become extinct.

---

[13] All further references to Atwood's *Oryx and Crake* as O&C.

Bertis, the fanatic sniper of *Player One*'s peak oil post-apocalyptic scenario, also believes that the pre-apocalyptic world is corrupt and about to be renewed through divine intervention. Just like Crake with the BlyssPluss pill, Bertis, *Player One*'s other characters notice, deploys rhythm and repetitions in his speech in order to indoctrinate (*PO* 187), for he sees himself as the prophet of the new world to come, 'plotting every moment to boil the carcass of the old order' (*PO* 189). The violence of this language signals the militant and divisive nature of apocalyptic discourse. Sustained by self-righteous absolute truth claims and moral dualism just like Tyler, Bertis conceives of his murders as partaking in a divinely sanctioned separation between the elect and the non-elect. It turns out, however, that he is also motivated by a much more mundane reason: he wants to kill his father, Leslie Freemont, who ran off with his wife. Freemont, a self-help guru who has become rich thanks to his $8,500 'Power Dynamics Seminar System', is *Player One*'s even more evidently parodic prophetic figure (we will return to both Bertis' and Freemont's apocalyptic rhetoric in Chapter 4). Freemont's ludicrous programme exploits human desire for radical renewal, as indicated by its inherently apocalyptic slogan, '*Are you ready to change, to join, to become part of What's Next?*' (*PO* 5; emphasis in original), thus signalling the self-referential nature of apocalyptic discourse, that is, how it serves the interests of those who articulate it.

This parodic emphasis on the self-referentiality of apocalypticism is at the core of Self's and Taylor's novels, to which the rest of this chapter is devoted. Both *The Book of Dave* and *The Island at the End of the World* deconstruct the apocalyptic paradigm from within, by parodically appropriating biblical apocalyptic tropes – from Revelation and the Genesis story of the Flood – and articulating critical temporalities that expose the apocalyptic construction of history as just a narrative, which is always self-referential and is particularly congenial for deranged minds. In underlining how reality is constituted by a web of narratives – a thread that runs throughout this study and to which we shall fully return in the Conclusion – Self's and Taylor's novels explore the dangers of closing off our narratives, that is, of granting them absolute truth value and epistemic primacy over others, passing off what is merely a construction as natural and universal, just as the apocalyptic metanarrative does.

The subtitle of *The Book of Dave*, *A Revelation of the Recent Past and the Distant Future*, unmistakably assigns the novel to the genre of apocalyptic writings, albeit with a parodic intent. For in telling the story of Dave Rudman, a cab driver in recent-past London, and of his crazed revelatory Book mistaken for a sacred text in the post-apocalyptic Ing Archipelago (the future UK, resulting from global warming and rising sea water levels), Self draws on apocalyptic motifs to parodically deconstruct them.[14] As Hunter M. Hayes aptly remarks, 'Rather than a new Iron Age the residents of Ham, Chil, New London and all of Ingerland exist in an Ironic Age, from the misprision stemming from the eponymous text to iron's renaming as "irony"' (2007: 173).[15] Irony, indeed, frames the critical distance between *The Book of Dave* and its parodied hypotext, Revelation, from which Self appropriates the defining elements of the apocalyptic plot: prophecy and revelation, misogyny, judgment and the New Jerusalem.

In his introduction to the Canongate edition of the Book of Revelation, Self defines it as a 'sick text' that 'has survived to be the very stuff of modern, psychotic nightmare' (1998: xii, xiv). This is the premise of *The Book of Dave*'s use of the apocalyptic tropes of prophecy and revelation. While apocalyptic prophecies reveal divine plans in history disclosed by otherworldly beings to human recipients, so that in the Book of Revelation John's prophecy is mediated by angels (Rev. 1:1), Dave's 'divine' revelation, in the parodic distance of the novel's critical temporality, is the product of a delusional state. It is after being prescribed Prozac for his post-divorce depression that Dave could hear his angelic messenger, 'the still, small, powdery voice of SmithKline Beecham ... *There is no god but you, Dave, It whispered, and you can be your own prophet*' (Self [2006] 2007: 345; emphasis in original).[16] This drug-induced parodic conflation of deity and prophet in the human person of Dave signals the self-referential nature of his apocalyptic Book.

The Book is partly made of the Knowledge, the test that all cab drivers in London have to pass in order to get their license and that creates in Dave's prophecy a map of a future and divine London, New London. But the Book also reveals the divine – or rather 'dävine' – Law, 'a set of doctrines and covenants' derived from Dave's working life and 'vindictive misogynism' (*BoD* 280-281) against his estranged wife.[17] Dave's divorce from Michelle, separation from his son Carl and ensuing breakdown parodically play the role of the crisis that

---

[14] For the sake of simplicity and to avoid confusion, Book, with a capital B, refers in this chapter to the Book written by Dave.

[15] It is important to note however that, more than a new Iron Age, Self's post-apocalyptic society is a neo-medieval 'feudal set-up, with a King, "guvners" (barons), and "chavs" (serfs), with the church proving the glue to hold the system together' (Robinson 2013: 99).

[16] All further references to Self's *The Book of Dave* as *BoD*.

[17] As the psychiatrists of the mental institution to which Dave commits himself remark, the 'doctrines and covenants' recall 'one of the Mormon holy books' (*BoD* 281). The very idea of writing the Book on metal plates and burying it in Hampstead, which is how it survives until it is found in post-apocalyptic Ing, comes from the Mormon faith, which Dave discovers through his pious aunt Gladys. Self intersperses this sort of information in the novel, showing through narrative fragmentation how Dave's unstable mind pieces together various elements from his life to produce his delusional revelation.

always triggers apocalyptic writing, and the Book includes a series of letters to Dave's Lost Boy – letters which recall Revelation, with its seven epistles to the seven churches of Asia Minor. Dave-the-god is no one but Dave-the-cabbie and His Law stems from his work and his life, an element that undercuts the absolute truth claims of apocalypticism, suggesting that, since the apocalyptic metanarrative is an attempt at temporal sense-making, its prophecies and revelations cannot but refer to the needs, desires and expectations of those who construct or deploy it.

This self-referentiality doubles up in the post-apocalypse, which interprets Dave's hallucinatory identification with god as revealed truth so that his revelation about the future is fulfilled, but only in the ironic mode of a self-fulfilling prophecy. Ing's way of life is thoroughly informed by Dave's worldview, for the Law and the Knowledge are ultimately instrumental to those in power, who exploit Dave's revelation to posit themselves as the only rightful interpreters of the Book and agents of its historical telos. Tellingly, on Ing, Dave-the-god and Dave-the-cabbie are joined by Dave-the-kings of the Dävidic dynasty, and all those related to the PCO – formerly the Public Carriage Office, now the priestly hierarchy – address other people through mirrors. This derives from Dave's work – as a cabbie he could only see his fares through the rearview mirror – but also stresses the self-referentiality of Dave's revelation. If 1 Corinthians prophesizes that 'now we see only a reflection as in a mirror; then we shall see face to face' (13:12), the post-apocalyptic population quite literally sees through the distorted mirror of Dave's crazed and myopic worldview, rather than with the 'face to face' clarity that should accompany the new world. In Dave's disturbed mind, 'the map, the territory and prophecy became as one' (*BoD* 347), a sentence which echoes Baudrillard's theory of simulation: 'The territory no longer precedes the map, nor does it survive it. It is nevertheless the map that precedes the territory – *precession of simulacra* – that engenders the territory' (1994b: 1; emphasis in original). The Knowledge is to Dave not merely a map of London, but also of New London, and because it is found and claimed to be a divine plan by the Ing's hierarchy, this map self-fulfillingly engenders the new city, it becomes territory, although, as we shall see, between London and New London there is a significant ironic distance, given by the post-apocalyptic misinterpretations of the Book and by Ing's limited technology. *The Book of Dave* therefore illustrates how even a deranged narrative about the future can become a metanarrative and how, to anticipate the terms of my discussion of David Mitchell's *Cloud Atlas* (2004) in Chapter 3, the simulacrum of a virtual future can influence the actual future, especially when it legitimizes those in power.

Since the Book, together with the figure of Dave and the readers' present, are thoroughly misinterpreted in the post-apocalyptic future, in a parodic inversion of the etymological meaning of 'apocalypse', Dave's revelatory text turns out to veil the truth. The Book itself is never fully revealed to its readers, for the only access they have to the text is through psychiatrists discussing Dave's delusions once he is hospitalized and the cabbie's rants and habits which, when contrasted with post-apocalyptic life, can gesture to the content of the absent revelatory text. Even the Second Book, which Dave writes to take back the 'hellish DESIGN FOR LIVING' (*BoD* 419; capitalization in original) of the first and which thus discloses to the post-apocalyptic Symun Dévúsh that the cabbie wrote his prophecy 'wen ee woz off iz rokkah' (*BoD* 81), does not impinge on Ing's misguided faith in Dave as god.[18] Tellingly, no one besides Symun ever sees the Second Book, since he claims that Dave took it away after showing it to him. This revelation is utterly partial, underscoring Self's ironic subversion of the sense-making function of apocalyptic discourse. That Dave's delusional and damaging revelation is seemingly the only book to survive in the post-apocalypse also signifies an ironic take on the trope of the post-apocalyptic archive, namely, as we shall see in the Conclusion, the anxiety over which texts, if any, would survive an apocalyptic catastrophe and how they would inform the future world.

The subtitle of *The Book of Dave*, *A Revelation of the Recent Past and the Distant Future*, reinforces Self's deconstruction of an apocalyptic revelation. In the pre-apocalyptic sections, which constitute the revelation of the recent past, 'the message seems to be that Dave's grumpy views of society are myopic and wrongheaded (though amusing) – a conclusion most readers will reach the first time they meet the blustering cabbie', Nathaniel Rich muses in his review of the

---

[18] The combination of roman type, sentences and words written in all capital letters and italics visually conveys Dave's psychological instability throughout the book. Symun's words are in Mokni, a 'phonetic transliteration of broad cockney' (Self 2007) that incorporates abbreviations and texting symbols. In the post-apocalyptic chapters, Self deploys two future versions of contemporary English: the Mokni dialect, spoken everywhere in Ing, and Arpee, the sacred language of the Book used by the people in power, which, as its name suggests (Received Pronunciation), is very close to standard English. Like Mitchell in the post-apocalyptic chapter of *Cloud Atlas*, Self takes the idea of a post-apocalyptic English from Russell Hoban's *Riddley Walker* (1980), entirely written in a post-apocalyptic dialect. Indeed, Self penned the introduction for the 2002 Bloomsbury edition of *Riddley Walker* and there are manifold similarities between Self's and Hoban's novels. Both *The Book of Dave* and *Riddley Walker* open with a map, which depicts a post-apocalyptic England, named Inland in Hoban's book, altered by flooding in its geography. Both narratives begin with a ritual, the slaughter of a moto and Riddley's naming day respectively. Both feature two twelve-year-old protagonists, Carl and Riddley, who are living at a time of transition. Both worlds are haunted by their past, whose scarce remaining written documents they misinterpret, and by the pre-apocalyptic myth of progress, which they foolishly pursue, even though this proves to be as destructive as when it led to the catastrophe centuries before. Both Carl and Riddley oppose the so-called progressive changes and, therefore, the people in power. Both books, finally, close with a glossary of their post-apocalyptic languages.

novel (2006). Arguably, the tautological and non-revelatory quality of these sections encapsulates Self's parody of apocalyptic logic. As for the revelation of the distant future, it is complicated by the novel's structure. Not only does the narrative constantly alternate between the future and the past, shifting from chapters set between 1987 and 2003 to chapters set between 509 AD and 524 AD – where 'AD', 'After Dave', ironically denotes a new form of dating which starts from the discovery of the sacred text – but neither the pre-apocalyptic nor the post-apocalyptic sections are in chronological order. Narrative strands begin, they are then interrupted, and after either an analepsis or a prolepsis, they are picked up considerably later. *The Book of Dave* actually starts with the post-apocalyptic story, so that the pre-apocalyptic explanations of the future customs are always belated and the result of a painstaking treasure hunt for correspondences between the two periods. The revelation promised by *The Book of Dave*'s subtitle is, again, partial at best and readers undergo interpretative difficulties that metafictionally parallel the misinterpretations of the Book's post-apocalyptic readership.

In his introduction to Revelation, Self identifies 'the visceral repulsion towards the bodily, the sensual and the sexual' as a primary characteristic of the biblical text (1998: xii). This is particularly evident in the misogynist imagery deployed by John for, as Keller remarks, in Revelation 'women appear only as whores and virgins, not as subjects of relationship but as abject emblems of male dread and desire' ([1996] 2005: 163). Tina Pippin reinforces this point by identifying the apocalyptic plot as 'a misogynist male fantasy of the end of time' and by summarizing the female presence in the biblical text as follows: 'the Bride is made into polis, city [the New Jerusalem], the Whore gang raped and burned and eaten, the Woman Clothed with the Sun is a reproductive vessel who is exiled subsequent to giving birth, and Jezebel is destroyed' (1999: 117, 119). Through the post-apocalyptic society, whose systematic oppression of women is the result of Dave's divorce-induced vengeful revelation, *The Book of Dave* brings to the fore, and disarms through parody, the misogyny of apocalyptic discourse, underscoring how the apocalyptic dualism between good and evil, the elect and the non-elect, is inherently gendered.

As Pippin observes (1992: 199), the gender politics of Revelation are based on the destruction of dangerous female sexuality and seductiveness, as exemplified by the horrible deaths of Jezebel (Rev. 2:18-2:29) and the Whore of Babylon (Rev. 17, 18), as well as by the control over the erotic power of the Woman Clothed with the Sun (Rev. 12) and the Bride (Rev. 19, 21). This patriarchal oppression is reflected in *The Book of Dave*'s post-apocalyptic chapters. On Ing, women are 'chavs', namely slaves, abused, raped and beaten, while bearing the brunt of the work required to support the community. They are forced to wear the 'cloakyfing', a garment which protects men from the sight of their 'chellish' immodesty – where 'chellish', from Michelle, means evil and, in its etymology, stresses, again, the self-referentiality of Dave's revelation. Dave's Law structures life in order to minimize women's power over children and hence over men. Children spend half of the week with their mothers and half with their fathers, as prescribed by the 'Changeover', and to avoid the contamination of the 'daddies' by the 'mummies', men and women live separated, as decreed by the 'Breakup'. Hardly by chance, the Drivers, namely the priests of Dävinanity, are 'queers – men who ha[ve] no desire to father children' (*BoD* 59) and hence, in the terms of Revelation and its 144,000 men who remain pure and chaste to follow the Lamb, cannot be 'defiled with women' (Rev. 14:4).[19]

The post-apocalyptic Breakup between the sexes signals the demonizing gender binary underlying the allegedly harmonic renewal at the core of apocalyptic teleology. As Pippin argues, 'The New Jerusalem is a woman, but women are not included in the utopian city' (1992: 195). Women are instead scapegoats, victimized, marginalized and controlled as the embodiment of seductive evil, so that the apocalyptic 'Utopia is not whole, but rather maintains this separation and hierarchy of power. The transformation of society in the Apocalypse is only partial transformation' (Pippin 1992: 204), and always a transformation that benefits men. With its origin in Dave's post-divorce fury, Self's post-apocalyptic society parodically exposes the misogyny of apocalyptic discourse as an 'engine of empowerment for socially marginalized male[s]' (Keller [1996] 2005: 59), something that also applies to Bruno in *The Flood* and Bertis in *Player One*. Apocalyptic discourse, with its promise of order and triumphant futurity, appeals to the disenfranchised, real or imaginary, but as the critical temporalities of the contemporary post-apocalyptic novel show, it ends up propping up oppressive power structures with its absolute truth claims and demonizing distinctions between good and evil.

These distinctions are foundational to the apocalyptic Last Judgment, after which the utopian New Jerusalem comes about in Revelation, and with it the final triumph of good over evil that is central to the sense-making function of the

---

[19] Iain Robinson points out how 'the amplification of Dave's anger at Michelle into an institutionalized misogyny' can also be read in terms of the novel's recontextualization of the Curse of Ham (Gen. 9), 'the way in which the crimes of the father go on to haunt subsequent generations' (2013: 95). As he explains, 'Genesis 9 describes how Noah, having been witnessed drunk and naked by his son Ham, and subjected to his ridicule, places a curse on Ham's son Canaan and his descendents [sic]. It seems like no coincidence that Self should have chosen Ham as the name for his future island community, and by doing so highlighted the theme of a son cursed for his father's sins' (2013: 90).

apocalyptic paradigm and its construction of history. Judgment is parodically transposed in the post-apocalyptic sections of *The Book of Dave* through the trials of Symun, his son Carl, and the latter's mentor Antonë Böm. After claiming he has found a Second Book by Dave, denying the Breakup and the Changeover, Symun is sent to New London to stand trial for 'flying' – where flying cannot but be heresy in a society entirely dominated by a cabbie's worldview – and Carl suffers the same destiny, together with Böm, when he attempts to find out what happened to his father. That Carl is brought to trial like his father already suggests a parodic inversion of the apocalyptic Last Judgment, for Self's post-apocalyptic judgment, made in the name of a preposterous god, never ends with its profound injustice, failing to establish the ultimate moral order at the core of apocalyptic logic. But it is the fact that the trials over flying are modelled on the present-day cab drivers' Knowledge test that most contributes to the parodic deconstruction of the apocalyptic plot and its sense-making function. The books of the Last Judgment – 'the dead were judged out of those things which were written in the books' (Rev. 20:12) – parodically correspond to the 'a4s' of the all too human Book of Dave. The deeds according to which the dead are judged in the Bible become the Knowledge of the streets of a city destroyed centuries before. The fearsome and tyrannical PCO, acting in place of the divine judge, has as its main principle that 'Objects in the mirror ... [m]ay appear larger than they are' (*BoD* 423). In other words, in the mirror of the PCO one looks even guiltier than one really is, a comic distortion of present meanings that emphasizes the unfairness of this judgment. Just as the Last Judgment of Revelation, the judgment of the fliers is allegedly meant to facilitate the advent of the celestial New London – a patent equivalent of the biblical New Jerusalem – as New London 'will only be restored by restitution of the pure and original Dävinanity' (*BoD* 178). But *The Book of Dave*'s critical temporality indicates how this apocalyptic construction of the future is just a narrative, a simulacrum that power deploys to preserve the status quo.

Through New London, Self parodically deconstructs the apocalyptic motif of the New Jerusalem and the utopian teleology it encapsulates. The adjective 'new' signals the connection with the divine kingdom of Revelation and its utopian renewal, but this connection is ironically subverted, since the adjective signifies a post-apocalyptic temporal inversion, namely, the future return to a past stage of human history, a critical temporality that recurs in many of the novels I consider in this book. In *The Book of Dave*, temporal inversion is made tangible by the fact that the catastrophe has interrupted the present year count, so that this is zeroed and has to start again, with the new meaning of 'AD' embodying the ironic distance of parody.[20] Although New London is supposed to be a replica of London, it is a neo-medieval city, whose 'winding, muddy lanes and narrow, cluttered alleys bore no more relation to the city of Dave than a child's drawing to what it depicts' (*BoD* 307). New London's society is regulated by constant and ridiculous misinterpretations of contemporary usages, while its streets are full of famished peasants made mentally ill by the Changeover who indicate how Dave's revelation has brought about misery, rather than the promised apocalyptic renewal. Notwithstanding this harsh reality, for the post-apocalyptic inhabitants of Ing, New London is the fulcrum of faith: people greet each other by saying 'Ware2, guv' and replying '2 Nú Lundun', while the city described by the Book is seen as 'a heavenly world of marvels that might be built here, on earth' (*BoD* 307), a veritable New Jerusalem on earth. Emphasizing the imbrication of apocalyptic logic and power, this apocalyptic faith is instrumental to the dystopian power of the PCO and the Dävidic dynasty. Since they elect themselves as the only ones capable of interpreting the Book and its plan for New London, this allegedly utopian telos ends up justifying their oppressions and allowing them to keep everyone in Ing subject to their despotic will.

Nowhere is the imbrication of apocalyptic logic and power clearer than in the relationship between New London and Ham, Symun's and Carl's native island. To the New Londoner Böm, Ham appears otherworldly: sick people come to this remote place to be healed by the oil of the motos, large animals which can be found only on Ham, where illness does not seem to exist. Old legends from a time before Dävinanity depict an even more 'veritable Arcadia' (*BoD* 59), which is later tainted by the new religion and establishment.[21] For Ham represents everything that the PCO and the Dävidic dynasty need to control in order to maintain their power. Not only does the island show that a better life is possible beyond the constraints of Dävinanity, but it is the place where Symun claims to have found Dave's Second Book, which denies the crazed precepts of the Book and, hence, the very basis of the power of the PCO and the Dävidic dynasty. The PCO thus sends a Driver to Ham who deploys the apocalyptic simulacrum of the 'imminent erection' of New London to 'sa[p] the will of the Hamstermen to

---

[20] This is another element Self appropriates from *Riddley Walker*: after a long period when 'no 1 write down no year count', the Government starts using 'O.C.', which means 'Our Count', as opposed to the pre-apocalyptic AD, which is tellingly interpreted as 'All Done' (Hoban [1980] 2002: 125).

[21] Self's parodic approach does not leave the utopia of Ham untouched, however. The 'rap' to the Mutha, the female goddess of the Hamsterwomen, is the children's song 'She'll Be Coming 'Round the Mountains' (*BoD* 303), which once again signals the comic post-apocalyptic misinterpretations of the readers' present.

maintain their own more laborious paradise' (*BoD* 130). The Driver imposes the most rigorous separation between men and women and the elimination of the motos, creatures which the PCO considers taboo. Arcadia becomes 'a torture garden' (*BoD* 304) and the last post-apocalyptic chapter sees the triumph of the PCO and of the dystopian New London on the utopian Ham: women wear their 'cloakyfing' very tight and sexual abuse is rampant, people are starving and all the motos are lined up to be killed. Even the final hint to a possible rebellion guided by Carl and Böm does not offer much hope, since it is not hard to imagine that the PCO and the Dävidic dynasty will retaliate with a gory repression – although it is significant to point out that the indeterminate note of the conclusion of the last post-apocalyptic section subverts the narrative sense of an ending, in line with the open conclusions that dominate the contemporary post-apocalyptic novel.[22] With its association to dystopian temporal inversion and oppressive state and religious power, New London parodically subverts the utopian teleology at the very core of apocalyptic discourse.

Indeed, as typical of the contemporary post-apocalyptic novel, *The Book of Dave*'s critical temporality presents us with a dystopian, rather than utopian, teleology to history, the fulcrum of which is the environmental catastrophe. Threatening images of water that prefigure the rising sea water levels generated by global warming recur in the pre-apocalyptic narrative (*BoD* 218, 263, 279, 404–405, 465). One of these images is an advertisement: 'water began to flood between the buildings, a tidal bore that came surging along the rivers of light …. Then the flooded concourse wavered, fragmented and was replaced by a slogan: DISANI MINERAL WATER, A NEW WAVE IS COMING' (*BoD* 294). The ad's ironic distance from the gravity of biblical doomsday prophecies assumes a bitter undertone, as it gestures to capitalism's environmental risks, to which we shall return in Chapters 3 and 4, while the incorporation of global warming into advertisement signals capital's 'fantasy structure', a 'presupposition that resources are infinite, that the earth itself is merely a husk which capital can at a certain point slough off like a used skin, and that any problem can be solved by the market' (Fisher 2009: 18). After all, global warming threatens the very foundations of capital, endless accumulation and expansion, which the ad unabashedly perpetuates.

Dave's clearest vision of the coming ecological apocalypse takes place when, after therapy, he is in full possession of his faculties, free from the Knowledge, the 'screen' and the 'mirror', and hence from his crazed revelation:

---

[22] The same indeterminate note features in the novel's concluding chapter, set in the pre-apocalyptic world, as Self ends the book with Carl pondering over his future.

The great wave came on, thrusting before it a scurf of beakers, stirrers...... [follows a long list of plastic objects] forming salt-bleached reefs, which would remain there for centuries, the lunar pull of the new lagoon freeing spiny fragments to bob into the cockle-picking hands of *know-nothing carrot-crunchers* who would scrutinize them and be filled with great awe by the notion that anything ever had – or ever would be again – Made in China. (*BoD* 404–405)

The 'MadeinChina', a symbol of contemporary global consumerism and capitalism, comes indeed to denote for the post-apocalyptic Ing the creation of the world 'out of the maelstrom' with plastic, 'the vital clay' (*BoD* 58, 75), so that, what is merely present-day waste, is interpreted as sacred residue of the primordial chaos. It is the above vision that compels Dave to write his Second Book, where he warns Carl that 'the family of humankind may have, at best, three or four more generations before the BREAKUP, before they find themselves sundered from the MUMMY EARTH' and that 'there cannot be – not now, not ever – a new London' (*BoD* 421). As Robinson argues, 'The language that Dave had previously applied to divorce and his relationship with Michelle is reapplied to a more fundamental split, that of man from nature. His appeal is that we should turn our backs on modernity's project of trying to achieve a better world – a New Jerusalem – through industry and capital' (2013: 96). If there is any revelation at all in Self's parodic *Revelation of the Recent Past and the Distant Future*, it is about the risks of the apocalyptic construction of history, in particular as encapsulated in the modern capitalist ideology of unfettered progress and accumulation, which is leading to the environmental apocalypse of consumer society.

The very plot of *The Book of Dave*, with its back and forth movement in time, complicates a linear narrative progression towards the sense of an ending and 'renders problematic the traditional idea of a temporal line orientated to the right towards progress' (Sorlin 2006: 102). Synchronic images of London reinforce this critical temporality. The city is a 'time tunnel, connecting the past with the present' (*BoD* 34) and, we may add, with the future, as the post-apocalyptic people work to re-erect it. London has 'ceased to evolve' in a linear and teleological fashion, but its history is defined by 'auto-cannibalism' (*BoD* 167, 95), in that the city continues to be built out of the materials of its past layers, so that its future is nothing other than its own past. This is also true of the post-apocalyptic future more broadly, which in the critical temporality of temporal inversion is a neo-medieval future, and of Dave's revelation, which in a hallucinatory synchronicity conflates present, past and future around the image of London, the fulcrum of the cabbie's life. The city's 'deep time' (*BoD* 95) is also that of the psyche, and the various uncanny similarities between pre- and post-apocalyptic chapters – from the parallels between the Skip Tracer employed by Dave (*BoD* 163–164) and the Chief Examiner of Carl's trial (*BoD* 425) to those between Gary Finch's pre-apocalyptic protest alongside the Fighting Fathers (*BoD* 398–454) and Gari Funch's post-apocalyptic protest against the final slaughtering of the motos (*BoD* 449), to the motos being marked with 'CalBio Tech' (*BoD* 19), the company for which one of Dave's fares is working (*BoD* 32), and their names replicating Carl's baby names, who is also described by the cabbie as a moto (*BoD* 419) – raise the nagging doubt that the post-deluge world should be read as a mere hallucination of Dave's. Self leaves the suspicion unanswered, but the hypothesis that Ing may just be a figment of Dave's imagination complicates to the extreme the possibility of reconstructing a linear and teleological development to the novel's history and ultimately reaffirms the key notion of this parodic critical temporality: apocalyptic logic is always self-referential and instrumental to the moment in which it is deployed. As Carl Dévúsh comments while contemplating the pit in which the Book was allegedly found, 'Its revelation was only in its emptiness – a void on to which any idea or belief might be superimposed' (*BoD* 384). As *The Book of Dave* illustrates, apocalyptic history is a technology of power/knowledge which serves the interest of those who self-referentially articulate this construction or exploit its 'absolute truth' to their advantage, positing themselves and their worldview as the culmination of history.

Taylor's *The Island at the End of the World* presents us with a similar self-referential apocalyptic construction of history. Seven years before the events recounted in the novel, the world was hit by the 'Great Flood' and Ben's family boarded the ark he had built. Ben and his children, Finn, Alice and Daisy, survived the deluge and managed to reach the titular island while Mary, Ben's wife, died saving their little child, Daisy – or so Ben's story goes. For with Will's arrival – sent by his aunt Mary, who, it turns out, did not die but fled the island – and Alice's rebellion against her father, Taylor progressively discloses that Ben invented the Flood story and created the island by digging a giant moat, so as to bring up his children far from the perverting influence of contemporary civilization. In exposing Ben's Flood as the product of a deranged mind, Taylor, just like Self, parodically foregrounds the dystopian implications of the apocalyptic paradigm and interrogates the world-making power of narratives.

As suggested by the epigraphs which introduce the novel's two parts, *The Island at the End of the World* parodically appropriates two apocalyptic narratives from Genesis, the Flood and the Fall, in addition to elements from

Revelation. The first epigraph is from Genesis 8:5, a passage in which the waters of the Flood start decreasing and land begins to be seen; the second is from Genesis 2:17, which establishes god's prohibition on eating from the tree of knowledge. The two epigraphs trace a narrative trajectory that is entirely internal to Ben's point of view: from the utopian Eden emerging after the Flood to a new Fall, where the forbidden knowledge, indicating the ironic distance of parody, is not the biblical knowledge of good and evil but, rather, the knowledge of the truth about the father's fictions. The gender distinction between the novel's two parts is significant, for it signals Ben's patriarchal oppression. While Ben's Flood story constitutes the uncontested premise of the first part of the book, narrated alternatively through Ben's and Finn's interior monologues, it is then deconstructed in the second part, narrated alternatively through Ben's and Alice's interior monologues. The voice of Alice, the Eve of Ben's paradise, comes to question her father's stories and seeks to pry them open, that is, to dispute their absolute truth value and epistemic primacy. But Ben's perspective takes over at the end of the novel, attempting to reinscribe apocalyptic logic and to reclose his narratives, after the narrowly escaped Fall of his 'utopian' society.

Taylor's choice of homodiegetic narrators and interior monologues limit readers to the characters' perspectives and, more specifically, to the point of view of those who are bound to the island and to the fictions which construct it, for Ben's voice is the dominant one in the novel's polyphonic narrative and his fundamentalist perspective informs the very structure of the book. Just as the children are tricked by Ben into thinking that they are the survivors of a catastrophic Flood, so are the readers, who only see things through the children's points of view and Ben's. In this sense, it is no coincidence that Will, the only character who is external to the island, is not a narrator at all. Taylor only gradually undermines Ben's reliability, making readers experience the world-making power of narratives, and in particular, how persuasive and despotic the apocalyptic metanarrative and its simulacra can be. This power is encapsulated by Ben's obsessive refrain *'They must never know'* (emphasis in original), which often appears in the short form *'They must never'*, as if, through this excision, Ben wanted to exorcize the possibility that his children managed to subvert his apocalyptic technology of power/knowledge. As Astrid Bracke argues, *The Island at the End of the World* underlines 'The role that narratives play in how we interpret the world', for Ben 'allows his children to read only a book of fairy tales, the Bible and a collection of Shakespeare's works', which 'literally shape how they perceive and interpret the world' (2017: 38). We find here another declination of the trope of the post-apocalyptic archive, namely, how power manipulates the archive of narratives accessible to the wider public in order to inform worldviews and strengthen its despotic hold.

The biblical Flood myth, upon which Ben heavily draws, is an apocalyptic narrative about beginnings and not merely about endings, for the collapse of the antediluvian world is followed by utopian renewal. As Norman Cohn underlines, for centuries exegetes interpreted the Genesis Flood as 'prefiguring the End of Time' (1996: 23).[23] The very reason for god's wrath in Genesis – humankind's wickedness (Gen. 6:5-6:13) – parallels Babylon's sins in Revelation (Rev. 17-18), while god's acting as 'a judge who is outraged at the infraction of the divinely established law' (Cohn 1996: 16) in the first book of the Bible is echoed by the Last Judgment of the final book (Rev. 20:11-20:15). Taylor makes this connection explicit by combining the imagery of destruction of the two biblical texts: 'the rains fell upon the earth and the waters rose and the thunder roared and the lightning flashed brighter than the sun illuminating horrors … and we watched through the portholes [of the ark] as Babylon fell and became the habitation of the devils' (Taylor [2009] 2010: 98), the latter part a direct quotation from Revelation 18:2, with Babylon typically signifying a corrupt civilization for Ben.[24]

At the same time, the way in which the post-diluvian age is presented in Genesis 'recalls – and was certainly intended to recall – the original creation of the world' (Cohn 1996: 14), with its pre-Fall Edenic qualities (Gen. 9:1-9:3), for what has drawn humankind for millennia to the Flood myth is not only the fear, mixed with fascination, of god's wrath, but also, and perhaps especially, the apocalyptic fantasy of being among the chosen ones who survive the deluge and are hence granted a new and better world. In Ben's Flood narrative, destruction and renewal are one. The post-deluge island is an 'UNCONTAMINATED' 'paradise', purified and washed clean of every sin by the waves of the Great Flood (*IEW* 3, 6) – where the words written in capital letters in the novel visually suggest Ben's deranged fundamentalism, as in *The Book of Dave*. The island is to Ben a new creation, a new 'Eden' (*IEW* 30) that also corresponds to the regeneration associated with the trope of the New Jerusalem. The image of the island, in Gilles Deleuze's terms, is itself suggestive of an apocalyptic dynamic: a violent cleansing leaving just enough behind – the island – for a 'second origin'

---

[23] This interpretation is reinforced by the Gospels of Matthew and Luke (Matthew 24:37-24:39; Luke 17:26-17:7), where one finds a parallel between the unexpectedness of the Flood and that of the Second Coming.

[24] All further references to Taylor's *The Island at the End of the World* as *IEW*.

(2004: 13), full of utopian possibilities. Deleuze indeed connects the image of the island to the myth of the Flood, for 'The ark sets down on the one place on earth that remains uncovered by water, a circular and sacred place, from which the world begins anew. It is an island or a mountain, or both at once .... Here we see original creation caught in a re-creation' (2004: 13). Taylor thus appropriates the apocalyptic tropes of the Flood and of the island to parodically deconstruct them from within.

Fuelled by a fundamentalist reading of the Bible, Ben is similar to those members of apocalyptic sects who, tired of the continuous deferral of the end and the ensuing utopian renewal, try to accelerate their advent by committing mass suicide.[25] Only, instead of committing suicide and similarly to Crake's Paradice project, Ben makes up his own end, the Flood story, and creates his own utopian New Jerusalem, the island. Ben's behaviour can be framed through what Baudrillard terms a 'fatal strategy of time' which, in seeking to 'shoot straight ahead to a point beyond the end', 'falsif[ies] ends and the calculation of ends, falsif[ies] time and the occurrence of things, hurr[ies] them along, impatient to see them accomplished, or secretly sensing that the promise of accomplishment is itself also false' – which it obviously is, since historical teleology constitutes, in Baudrillard's terms, the 'immense simulation model' (1994a: 8, 7) at the core of both religious and modern temporality. Worried that the divine pledge of salvation might be just, as Finn reports, a 'lusion' (*IEW* 65), Ben paradoxically produces his own apocalyptic simulacrum.[26]

This fatal strategy of time derives from the 'tension between [the] desire and deferral' (Keller [1996] 2005: 94) of the end inherent in apocalyptic temporality, for while the succession of events is rendered meaningful and coherent by teleology, it is essential to the existence of history itself that the end which sustains its systematization of time does not take place. The apocalyptic end is an aporetic notion, where 'aporia', in Derrida's terms, from the Greek '*a*' (without) and '*poros*' (passage) is etymologically 'the difficult or the impracticable, here the impossible, passage, the refused, denied, or prohibited passage, indeed the nonpassage, which can in fact be something else, the event of a coming or of a future advent which no longer has the form of the movement that consists in passing, traversing, or transiting' (1993: 8). Applying Derrida's reflections on the aporia of the end as death to the apocalyptic end we could argue that the latter

---

[25] See Bromley and Melton (2009), for instance, on the mass suicides of the Order of the Solar Temple, the Branch Davidians and Heaven's Gate.
[26] Finn's peculiar phonetic spelling is aimed at 'get[ting readers] inside his mind. He's not writing those words – he's thinking them' (Taylor 2008).

is aporetic in that 'The coming or the future advent of the event would have no relation to the passage of what happens or comes to pass' (Derrida 1993: 21), for the apocalyptic end brings about the end of time itself. The end is a liminal notion, which can guide our interpretations of the flow of time but which cannot be experienced or represented, as we shall see further in Chapter 2 with the absent apocalypses of Cormac McCarthy's *The Road* (2006) and Jim Crace's *The Pesthouse* (2007). In other words, as Taylor's critical temporality suggests, the end cannot but be a self-referential construct, just like Ben's Flood.

The Island at the End of the World parodically exposes the temporal mechanisms which are central to the functioning of the apocalyptic metanarrative, namely, the foreshadowing of the end and the discontinuity between the pre-apocalyptic and the post-apocalyptic era, as the manipulative fabrication of an unhinged mind. In apocalyptic history, as we have seen in the *Left Behind* and dispensationalism, the flow of time is relevant merely insofar as it is relentlessly advancing towards its telos, and past and present are interpreted as replete with signs foreshadowing this end and the ensuing utopian renewal. Through parody, however, Taylor emphasizes how these interpretations are always articulated from the viewpoint of an end which can only be a self-referential narrative construct, as it is beyond human epistemic possibilities. Ben occupies a fictitious post-apocalyptic position, and his equally fictitious analepses illustrate how apocalyptic logic constructs a sense of an ending to history through what Bernstein and Morson term 'backshadowing', that is, 'a kind of retroactive foreshadowing' (Bernstein 1994: 16), which effectively 'turns the past into a well-plotted story. Everything conspires to produce the outcome we know; loose ends, which intimate other possibilities, are drastically reduced or entirely eliminated' (Morson 1994: 236). Ben, indeed, retrospectively superimposes on his past a teleological and deterministic order which serves his own ends by allegedly foreshadowing the Flood and the 'utopia' of the island.

As his story goes, an earthquake, part of a series of disasters that Ben backshadows as divine 'warning[s] … of what was to come' (*IEW* 34), prompts the man's conversion. This event is described by appropriating Revelation 6:12-17:

> [A]nd lo the sun became black and the moon became as blood, and the stars of heaven fell unto the earth, and every mountain and island were moved out of their places, and the president and the senators and the shareholders and copywriters hid themselves in the lobbies of skyscrapers, and said to the skyscrapers, Fall on us and hide us from the face of Him that sitteth on the throne, for the great day of His wrath is come. (*IEW* 33)

In the ironic distance of parody, the 'kings', the 'great' and 'rich men' of Revelation, hiding 'in the mountains', become in Ben's version the 'president', the 'shareholders' and 'copywriters', hiding in 'the lobbies of skyscrapers', thus identifying Western, and in particular American, capitalism as responsible for divine wrath, an element further emphasized by Ben's use of the trope of Babylon. In Revelation, the sins of Babylon, the 'great city, which reigneth over the kings of the earth' (Rev. 17:18), are 'less traditionally religious than economic. The spiritual foulness of the empire emanates from the gross capital accumulation of its elites' (Keller [1996] 2005: 75). The city is described predominantly through its commercial activities (Rev. 18) and the causes of the system's collapse are its internal contradictions, for 'Babylon will be burnt and devoured by "her" own beasts, an apt allegory of the voracious power drives at the top of the pyramid as well as of the nonsustainable practices which eat up its base' (Keller [1996] 2005: 75).[27] Drawing on these elements, in Ben's memories of the past 'money answered all things', 'all was vanity and lies' (*IEW* 34, 33), and he backshadows America as 'prideful and doomed', destined to be destroyed at the hands of god because of its defining features: spiritual 'emptiness and greed' (*IEW* 163, 32). After the earthquake, Ben sees 'the Light': he quits his job in advertising and converts to Christianity, finally feeling 'a sense of freedom, of rightness' (*IEW* 34).

It is then that God reveals to him that 'Behold I, even I, do bring a flood of waters upon the earth, to destroy all flesh, wherein is the breath of life and everything upon the earth shall die, all but YOU' (*IEW* 97) – a sentence which echoes Genesis 6:17-6:18. Ben indeed constructs his character in his own Flood story as the just Noah (Gen. 6:8-6:9), whose moral and god-fearing behaviour foreshadows his deliverance from the deluge and his admittance to the New Jerusalem of the island. But in the ironic distance of parody, the divine revelation of the imminent Flood is conveyed to Ben through 'the lightwaves and the pixels' of the TV and 'the hissing baby monitor' (*IEW* 97). Instead of receiving precise instructions by god on the dimensions and shape of the ark, as happens in Genesis (Gen. 6:14-6:16), Ben borrows a manual from the library, called *How to Build an Ark*, while the animals saved from the deluge are only a dog, a cat, a few goats and chickens – a far less heroic feat than Noah's. It is the very identification of Ben with Noah which strikes the readers as parodic, for the former's behaviour is the opposite of the righteousness central to the biblical figure in the Flood story.

[27] Here we can see the 'strange doubleness' of Revelation (Keller [1996] 2005: 18), and by extension traditional apocalyptic logic, that is, its revolutionary potential to critique imperialist and capitalist practices, which coexists with its potential to prop up these same oppressive structures, as we shall further see in the following chapters through my analysis of the import of apocalyptic logic on American imperialist ideologies, the nexus of colonialism and the Anthropocene, and neoliberalism.

Violent and subject to outbursts of rage which get even worse when he is drunk, Ben appears in the novel as unhinged and a 'tyrant', as Alice calls him.[28] Indeed, he explicitly associates his own actions with 'righteousness' when he hits the girl and denies her access to the 'Knowing Tree', which, by affording a panoramic view over the fake island, would reveal his lies (*IEW* 52–53).

In *The Island at the End of the World*'s critical temporality, apocalyptic foreshadowing is a mere narrative strategy that deploys the simulacrum of a utopian teleology to conceal and enforce despotic practices. Similarly to Crake's and Bertis's manipulative use of apocalyptic discourse, Ben's backshadowing is aimed at persuading his children that every event in the past built up to their presence on the island, the New Jerusalem granted to them by god, where they can live 'happily ever after', as Daisy is fond of repeating (*IEW* 119, 151, 215). Ben claims his stories are aimed at making 'their lives better safer freer more beautiful' (*IEW* 197), but the New Jerusalem Ben constructs is a projection of his hopes and dreams – an 'I-land' in Finn's peculiar spelling – and a dystopian space of confinement to the rest of the family, especially to Alice, who feels that this 'life ISN'T worth living' (*IEW* 52). The apocalyptic 'oneness of truth' (Keller [1996] 2005: 88) articulates a self-referential totalizing/totalitarian temporality, which in its closure claims to know what is best for everybody, deterministically erasing alternative accounts, events and people that transcend its teleology. 'I-land' captures the solitary and tyrannically enclosed nature of the place, keeping at bay any 'you' who does not belong to the family and to what Ben considers a utopian world. As Ben replies to Alice, it is life out of the island which is not worth living (*IEW* 52). And when Alice and Will attempt to contest Ben's apocalyptic narrative, they likely pay for this betrayal with their life (the novel is not explicit on the children's disappearance).

Where in the traditional apocalyptic paradigm it is the catastrophe that brings about a temporal discontinuity, in *The Island at the End of the World*, with the ironic distance of parody, it is Ben's fictitious Flood narrative that creates a clean break from the pre-apocalyptic world. 'Ben's control over his children', Caroline

---

[28] Ben is thus closer to the post-Flood Noah, who gets drunk and then curses his son Ham (Gen. 9:21-9:27), although this episode, according to Cohn, may describe 'someone other than Noah the hero of the Flood' (1996: 14). Yet it is significant to note that it is on this episode that parodic deconstructions of the Flood myth, such as Taylor's, Timothy Findley's *Not Wanted on the Voyage* (1984) and David Maines's *The Flood* (2004), often draw. Cf. for instance Julian Barnes's *A History of the World in 10½ Chapters* (1989), which explicitly confronts the issue: 'Perhaps this is why your scholars are so jumpy, so keen to separate the first Noah from the second: the consequences are awkward. But the story of the "second" Noah – the drunkenness, the indecency, the capricious punishment of a dutiful son – well, it didn't come as a surprise to those of us who knew the "first" Noah on the Ark. A depressing yet predictable case of alcoholic degeneration, I'm afraid' (Barnes [1989] 1990: 30).

Edwards argues, 'depends on his control of time and on their understanding of their own pasts' (2012: 490). The apocalyptic renewal can be entered only by leaving behind, once and for all, the past. As Ben explains in an entry of his journal, 'you can't live in paradise with the stains and burns of hell still clinging to you. You have to wash yourself clean, to grow a new skin – you have to bathe in the waters of Lethe' (*IEW* 197). By concealing the knowledge of the events which brought the family to the island, the Flood plays the role of Lethe, the river of forgetfulness of Greek mythology, and, just like Dave's Book, Ben's narrative is exposed as an apocalyptic technology of power/knowledge that veils, rather than unveils, the truth.

Ben's journal entry also signals how the discontinuity between the pre- and post-apocalypse is a moral one at its heart. As Keller argues, the apocalyptic 'polarity of good versus evil was from its incipience inseparable from a linearizing temporality in which the past and present were subsumed under the power of evil, while the imminent future remained pristine' ([1996] 2005: 94). Ben's 'I-land' frames a way of thinking about time, as well as space, in terms of moral dualism, where the 'I' embodies goodness, purged from the evil 'you' of the antediluvian world. Drawing on the connection of Babylon with femininity and sex, Ben depicts the 'past' civilization to his children as a temptress, whose sinful lure was performed by making people addicted to her seductions. As Finn dutifully reports, emphasizing, yet again, apocalyptic foreshadowing, 'all them things the tall houses an the bright lights an the shiny metals all them things wer dictive. People grew sest with em they came greedy an dicted an thats what made the bad things happen thats what made the flood' (*IEW* 78). But Babylon has of course not fallen and its evil 'you' encroaches upon the pure 'I' of the 'I-land', as signified by Will's arrival. Alice, who falls in love with her cousin, in her father's eyes 'defil[es] [his] land ... with the carcasses of [her] abominable deeds' (*IEW* 113). Ben's misogynist language foregrounds the imbrication of apocalyptic logic with patriarchal power. As discussed, the apocalyptic paradigm is 'a quintessentially male product', in which 'the extremes of innocence and of vice are coded as impersonally feminine' (Keller [1996] 2005: 28, 11). While Ben associates Daisy, 'sweet and lazy', with innocent perfection because, given her young age, she is sexless (*IEW*, 57, 191), Alice, 'the poisoned chalice', is a sinful 'harlot' (*IEW* 58, 136) who contaminates the 'I-land' through 'the lewdness of [her] whoredom' (*IEW* 150) – an image that frames how Alice morphs into Babylon to Ben's eyes. As a male, Finn is, instead, his father's ally. The 'I-land' is so important to the boy that, when his cat dies, he expresses his sadness in terms of it – 'Like some body took the I out of I-land' (*IEW* 14) – and when he discovers Alice and Will kissing, with a sentence that recalls the Genesis Fall and his father's patriarchal perspective, he muses that they should be 'banisht from the I-land' (*IEW* 116). *The Island at the End of the World*'s critical temporality thus debunks the temporal and moral dualism central to apocalyptic history as a narrative strategy bound up with self-righteous, misogynist and coercive elements. Ben not only seeks to disconnect the present from the past but to make the latter unreachable and sinful, so that the children's only possibility in life should be the future he has designed for them, his 'I-land' at the end of the world.

Contrary to the Genesis Fall, the knowledge that Will, the 'serpent' (*IEW* 201) of Ben's Eden, promises Alice/Eve is inherently temporal, consisting as it does in a revelation that fissures the deterministic inevitability of Ben's apocalyptic history by disclosing its self-referentiality. Alice remembers good things about the past world and, more importantly, elements that do not fit the official Flood story, such as Mary on the island. In other words, Alice remembers elements that subvert the totalizing closure of Ben's apocalyptic history and its absolute truth claims. Yet, drawing on apocalyptic moral dualism, the man tries to brainwash her into thinking that those memories depend on the fact that she has been corrupted by the pre-apocalyptic world. Alice's sections unfold while she attempts to go beyond Ben's sense of an ending and break free from the web of coercive narratives in which she is entangled. Tellingly, Alice's sections are mostly turned towards the past, the temporal dimension that Ben has closed by narrating it as apocalyptically discontinuous from the present and by providing a totalitarian narrative which is not open to any alternative version. Her interior monologues slow the linear succession of events down by revolving solely around the last few hours of her life, and continuously interrupt a teleological narrative chronology by returning, through flashbacks, to the salient moments of her love story with Will and her conflict with her father. Alice's monologues thus exhibit a structural resistance to apocalyptic history. Yet they also illustrate the insidiousness and determinism of Ben's apocalyptic fiction: her narrative hardly conceives of any future at all, but for the very immediate one, gesturing to the difficulty in imagining something beyond the world Ben has constructed.

As in *The Book of Dave*, if there is any revelation in *The Island at the End of the World*, this is about the constructedness and dangers of apocalyptic history, specifically, the deterministic and totalitarian closure of apocalyptic teleology, which obliterates any alternative version of events and possibilities. Perched on top of the Knowing Tree, Alice receives confirmation of what Will has told her, that there was no mighty deluge and that the island is not an island. Ben, though, conceives of this climactic moment by drawing on Genesis 3:3-5 and identifying himself with the enraged god of the Fall (like Dave, he is prophet and god of this post-apocalyptic world):

> But of the Tree which is in the midst of the garden, I have said, Ye shall not climb it, neither shall ye look from it, lest ye DIE. But the serpent said to my daughter, Ye shall NOT surely die. For your father doth know that in the day you look from this Tree, then your eyes shall be opened, and you shall KNOW .... She sees. She knows. Behold, the girl is become as one of us. (*IEW* 201)

In Ben's euphemistic terms, Alice then 'ha[s] to go' (*IEW* 206), because she has forced open the absolute closure of her father's history, challenging it as a self-referential construct. Her narrative stops mid-sentence and is never resumed. The male perspective of the 'I-land' takes over and Ben seeks to close his apocalyptic fiction once more by destroying the Knowing Tree in the hope that the truth about the outside world will be inaccessible to Finn and Daisy. His last words in the novel are a quotation from Revelation 21:4, which re-establish the apocalyptic utopia of the island: 'For He will swallow up death in victory and wipe away tears from all faces. And there shall be no more death, neither sorrow, nor crying. Neither shall there be any more pain' (*IEW* 210).

Taylor's last chapter, however, challenges this deterministic closure. In the final pages, Finn reports that Ben is crying, which directly contradicts Ben's utopian faith that 'there shall be no more death, neither sorrow, nor crying' and indicates that the 'I-land' has undergone a Fall for his creator as well. Even to Finn the 'I-land' is no longer utopian. The opening of the boy's last section recalls the opening of his first. But while in the latter Finn cheers because spring is coming, at the end of the novel the boy grieves for the approaching winter, symbolizing the end of a happy period in his life. For if at the beginning Finn feels sure of his own identity as much as he is 'Shure ... [he] lives on an I-land and [his] Ma died wen [he] wer lil. Shure as ... the seas the sea' (*IEW* 7) – namely, as much as he is sure of all the things about which his father is lying – by the end of the book Finn realizes that 'theres no thing you can ever truly no' (*IEW* 211), debunking the totalizing truth-claims of apocalypticism. The ominous enjambement of the very final sentence of *The Island at the End of the World* – 'Weare all go-ing to live haply/Everafter' (*IEW* 215) – appropriates the endings of fairy tales only to subvert it by reinforcing the disturbing coercion of the 'happy' life Ben has imposed upon his children, signalling the dystopian dangers of absolutizing one's own values and closing one's own narratives, granting them epistemic primacy over others.

As I have argued in this chapter, in opposition to prophecy fiction like the *Left Behind*, the contemporary post-apocalyptic novel draws on biblical apocalyptic discourse to subvert it through the critical distance of parody, foregrounding the violence and misogyny of its absolute distinctions between good and evil, its self-referential constructedness and the deterministic coercion of its teleology. The import of apocalyptic history, these fictions' critical temporalities show, is that agency and contingency are replaced by a Manichean script where everything happens for a reason, prefiguring the destruction of evil and the triumph of good. Thus, those who appropriate this script, like the PCO and the Dävidic hierarchy in *The Book of Dave*, Ben in *The Island at the End of the World*, and the various prophetic figures of *The Leftovers*, *Station Eleven*, *The Flood*, the *MaddAddam* trilogy, and *Player One* can justify oppressions in the name of that utopian renewal which awaits them, the self-appointed pure. As many of the fictions discussed in this chapter suggest through their American setting, this script is particularly pernicious in the United States, where the influence of Christian fundamentalism, and apocalyptic logic more broadly, is extensive. It is to this pervasive American apocalypticism, which I term Apocalypse America, that the next chapter turns.

2

Apocalypse America

On a desolate shore, it is the ruins of the Statue of Liberty sticking out of the sand that reveal that the 'alien' planet, currently inhabited by intelligent apes, is Earth in the far future. The message of this iconic scene from the movie *Planet of the Apes* (1968) is clear: humankind destroyed itself – 'you finally blew it all up', Colonel Taylor screams in despair – and the Statue testifies to the end of the ideals of American freedom, democracy, justice, and more broadly, American exceptionalism, of which the Statue is a symbol. The appearance of the Statue of Liberty in *Planet of the Apes* is not an isolated occurrence. As Gerry Canavan (2008) writes in a blog post collecting images of the wrecked Statue of Liberty in popular culture, this has been 'the quintessential icon of disaster since the 1940s', with recent examples in films like *The Day After Tomorrow* (2004), *Cloverfield* (2008) and *Independence Day* (1996).[1] Indeed, America is itself the quintessential setting for post-apocalyptic narratives, even by non-American authors.[2] This predominance of narratives of an American wrecked future is hardly coincidental, for, I argue in this chapter, apocalyptic time is central to the American project from modernity to the contemporary moment. Considering examples of post-apocalyptic novels set in the United States and focussing on Cormac McCarthy's *The Road* (2006) and Jim Crace's *The Pesthouse* (2007), which I discuss drawing on the archival materials of the Jim Crace Papers held at the Harry Ransom Center (University of Texas at Austin), I show how the texts' critical temporalities foreground and question

---

[1] In literature, an example of the ruined Statue of Liberty trope is J. G. Ballard's *Hello America* (1981), where the statue is under water. Matthew Sharpe's *Jamestown* (2007), which we shall discuss in Chapter 3, opens instead with the collapse of another New York City landmark, the Chrysler Building, signalling the novel's critique of capitalism.

[2] In addition to the novels discussed in this chapter, examples of contemporary post-apocalyptic novels set in America include Emily St. John Mandel's *Station Eleven* (2014), Edan Lepucki's *California* (2014), Chang-rae Lee's *On Such a Full Sea* (2014), Margaret Atwood's *MaddAddam* trilogy (2003–2013), Nathaniel Rich's *Odds Against Tomorrow* (2013), Karen Thompson Walker's *The Age of Miracles* (2012), Thomas Mullen's *The Revisionists* (2011), Sam Taylor's *The Island at the End of the World* (2009), Lee Konstantinou's *Pop Apocalypse* (2009), Michael Cunningham's *Specimen Days* (2005) and David Mitchell's *Cloud Atlas* (2004).

the apocalyptic foundations of nationalist and imperialistic ideologies that construct America as the culmination of history.

The chapter opens by charting the typical critical interpretation of the contemporary flourishing of the post-apocalyptic genre as a response to the perceived sense of crisis and heightened fragility in the West following the terrorist attacks on the World Trade Center and the Pentagon on 11 September 2001, as well as the construction of 9/11 itself as an apocalyptic event in the contemporary sense of 'apocalypse'. This construction, however, risks obscuring the far more pernicious resurgence of traditional apocalyptic logic and its self-righteous moral dualism in the War on Terror. I trace this resurgence, while positioning it in the longer history that characterizes Apocalypse America, that is, the nation's self-legitimation through the utopian teleology of apocalyptic logic. From the colonial myth of a New World to the image of a 'city upon a hill', an example set by the early Puritan communities to the rest of the world; from Manifest Destiny, the belief that westward expansion in the continent was divinely sanctioned, to American exceptionalism, the belief that American values are unique and superior, to the good versus evil rhetoric of the War on Terror, I show how America's conception of its own history and hegemony is intrinsically apocalyptic. The chapter then turns to a survey of post-apocalyptic novels set in the United States and written by both Americans (Louise Erdrich, Colson Whitehead and Cormac McCarthy) and non-Americans (Egyptian-Canadian Omar El Akkad and British Jim Crace) to reflect upon the nation's global hegemony. I argue that El Akkad's *American War* (2017a), Erdrich's *Future Home of the Living God* (2017), Whitehead's *Zone One* (2011), McCarthy's *The Road* and Crace's *The Pesthouse* do not merely respond to the sense of a growingly insecure post-9/11 world but, through their critical temporalities, undermine the apocalyptic vision of history at the core of American ideologies, bringing to the fore its constructedness and how it is instrumental to American imperialistic projects, including the War on Terror.[3]

Since, as Will Self writes, 'Every generation gets the end-of-the-world anxiety it deserves' (2002: vi), it is no surprise that the twenty-first-century flourishing of post-apocalyptic novels set in America, and indeed the bourgeoning of the

---

[3] There is a long history of texts which undercut exceptionalist ideologies by depicting a ruined American future. See P. Williams, for instance, for an analysis of fictions where 'the polarity of the frontier is reversed, and the United States is pushed back or recolonized after a nuclear war' (2011: 16–17) and Seed for a discussion of invasion narratives in which 'the underside of manifest destiny is explored – the fear of failure, defeat, subversion' (2007: 64). My analysis of the contemporary post-apocalyptic novel shows, however, how these post-apocalyptic reversals should be read as critiques of the apocalyptic conception of history that props up the nation's ideologies.

genre more broadly, has been related to the cultural atmosphere of trauma and risk after 9/11. Claire Colebrook, for instance, qualifies the post-9/11 novel as having a 'dominant post-apocalyptic mode', arguing that in this genre 'the concrete historical event of 9/11 intensified and captured a broader shift toward a terror that could not be figured in terms of human-to-human violence, but would instead take the form of a certain violence and violation of humanity as such' (2015: 4, 5–6). Turning to the trauma paradigm that dominates many analyses of the American novel after the terrorist attacks, Richard Gray reads the indeterminate nature of *The Road*'s apocalypse through the unrepresentability of the traumatic experience:

> The unnameable remains unnamed, except in its human consequences. The reason for this indeterminacy is simple. McCarthy is dealing with trauma; and, in the first instance, with trauma of a very immediate kind. It is surely right to see *The Road* as a post-9/11 novel, not just in the obvious, literal sense, but to the extent that it takes the measure of that sense of crisis that has seemed to haunt the West, and the United States in particular, ever since the destruction of the World Trade Center. (2011: 39–40)[4]

Similarly, Lydia Cooper claims that 'The apocalypticism of *The Road* seems to be a response to an immediate and visceral fear of cataclysmic doom in the United States after the terrorist attacks on 9/11' (2011: 221). Erica Sollazzo also reads *Zone One*, set in Manhattan, in the financial district where the attacks took place, as reflecting a 'moment in which the city is a hotbed of anxieties and possibly the biggest locus of national uneasiness' (2017: 459).[5] Novelists themselves trace a link between their post-apocalyptic writings and the terrorist attacks. Whitehead observes that 'Since 9/11, I've had a heightened sense of insecurity and anxiety, and I think that definitely plays out [in *Zone One*]' (Schulman 2011). By the same token, on the subject of *The Pesthouse*, Crace comments that 'The idea of America's apocalypse is in the air and it has been since 9/11, and especially since the War in Iraq' (Balée 2007: 518).

It is not only that twenty-first-century post-apocalyptic fiction, especially when it is set in America, is inevitably read as informed by 9/11. Rather, in a hermeneutic circle, the terrorist attacks are themselves read through apocalyptic imagery of catastrophe. Slavoj Žižek asks: 'when we watched the

---

[4] For other analyses of the 9/11 novel informed by trauma theory see, for instance, Keeble (2014) and Versluys (2009). As explored later on in the chapter, against Gray's interpretation (2011), I read *The Road*'s absent apocalypse as a critique of the epistemic primacy of the end in apocalyptic logic.

[5] Cf. also Kyle William Bishop's argument that '*Zone One* transcends pulp fiction by piercingly exploring the national trauma of September 11 through the depiction of New York City as an infected biological body' (2015: 90).

oft-repeated shot of frightened people running toward the camera ahead of the giant cloud of dust from the collapsing tower, was not the framing of the shot itself reminiscent of spectacular shots in a catastrophe movie[?]' (2002: 11). His question is echoed by Baudrillard's observation that 'The countless disaster movies bear witness to this fantasy [of the collapse of the West, embodied by the collapse of the Twin Towers]' (2003: 7). September 11 is thus construed as apocalyptic in the contemporary sense of the term as 'catastrophe', as perfectly captured by the 12 September 2001 cover of the *Daily Mail*, featuring the word 'Apocalypse' emerging out of the dust of the crumbling Twin Towers, as well as by the term 'ground zero', which typically denotes the centre of a nuclear explosion and then comes to be the moniker for the destroyed World Trade Center site.

A post-apocalyptic sensibility, far from the utopian renewal of the traditional apocalyptic paradigm, dominates indeed literary and theoretical responses to the attacks. Don DeLillo writes in *Falling Man* that 'These are the days after. Everything now is measured by after' (2007: 138). Jonathan Franzen (2001) describes 9/11 as an end that precipitates a shift from an old world to a new, dangerous world: the survivors 'were stumbling out of the smoke into a different world. Who would have guessed that everything could end so suddenly on a pretty Tuesday morning?'.[6] René Girard similarly defines the attacks as a 'seminal event' that is impossible to see as the 'mere continuation of the violence of the twentieth century' but that instead inaugurates a 'new world dimension' (Doran and Girard 2008: 20–21), something reinforced by Kristiaan Versluys, who claims that 9/11 is 'ultimately a semiotic event, involving the total breakdown of all meaning-making systems' (2009: 2). These reflections are steeped in an exceptionalist rhetoric compounded by the very idea of '9/11', where the year of the event is elided – and note of course, too, how the term subscribes to the American convention of putting the month before the day.[7]

---

[6] Cf. a similar post-apocalyptic image in President George W. Bush's speech on 20 September 2011: 'All of this was brought upon us in a single day, and night fell on a different world, a world where freedom itself is under attack' (2001b).

[7] As Marc Redfield observes, '"September 11" presupposes and demands knowledge: "September 11" – the year understood, the attacks understood. Imperatively and imperialistically, the empty date suggests itself as a zero-point, the ground of a quasi-theological turn or conversion: *everything changed* that day, as the US mainstream media so often tells itself. A new history begins here, at this calendrical ground zero: previous September 11ths disappear into that zero, from the bureaucratically trivial ("9-1-1 Day") to the historical and tragic (September 11, 1973, the date of Salvador Allende's overthrow in a US-backed coup that ushered in one of the worst reigns of terror in the twentieth century) .... the global hegemony of American media and culture imposes the sign of th[is] erasure worldwide' (2007: 58–59). For a critique of the 'aesthetic of noise' which is used to reinforce the exceptionalism of 9/11 in contemporary American fiction, see Sykes (2018).

As the above repetition of the term 'event' suggests, pronouncements over the apocalyptic/catastrophic exceptionalism of the terrorist attacks gesture to the philosophies of the event, whereby the latter is conceived as 'something shocking, out of joint, that appears to happen all of a sudden and interrupts the usual flow of things; something that emerges seemingly out of nowhere, without discernible causes' (Žižek 2014: 2).[8] An event is, in other words, something radically new, exceptional, unpredictable, that cannot be reduced to previous conceptual categories and a linear and univocal trajectory of causes and effects – something in itself problematic in the case of 9/11, as it risks obscuring the geopolitical situation from which the terrorist attacks were born. Thus, the contemporary apocalyptic rhetoric that underlies the reflections above serves to convey the seismic change that 9/11 is supposed to have heralded in relation to history. As Baudrillard writes, 'The whole play of history and power is disrupted' by this 'absolute event, the "mother" of all events' (2003: 4). What is being disrupted is the triumphant apocalyptic history traced by the neoliberal order, whereby, in Fukuyama's formulation (1992) and as we shall further see in Chapter 4, the whole world is, allegedly, peacefully and naturally converging upon the telos of history, the global free market and an American-style liberal democracy. 'What is at stake', Baudrillard continues, is 'globalization itself', 'that order which has virtually reached its culmination' (1992: 11, 12). Thus, in the face of 9/11's threat to an understanding of history informed by traditional apocalyptic logic, political discourse not only evokes an apocalyptic sense of catastrophe but also resurfaces a far more insidious traditional apocalypticism.

The aftermath of the attacks saw the United States reasserting the belief in their exceptional role in history as the nation which would free the world from terrorism and realize the historical telos of universal democracy and freedom through an operation that, with its name 'Enduring Freedom', recalled the eternal utopianism of the New Jerusalem. As Gray maintains, 9/11 brings traditional 'apocalyptic thinking to the centre of American politics' (2007: 107). Apocalyptic discourse satisfies the need for an overarching metanarrative that allows one to construct the crisis of 9/11 in the reassuring terms of moral dualism – the good American elects versus the evil others, the 'enemies of freedom' (Bush 2001b) – and make sense of it as a phase in a preordained teleology. As ever, apocalyptic logic, with its divisive and totalizing moral binaries – 'Either you are with us or you are with the terrorists' (Bush 2001b) – also fuels violence, namely, the

---

[8] On the notion of event, see also Badiou (2005).

War on Terror. The war was framed by the Bush administration as a 'conflict between good and evil' (Bush 2002), where the United States' 'responsibility to history' was 'to answer these attacks and rid the world of evil' (Bush 2001a).[9] But as suggested by the ruse about Iraq's weapons of mass destruction, which the country did not possess, as opposed to its abundant oil reserves, global neoliberal hegemony and oil control were also at stake in the 'messianic imperialism' of the War on Terror, aimed at ensuring a 'pax Americana', which is, at once, a 'pax apocalyptica' and a 'pax economica' (Keller 2005: ix, 4, 48). Apocalyptic logic, that is, effectively serves power's interests – notice, in this sense, how the apocalyptic rhetoric around an enduring global freedom chimes with neoliberalism, whose cardinal assumption, rife with contradictions (Brown 2015), is that individual freedoms and democratic rights are best guaranteed through the logic of the free market. Thus, the combination of this rhetoric and assumption led the US-appointed Coalition Provisional Authority to impose on Iraq a neoliberal state apparatus aimed at facilitating foreign capitalist accumulation (Harvey 2005: 5–7). The Iraqis, in other words, were finally made 'free' to become neoliberal. While the adoption of the apocalypse pattern in response to 9/11 derived from an alliance between neoconservatives and the Christian Right, which, as explored in Chapter 1, is profoundly influenced by the apocalyptic beliefs of dispensationalism and the Rapture (Bush is himself a born-again Christian who adheres to postmillennialism (Gray 2007: 116–117)), the presence of apocalyptic beliefs in American culture and politics is hardly new.

Signalling how foundational apocalyptic logic is to the nation, Keller speaks of 'The United States of Apocalypse' (2005). Indeed, as Douglas Robinson states, 'the very idea of America in history *is* apocalyptic' (1985: xi; emphasis in original), and it has been so ever since the colonization of the significantly named New World, an image we shall further explore in Chapter 3. Christopher Columbus's 'conviction that his mission represented the fulfilment of apocalyptic prophecy ... initiated what was to become a perennial imaginative association of America with the promise of apocalyptic historical renewal' (Zamora 1989: 7). John Winthrop's famous sermon of 1630 about a 'city upon a hill' cemented this promise by conceiving of America as a virtuous new beginning in history, granted to the Puritans by god, far from the corruption of the Old World (Zakai [1992] 2002) – the usual apocalypse pattern we have seen in Chapter 1 translated into

---

[9] The latter extracts features in a speech which asserts the belief in an intrinsically apocalyptic understanding of history where, in god's 'moral design', 'Grief and tragedy and hatred are only for a time. Goodness, remembrance and love have no end' (Bush 2001a). For other instances of political uses of apocalyptic rhetoric post-9/11, see Gray (2007) and Lincoln (2006).

spatial terms. The Revolutionary War 'was used to rekindle a sense of... the new nation as a place of rupture with history, a newly made lantern that would beam the doctrines of enlightened democracy to the rest of the world' (Quinby 1994: xviii–xix). American exceptionalism and Manifest Destiny represent, indeed, the 'Americanization of an apocalyptic myth', for in these two metanarratives 'The idea of a messianic saviour, which was at the core of early Christianity, became the idea of a Redeemer Nation' (Gray 2007: 112) guided by the ideals of freedom and democracy – a sense of universal mission that continues to underwrite post-9/11 politics.[10] The religious apocalyptic narrative has gradually become a secular metanarrative – by taking the form of the modern myth of material and technological progress or of the neoliberal convergence, for instance – but the premise remains the same: the United States self-legitimizes as the culmination of a progressive history and as the true agent of the historical telos, variously conceived throughout the centuries.

It is this Apocalypse America that the critical temporalities discussed in this chapter deconstruct. El Akkad's *American War* challenges the apocalyptic discourse of messianic innocence surrounding the American intervention in Afghanistan and Iraq; Erdrich's reverse evolution in *Future Home of the Living God* targets the exceptionalist image of America as the culmination of history; the delusional operation 'American Phoenix' in Whitehead's *Zone One* compounds the constructedness of the nation's self-legitimation through apocalyptic utopian teleology; while McCarthy's *The Road* and Crace's *The Pesthouse*, on which the chapter focusses, rupture Manifest Destiny and the very image of the New World with their post-apocalyptic journeys and the temporal inversion of their future old worlds.

El Akkad's *American War* is set in the last decades of the twenty-first century, in an America that is not the *United* States anymore, for part of the South is a protectorate of Mexico and part has again seceded, forming the Free Southern State and bringing about the Second American Civil War. The cause of this war is fossil fuels: in a world ravaged by global warming, where entire areas of America are under water – Florida, for instance, is now the Florida Sea – the South opposes the Sustainable Future Act Bill, which prohibits the use of fossil fuels, and state intervention in its core business. As its generic

---

[10] Cf. J. Beck on the analogies between Manifest Destiny and post-9/11 politics: 'George W. Bush's declaration of a global "war on terror," not to mention his early, misguided but revealing preference for Wild West analogies – Osama bin Laden is wanted "dead or alive" and will be "smoked out"; Afghanistan is "wilder than the Wild West" – ... relies on a collective memory of the West as the overdetermined site of American becoming, where legitimate force is invoked in the name of justice and freedom' (2009: 285).

title suggests – which American War? – this novel is not only concerned with the fictional Second Civil War. Indeed, while the key role played by fossil fuels in the novel's post-apocalyptic scenario signifies the Anthropocene's environmental risks, it also arguably gestures to the politics of oil underlying the War on Terror. El Akkad explains that the idea for *American War* came to him when listening to a foreign policy expert discussing the invasion of Afghanistan and the question 'why do they [Afghans] hate us [Americans] so much?' (El Akkad 2017b). This question, posed by Bush himself in his address to the nation on 20 September 2001 (2001b), encapsulates the discourse of messianic innocence at the core of post-9/11 politics. 'They hate our freedoms', Bush claimed (2001b), an answer that cements the apocalyptic binaries good versus evil, us versus them, and reinforces America's sense of its universal mission to defend 'our' freedoms from 'their' evil threats. El Akkad's novel, however, challenges this apocalyptic stance of messianic innocence.

Troubling the binary us versus them, *American War* 'tak[es] these conflicts that have happened very far away, and to people who don't have much of a voice, and recast[s] them as elements of something very close to home' (El Akkad 2017b). Drones, known as the 'birds', no longer strike far away countries but the South of the United States, and a prison camp styled after Guantanamo Bay now tortures American citizens, invoking the same rhetoric of the state of exception, that is, 'set[ting] aside the normal guidelines [of the law] because the circumstances themselves [a]re far from normal' (El Akkad 2017a: 225).[11] Rupturing the discourse of America's messianic innocence and apocalyptic mission, Albert Gaines, who fought in Iraq and Syria in wars that, *American War* implies, were the fallout of post-9/11 American foreign policy and were later declared wrong, muses: 'they'll use words like democracy and freedom and equality and the whole time both you and they know that the meaning of those words changes by the day, changes like the weather' (*AW* 142). In an inverted geopolitical situation that spells the end of American exceptionalism and of the nation's apocalyptic vision of itself as the culmination of history, the United States' role of defender of freedom and democracy is taken over by the Bouazizi Empire, formed of a collection of nations across the Middle East and North Africa after the Fifth Spring Revolution.[12] Just like the United States previously, however, the Empire is hardly acting to protect freedom and democracy. '[W]e

---

[11] All further references to El Akkad's *American War* as *AW*. On the post-9/11 state of exception and the contemporary novel, see De Boever.

[12] In its name, the Empire pays homage to Mohamed Bouazizi, a Tunisian street vendor whose self-immolation protesting police abuses helped kick-start the Tunisian Revolution and the Arab Spring of 2011.

intend [the Bouazizi Empire] to be the most powerful empire in the world. For that to happen, other empires must fail' (*AW* 306), Joe explains upon giving the protagonist Sarat a lethal biological weapon that will decimate the American population, decry the failure of America's apocalyptic project once and for all and affirm the Bouazizi Empire's similarly teleological conception of its own history. *American War* thus exposes the apocalyptic construction of history in all its deadly complicity with power.

The critical temporality of Erdrich's *Future Home of the Living God* undermines, instead, the progressive history of American exceptionalism. In a very literal form of temporal inversion, in a near-future America evolution has seemingly reversed, though nobody knows what is going on, so much so that people are taking to the streets with question mark signs. As one of the characters puts it, 'the first thing that happens at the end of the world is that we don't know what is happening' (Erdrich [2017] 2018: 93).[13] Similarly to *The Road* and *The Pesthouse*, as we shall see, and subverting the sense-making function of the end, Erdrich's apocalypse remains obscure. Prehistoric animals begin to appear, while domestic animals stop breeding. Human reproduction itself is at risk: fewer and fewer 'originals', that is homo sapiens children, are born and manage to survive, and there are confused rumours that women are now giving birth to more primitive human species.[14] In an attempt to perpetuate homo sapiens, just as in Margaret Atwood's dystopian classic *The Handmaid's Tale* (1985), a theocratic government, the Church of the New Constitution, takes hold of pregnant and fertile women, including the novel's narrator Cedar, for 'womb volunteering'. The Patriot Act, born soon after 9/11 'to protect innocent Americans from the deadly plans of terrorists dedicated to destroying America and our way of life' (Department of Justice 2001; note once again the apocalyptic discourse of messianic innocence), is now invoked by the new government to seize medical data, showing just how effective and versatile apocalyptic logic is in propping up power structures. Erdrich, indeed, began writing *Future Home of the Living God* 'during the George W. Bush era prompted partly by the use of fear to limit debate following the 9/11 terror attacks and partly by his stance on reproductive rights' (Welsh 2018), she then moved to other projects during the Obama administration, returning to the novel only after the 2016 election of Donald Trump, 'feel[ing] like things [we]re

---

[13] All further references to Erdrich's *Future Home of the Living God* as *FHLG*.
[14] A process of devolution also lies at the heart of Lidia Yuknavitch's *The Book of Joan* (2017), to which we shall return in Chapter 3 and the Conclusion: because of a 'geocatastrophe' and its radiations people lose all bodily hair and sexual markers, including genitalia, so that reproduction is impossible.

going backward again' (Atwood and Erdrich 2017). But while the inspirations for Erdrich's novel are clearly post-9/11 politics, issues around reproductive rights, as well as global warming (*Future Home of the Living God* is set at a time in which snow is a rare occurrence), it is important to note the shape that her American end times take.

Instead of the rhetoric of steady technological advancement, progress and the exceptionalist image of the nation as the culmination of history, when watching the news, people are confronted with graphics depicting 'humanoid figures growing hunched as they walked into the mists of time, while in the background Beethoven's Fifth Symphony dissolves into a haunting series of hoots and squawks' (*FHLG* 52). Even this despairing graphic of temporal inversion is, however, still too much of a linear narrative, an attempt at imposing a sense-making order, albeit a negative one, on a time of disorder. As a palaeontologist puts it, 'if evolution has actually stopped ... Life might skip forward, sideways, in unforeseen directions. We wouldn't see the narrative we think we know. Why? Because there was never a story moving forward and there wouldn't be one moving backward .... We might actually see chaos' (*FHLG* 54–55). There is no teleology, no meaningful narrative, governing human history, not even evolution, which is made of 'genetic mishaps' and 'agonizing failures' (*FHLG* 107). *Future Home of the Living God* is thus structured around the tension between Cedar's attempt at a chronological and linear narrative of her foetus's development in her diary and her knowledge that this narrative is a mere construction she is articulating to preserve her sanity and avoid confronting the chaos of historical contingency surrounding her.[15] For one thing, her baby might even not be an 'original' and thus their development would be impossible to chart. As Cedar writes in her diary, 'I want to see past my lifetime, past yours, into exactly what the palaeontologist says will not exist: the narrative' (*FHLG* 67) – notice the parallels with Kermode's theorization of the sense of an ending as a construct in which we project ourselves 'past the End, so as to see the structure whole, a thing we cannot do from our spot of time in the middle' ([1966] 2000: 8). But *Future Home of the Living God* frustrates this desire for an apocalyptic sense of an ending. Not only does the novel refuse to solve the mystery of the evolutionary catastrophe but Cedar, sedated as soon as labour is completed, can never know what species her baby belongs to nor if they survive, and the book closes, open-endedly, on Cedar musing on an unknowable and unimaginable future in which

---

[15] As we shall further discuss in the Conclusion, in recording an account of the times in which she is living, Cedar joins the ranks of many other characters in dystopian/apocalyptic fictions who find solace from their precarious situations in writing.

the last snow falls on Earth. Similarly to the temporal inversions of *The Road* and *The Pesthouse*, *Future Home of the Living God*'s critical temporality serves to debunk the sense-making function of the end and the apocalyptic understanding of history at the heart of American ideologies as mere constructions.

It is to the 'narrative of America', and especially to the 'American dream of reinvention' that, as Whitehead states in an interview (Fassler 2011), *Zone One* speaks. Taking place over three days a few years after a zombie plague has decimated the world's human population, *Zone One* revolves around the attempts of the American post-apocalyptic government, now based in Buffalo, to rewind the catastrophe and bring back the old ways. Apocalyptic imagery of renewal is at the core of the project and of the buzzwords specialists in Buffalo create to prop up the effort of reconstruction: 'It was a new day. Now, the people were no longer mere survivors, half-mad refugees, a pathetic, shit-flecked, traumatized herd, but the "American Phoenix"' (ZO 79), guided by the omnipresent slogan 'We Make Tomorrow!' and by the 'pheenie', short for Phoenix, anthem 'Stop! Can You Hear the Eagle Roar? (Theme from *Reconstruction*)'.[16] As the image of the eagle – the national animal of the United States – suggests, the pheenie optimism about the possibility of reconstruction taps into the myth of American exceptionalism. New York, and specifically the area of Lower Manhattan named zone one, is the symbolic heart of the American Phoenix operation and a messianic model for the rest of the world, for 'If you can bring back New York City, you can bring back the world' (ZO 97). Improbable icons of the exceptionalist mythology punctuate *Zone One*: a Rosie the Riveter manifests as soccer mom turned deadly zombie killer after her husband and children were eaten on Last Night (ZO 18), the night the plague began; a rugged 'cowboy right-winger … was going to show this vermin who was boss' (ZO 181); self-reliant American heroes, parodying Emerson, live for months in isolation on a catamaran in a Michigan lake or battle zombies with a pitchfork while barricaded in grain silos (ZO 43); and post-apocalyptic pioneers, the 'true homesteader[s]', lock themselves up in their Manhattan apartments (ZO 208). Not only does Whitehead satirically undermine these images of American exceptionalism but zone one's reconstruction fails, undercutting the apocalyptic discourse of renewal so foundational to the American New World and to the

---

[16] As Hurley points out, 'Reconstruction', with its echo of the post–Civil War period, carries with it 'the disavowed history of white supremacy' (2015: 314). Indeed, drawing on the Haitian heritage of the figure of the zombie and emphasizing *Zone One*'s 'postracial (in the sense of deracinated) protagonist, a character named after a white swimmer who is revealed to have been black only in the final pages of the novel', Hurley develops a reading of Whitehead's zombies as the 'nightmare that haunts the postracial dream: a nightmare of the [racist] past come to life' (2015: 313).

'Enduring Freedom' of post-9/11 politics – notice how 'zone one' echoes 'ground zero', metaphorically signifying the latter's potential renewal, which is then denied.[17]

Whitehead juxtaposes the deceitful apocalyptic promise of the American Phoenix's rebirth with the protagonist's mediocrity and scepticism about the very possibility of a future in this ruined world. It is telling that Mark Spitz is just the protagonist's post-apocalyptic nickname, for the catastrophe strips him of his identity, emphasizing his utter unexceptionality, a quality the narrative returns to time and again. As Mark Spitz muses, subverting the myth of the exceptionalism of the American hero and the nation itself, 'He had led a mediocre life exceptional only in the magnitude of its unexceptionality. Now the world was mediocre, rendering him perfect' (*ZO* 148).[18] While through their exceptionalist buzzwords and 'By processing the sweeper data [produced by those who sweep, i.e. kill, the zombies], the technocrats in Buffalo create prophetic projections that make the future imaginable, knowable, and subject to human control' (Sorensen 664–665), Mark Spitz rejects the lure of this apocalyptic sense-making pattern. The slogan 'We Make Tomorrow!' is for him a 'malware', a 'contagion in its own right' (*ZO* 24; 13) that he needs to eliminate in order to survive. Paralleling the static critical temporality that we shall find in *The Road*, where there is no future dimension possible for the survivors, to Mark Spitz, 'There was no when-it-was-over, no after. Only the next five minutes', for to make those next five minutes all delusional projections about the future need to be banished (*ZO* 59). Mark Spitz's scepticism about the government's apocalyptic narrative proves to be correct. Once the wall that had kept the zombies out of zone one falls, the apocalyptic promise of renewal of the American Phoenix out of the pervasive ash of the incinerated living dead is revealed to be a mere 'public relations stunt' (*ZO* 249), concocted to keep the dwindling population in check and motivated. The apocalyptic understanding of history, and the American myths it props up, is exposed to be as fragile as the barricades which temporarily allow the post-apocalyptic survivors to stay alive.

The barricade around zone one 'Keep[s] chaos out, order in' and, Mark Spitz muses, only makes literal those divisions upon which the country is founded

---

[17] 9/11 is evoked in the novel when Mark Spitz happens upon the World Trade Center subway station (*ZO* 212) and, as Bishop suggests, the omnipresent ash also 'clearly recalls the debris resulting from the fall of the twin towers' (2015: 92).

[18] Hurley also stresses that 'Mark Spitz's avowed averageness' is a 'recognizable means of black survival in a white world that places a high premium on the ability to live in between the poles of what Patricia Hill Collins has called a "simultaneous invisibility and hypervisibility"' (2015: 322).

(ZO 97, 102), from the binary Old/New World to the Us/Them of post-9/11 politics. Similarly to these apocalyptic binaries, the humans versus zombies distinction, in conjuncture with the historical teleology constructed through the PR operation of the American Phoenix, allows the survivors to impose a semblance of order on a time of disorder. But just like the American Phoenix, this binary does not hold, and not only because the wall around zone one falls heralding the widespread contagion of the scattered survivors. Rather, Mark Spitz repeatedly foregrounds similarities between the pre- and the post-apocalypse, humans and zombies, in particular, as we shall see in Chapter 4, through parallels between the zombified world and the pre-apocalyptic neoliberal system. In a variation of the wrecked Statue of Liberty trope, the Statue itself appears zombie-like in *Zone One*, rather than as the guarantor of freedom. Glossing Emma Lazarus's poem 'The New Colossus' (1883), 'Give me your tired, your poor,/Your huddled masses yearning to breathe free', engraved on a plaque in the Statue's pedestal, Mark Spitz, upon seeing Lady Liberty, comments 'Give me your poor, your hungry, your suppurating masses yearning to eat' (ZO 57). To Whitehead's protagonist, New York appears as a cannibalistic organism whose message to its citizens has always been, even prior to the plague, 'I am going to eat you up' (ZO 244). Just as the infectious zombies erode the mentality us versus them, the binary pre- versus post-apocalypse is continuously troubled by the narrative, challenging the very structure of apocalyptic temporality and its promise of a radical renewal after the end. 'The plague had a knack for narrative closure' (ZO 130), a closure that is of course far from the plenitude of the apocalyptic sense of an ending, for similarly to *The Road*, these are truly the end times, with no possibility of a rebirth, not even for America.

Both McCarthy's *The Road* and Crace's *The Pesthouse*, to which the rest of this chapter is devoted, depict journeys towards the coast in a dystopian post-apocalyptic America that is far from the utopian culmination of history at the core of Apocalypse America. *The Road*'s journey subverts Manifest Destiny with its lack of destination, while the man's precarious narrative that identifies him and his son as the 'good guys' who are 'carrying the fire' resonates with the exceptionalist discourse of the War on Terror to undermine it from within. Similarly, *The Pesthouse*'s post-apocalyptic pioneers not only represent the future-past of temporal inversion – something that parallels the wasteland's challenge to the apocalyptic trope of the New World in *The Road* – but reverse the direction of Manifest Destiny, as they travel east hoping to leave their American nightmare behind. Both texts refuse to disclose the nature of their apocalypses, and indeed hardly mention these catastrophes at all, elements that undermine the sense-making function of the end in apocalyptic logic and stand in stark contrast to the exceptionalist rhetoric surrounding the 'apocalypse' of 9/11.

The Road's subversion of apocalyptic utopian teleology through its uncompromisingly dystopian future is inextricably linked with the questioning of the apocalyptic role of America in history. Following John Cant, who considers McCarthy a 'mythoclast' because of the novelist's 'attack on the American metanarrative of exceptionalism' (2008: 74) throughout his oeuvre, I argue that McCarthy's ongoing concern with the debunking of national mythologies of history and the power structures they sustain – a concern most notable, among the earlier works, in the revisionist western *Blood Meridian* (1985) – reaches its apex with *The Road*, where the post-apocalyptic scenario allows the novelist to target the apocalyptic ideological core of America.[19] Set after the end of American exceptionalism, indeed of the United States themselves, *The Road* exposes the apocalyptic construction of history as a narrative which is complicit with power structures and is dangerously illusory. There is no New Jerusalem after the end, not even for the American 'good guys', the unnamed father and son who 'carry the fire' of civilization on their desolate journey, but only the 'borrowed world' of the wasteland (*TR* 130), a lack of futurity reinforced by the novel's circular plot.

'Borrowed time and borrowed world and borrowed eyes with which to sorrow it' (*TR* 130): the spatio-temporal connection in this sentence invites a reading of *The Road*'s landscape through the Bakhtinian notion of 'chronotope', that is, 'the intrinsic connectedness of temporal and spatial relationships that are artistically expressed in literature' (Bakhtin 1981: 84). In a chronotope 'time, as it were, thickens, takes on flesh, becomes artistically visible; likewise, space becomes charged and responsive to the movements of time, plot and history' (Bakhtin 1981: 84). I argue that *The Road*'s critical temporality is spatially embodied in two chronotopes central to the post-apocalyptic journey of the unnamed father and son: the wasteland and the road. These make tangible the survivors' 'sorrow', as in the dystopian post-apocalyptic America time and space are 'borrowed', that is, the survivors live precariously, without a real future perspective. The wasteland and the road signify a static critical temporality, akin to what Eric Cazdyn (2012) describes as the 'meantime' of the 'already dead', for although time objectively continues to flow, survivors perceive it as stuck in an uncertain and bleak present that does not lead anywhere, a present which is devoid of the possibility of significant change, eventfulness and, hence, futurity itself.

---

[19] In addition to Cant (2008), on McCarthy's revisionist approach to American history, see J. Beck (2009).

In discussing the chronotope of the apocalyptic narrative, Elana Gomel notes how this culminates in the death of time and the triumph of space since, in its perfection, 'the millennium is *static*. Situated beyond history, the millennium is free of flux, contingency and chance; its representations are always couched in spatial terms, as avatars of the New Jerusalem' (2010: 122; emphasis mine). The wasteland and the road, however, are dystopian spaces that convey an equally dystopian static temporality, which foregrounds the absence of a utopian renewal after the end, and hence the collapsing of the sense-making order the traditional apocalyptic paradigm projects onto history through utopian teleology. *The Road* is set at the end of (American) history, but this is very much unlike Fukuyama's formulation of 'global democratic capitalism' as the 'end point of mankind's ideological evolution' (1992: xi). Indeed, the novel's sense of a stalled present chimes, as we shall see in Chapter 4, with the temporality identified by critiques of neoliberalism, signalling the spectre of no future that haunts the current system and its 'utopian' end of history.

The Road's unspecified catastrophe has left America a 'wasted country', 'barren, silent, godless' (*TR* 6, 4), where barrenness is key to the image of the wasteland, from the grail stories onwards. Indeed, the novel's early title was *The Grail* (Cooper 2011). But *The Road*'s wasteland is clearly irrecoverable, as opposed to the possibility of regeneration central to the grail stories.[20] Thus, I argue that rather than being 'an apocalyptic grail narrative' (Cooper 2011), *The Road* subverts the traditional grail narrative to critique apocalyptic history. The fact that McCarthy qualifies his wasteland as 'godless' already indicates his subversion of the grail myth. The connection between the recovery of the Fisher King and that of the wasteland is severed, in that the father – the Fisher King, in Cooper's reading (Cooper 2011: 226–227) – dies towards the conclusion of the novel. And while the man, as Cooper underlines (Cooper 2011: 224–226), repeatedly describes the boy in terms evocative of the grail, the healing traditionally granted by the cup of Christ is absent. The depictions of *The Road*'s wasteland never provide the readers with any hope that the ecosystem can regenerate: 'everything [is] dead to the root' (*TR* 21); the trees are 'charred'

---

[20] Dhira B. Mahoney summarizes the various versions of the grail myth in relation to the motif of the wasteland as follows: 'the Waste Land [is] closely connected with the wound of the Maimed King [who coincides with the Fisher King in some versions]. The land is devastated, infertile, or at war. In the Perceval strain, the Waste Land is linked to the Question Failure [the failure to ask the right question, either about the king or about the grail itself], which either causes the devastation or prevents its recovery. (In the *Perceval* Continuations, Gauvain and Perceval do, respectively, restore the Waste Land by asking the Question.) In the *Queste* strain, on the other hand, the Waste Land is caused by the Dolorous Stroke [to the king] …. Whereas in the Vulgate *Queste* the restoration of the land is separated from the healing of the Maimed King, in the Post-Vulgate Cycle Galaad's action of applying blood from the Lance to the wound heals both King and land simultaneously' (2000: 8).

because of the fires that followed the catastrophe and 'limbless' (*TR* 8); the whole country is 'burned away' and 'cauterized' (*TR* 14); animals appear to be nearly extinct, and the novel's final paragraph, to which we shall return later in this analysis, powerfully restates the irrecoverable end of nature through the image of the bygone brook trout. By undercutting the possibility of regeneration traditionally associated with the image of the wasteland, McCarthy's wasteland, with its stunted growth, is a chronotope for the novel's static critical temporality, spatially embodying the lack of a post-apocalyptic utopian renewal and of futurity itself.

To further the unrelenting dystopian depictions of the wasteland, *The Road*'s landscape is almost monochromatic, as, similarly to *Zone One*, 'everything [is] covered with ash and dust' (*TR* 12). Black and grey dominate the post-apocalyptic scenario, with only sparse glimpses of other colours: the blue plastic tarp, yellow vests, the red scarves of the 'bad guys'. Apart from the father's dreams of the pre-apocalyptic world – dreams which are rich in colours and natural details, in stark contrast to the post-apocalyptic wasteland – the only different hues in the text are related to man-made objects. Nature has become devoid of the variety of its colours and the wasteland is characterized by an encroaching darkness, with 'Nights dark beyond darkness and the days more gray each one than what had gone before' (*TR* 3). The quasi-absence of light evokes, by inverting it, the biblical *fiat lux*. Where in the Book of Genesis (Gen. 1:3) the separation of light from darkness marks the beginning of god's creation of the world, here the advancing darkness suggests the unmaking of this creation after the apocalypse, a movement towards non-differentiation and the ultimate erasure of futurity. Rather than an apocalyptic renewal, what the readers witness is 'The ponderous counterspectacle of things ceasing to be. The sweeping waste, hydroptic and coldly secular. The silence' (*TR* 274), where the reference to the 'coldly secular' and silent 'waste' echoes the opening 'barren, silent, godless'.

This encroaching darkness subverts the 'unveiling' which is the etymological meaning of 'apocalypse'. The Book of Revelation is structured around acts of vision, emphasized by the recurrent expression 'And I saw', for Revelation is the product of god's injunction 'What thou [John] seest, write in a book' (Rev. 1:11). One of the motifs which recur in *The Road*, instead, is that of compromised vision. The dark and monotonous ashen wasteland, where there is 'nothing to see' (*TR* 4, 8, 9), continuously frustrates the sense of sight and, appropriately, in the opening sentences of the novel, McCarthy parallels the dimness of the post-apocalyptic world to a glaucoma, an eye condition which may lead to blindness. Indeed, both Ely and a man struck by lightning, whom the protagonists encounter on the road, are blind or nearly so. As Kevin Kearney argues, *The Road*, in its continuous denial of the possibility to see, 'ends up being speculative fiction that subverts speculation', especially given that at the text's core lies the 'structural absence' of the apocalypse itself (2012: 161). This gap in the narrative frustrates the readers' desire to see, their desire for an apocalyptic unveiling, and, therefore, undermines the apocalyptic epistemic primacy of the end, which, unspecified, cannot perform its sense-making function.

The only description McCarthy gives of the catastrophe is that of 'A long shear of light and then a series of low concussions' (*TR* 52). This single terse reference to *The Road*'s apocalypse, which is certainly an event in the sense of 'something shocking, out of joint, that appears to happen all of a sudden and interrupts the usual flow of things' (Žižek 2014: 2) in its both occurrence and consequences, stands in stark contrast to the barrage of exceptionalist rhetoric surrounding the alleged eventfulness of 9/11. The flash of light of *The Road*'s apocalypse is certainly not revealing in the traditional apocalyptic sense, in that it does not disclose a utopian renewal nor, indeed, the very nature of the disaster.[21] If anything, it sheds light on the novel's critique of apocalyptic history as just a myth, like the anti-apocalyptic revelations of Will Self's *The Book of Dave* (2006) and Sam Taylor's *The Island at the End of the World* (2009) discussed in Chapter 1. McCarthy signals this reversal of traditional apocalyptic unveiling through the interplay between light and darkness, vision and blindness. It is in the 'gray light' that the father 's[ees] for a brief moment the absolute truth of the world', that is, that the survivors are living on 'borrowed time' in the 'Darkness implacable ... [of] The crushing black vacuum of the universe' (*TR* 130). The 'absolute truth' of the 'black vacuum of the universe' is the opposite of the 'truth' of Revelation and of the plenitude of meaning given by the fact that 'there shall be no night there [in the New Jerusalem]; and they [the elect] need no candle, neither light of the sun; for the Lord God giveth them light' (Rev. 22:5). As Peter Boxall writes, the father's is 'the encounter with truth that is as unenlightening as death, and that is only thinkable as death' (2013: 219), as the end of the world, without any possibility of long-term human survival, let alone utopian renewal. The same critique of apocalyptic history as mere narrative features in the words of Ely. The character's name – the only name which appears in the novel – is replete with biblical echoes (Broncano 2014: 137–138). Yet, recalling

---

[21] Critics have often speculated on the nature of *The Road*'s apocalypse. Tim Blackmore (2009) and Cant (2008), for instance, read the novel as set in a nuclear winter scenario, Dana Phillips (2011) suggests the hypothesis of a comet, while Susan Kollin (2011) that of environmental crisis. The crux of the matter, however, is that all these interpretations are equally possible and that the event remains unspecified, which, I argue, encapsulates *The Road*'s critique of apocalyptic logic.

the critical distance of the prophetic figures analysed in Chapter 1, Ely sees, notwithstanding his compromised vision, that 'There is no God and we [the post-apocalyptic survivors] are his prophets' (*TR* 170), for they bear witness to the failure of utopian teleology and its sense-making project. In particular, since America's motto is 'In God We Trust', Ely's statement gestures to the demise of the nation's apocalyptic ideologies.[22]

As the father realizes, everything is 'predicated on a world to come' (*TR* 187), but it is this future dimension that is negated by *The Road*'s static temporality. When the end reveals itself to be a final catastrophe and the apocalyptic expectation for a better world to come a lie, the survivors' perception of time is deprived of order, meaning and even futurity itself. Time is frozen in a precarious present devoid of future perspective, a 'borrowed time' connected to a 'borrowed world', as the irrecoverable biosphere grants merely temporary survival. Indeed, the chronotope of the wasteland, with its stunted growth, reflects and reinforces this static temporality. Hardly by chance, the novel's only reference to the unspecified catastrophe begins with a memory in which 'the clocks stopped at 1:17' (*TR* 52). From that moment onwards 'Every day is a lie' (*TR* 238), as the objective flow of time does not truly signify the possibility of a future. Rather, in this hopeless situation, 'The day [is] providential to itself. The hour. There is no later. This is later' (*TR* 54) and it makes little sense to mark the objective passing of the days, which 'sloug[h] past uncounted and uncalendared' (*TR* 273).

Cant remarks how the wasteland is a recurrent motif in McCarthy's fictions, and defines it as a 'counter-mythic landscape' to the wilderness which 'offered the intrepid white man, whether Puritan or pioneer, the escape to freedom and the opportunity for conquest' central to American exceptionalism and Manifest Destiny (2008: 11–12). But, as we have seen, these two metanarratives articulate an apocalyptic understanding of American history. What is at stake in *The Road*'s 'counter-mythic' wasteland is, then, the critique of this conception of history. As Robinson points out, American apocalyptic ideologies are 'concerned with the end of old eras and the beginning of new eras, with the transition in space and time from an Old to a New World, from the Age of Europe (decadence, decay, death) to the Age of America (rebirth, return to primal innocence), in which America becomes the messianic model for the world' (1985: 2) – a conception

---

[22] Cf. the cover of Lionel Shriver's *The Mandibles: A Family, 2029–2047* (2016), where the motto becomes 'In God We Trusted'. In the world of Shriver's novel, American exceptionalism has been completely crushed by a series of economic crises and, symbolizing the end of this ideology, the United States have to give up their country code, 1, to China, which has replaced the United States as the world's biggest economy.

that, as discussed, continues to play a key role in twenty-first-century United States. Robinson's 'transition in space and time' resonates with the notion of chronotope central to my analysis. If one could frame the traditional conception of America as an apocalyptic chronotope, in that the nation represents the 'objectification of the apocalyptic millennial future' (Keller [1996] 2005: 141), *The Road*'s wasteland encapsulates an anti-apocalyptic American chronotope that critiques the image of the nation as the culmination of history. The wasteland reverses the trope of the New World as a bountiful territory where, in Robinson's terms, one can leave behind the Old World's 'decadence, decay, [and] death' – indeed, the wasteland reverses the trope of the New World *tout court*.

McCarthy's wasteland does not regenerate, and is therefore far from granting the 'rebirth, [and the] return to primal innocence' Robinson posits as characteristic of the New World. Rather, the end of nature, combined with the grey colour palette and the omnipresent ash, which leaves everything 'faded and weathered' (*TR* 8), suggest that this post-apocalyptic America is no New World but an old world, devoid of any future. The novel's recourse to the critical temporality of temporal inversion gives us a world that has reverted to a pre-technological and barbaric state: the government and all its infrastructures have collapsed, humankind is back to the basics of mere survival and reduced to scavenging for food amidst the ruins of the pre-apocalyptic society, while some people – the 'bad guys' – even resort to cannibalism. Language itself is losing its complexity, with 'The names of things slowly following those things into oblivion' (*TR* 88), and the wasteland features messages in runes and patterans which suggest that people are forgetting the pre-apocalyptic alphabet and are reverting to past systems of communication. To strengthen the impression of an old rather than New World, *The Road*'s temporal setting is as vague as its spatial one, and the novel appears at times to be set before the readers' present. One finds no recent technological objects; instead, the wasteland is scattered with 'traces from a pre-industrial past that have moved inexplicably to the surface' (Giggs 2011: 212), from a sextant to arrowheads and Spanish coins. These relics complicate a linear apocalyptic history and the temporal confusion thus generated, together with the unspecified apocalypse, efface the possibility of connecting the readers' America to the novel's wasteland through a coherent temporal plot, undercutting, once again, the sense-making function of the apocalyptic paradigm.

Just like the wasteland, the novel's road signifies that time is lived as if it is not flowing towards a possible future but as if it is static. Bakhtin defines the road as the 'chronotope of encounter', 'appropriate for portraying events governed by chance' and for conveying the idea of the flow of time, as 'time, as it were, fuses together with space and flows in it (forming the road)' (1981: 243–244). By providing the fictional place where the father and son meet other characters and face trials, the road drives McCarthy's plot forward – indeed, the journey on the road constitutes the entire narrative. This narrative forward motion might initially appear to suggest the road as a chronotope for the flowing of time, in consonance with the Bakhtinian understanding. And, since the conclusion of the novel coincides with the end of the journey on the road, given that the new family the boy joins after his father's death keeps away from the road, the temporal flow the road seemingly embodies would be teleological, in accord with the apocalyptic conception of history. Yet one only needs to pay closer attention to what actually takes place on McCarthy's road to see that the novelist subverts the teleological understanding of this chronotope. On the one hand, the road, strictly speaking, does not take the characters anywhere, and the journey is pervaded by a sense of futility and lack of direction that challenges the idea of a telos to the father and son's wanderings. As Boxall writes, 'Where the idea of the road offers the prospect of direction, a movement from A to B, the road here has thickened, coagulated, like the cold oleaginous sea that breaks leadenly on the novel's grey shore, so that neither the sentences in this work nor the world it describes has any forward momentum, any future orientation' (2013: 220). Boxall indeed notes that the sentences' sparseness of finite verbs 'carries an extraordinary stasis, a freezing of the kinetic energy that pushes narrative forward, that gives a sentence its direction and movement' (Boxall 2013: 219), a stasis that compounds what I have identified as the novel's static critical temporality. On the other hand, the novel's narrative structure, which reflects the journey on the road, consists of textual fragments and of the cyclical repetition of almost identical events, elements which complicate the sense of an ending and convey the idea that no significant change is possible for the man and the child after the apocalypse. Where the motif of the wasteland, traditionally associated with regeneration, serves in the novel as a chronotope that challenges the apocalyptic utopian renewal, the seemingly teleological chronotope of the road serves to subvert apocalyptic teleology.

Critics have attempted to locate the father and son's journey on the map of the United States (Morgan 2008; Rambo 2008) but, just like with the unspecified apocalypse, McCarthy is reticent in providing textual clues that unmistakably establish the route of the road. The lack of clear geographical details – a lack accentuated by the monotony of the wasteland, where the ash appears to have stripped the landscape of its identifying traits – conveys an impression of directionlessness, which paradoxically reaches its apex when the protagonists get to their destination, a southern coast. For, indeed, the only unambiguous geographical indication the text gives the readers is that the two are moving south, looking for a warmer climate – a direction, that of the south, which is relevant to the novel's critique of apocalyptic logic, as the following pages argue. The southern coast proves, however, to be as dead and inhospitable as the lands they cross to get there. The sea is not blue anymore but 'bleak [...]. Cold. Desolate. Birdless', 'one vast salt sepulchre. Senseless. Senseless' (*TR* 215, 222), descriptions which echo those of the irrecoverable wasteland. The term 'senseless' is revealing, as it denotes both the absence of sentient life in the 'sepulchre' of the post-apocalyptic sea and the futility of the journey to the coast, namely, the lack of a proper telos to their travelling beyond the father's desire to keep the child alive. Even this goal appears hardly sustainable in the long run. As the boy's mother knows only too well, for she commits suicide some time before the narrative begins, the father and son are living on the 'borrowed time' of the already dead as it is only a matter of time until the 'bad guys' find them and eat them, or until they are unable to find any more edible remains of the past civilization and die of starvation.

Thus, after reaching the inhospitable coast, the two protagonists go on walking and, this time, with no apparent destination. This sense of an open road and journey is not liberating. Rather, the impression conveyed is somewhat claustrophobic, in that no road could ever take the survivors anywhere. People are condemned to be always on the move, for the wasteland cannot provide them with an enduringly safe shelter – with a home – as epitomized by the episode in which the protagonists go back to the house where the man grew up, only to realize that they should not have gone there at all as that past is lost forever, or by the episode of the well-stocked bunker the two have to abandon because it is too exposed. The impossibility of ever reaching a telos in the father and son's travelling – and certainly not a utopian telos – frames the road as a chronotope for the novel's subversion of apocalyptic teleology. The apocalyptic end has come in the world of *The Road* but, rather than bringing about a utopian renewal, it has condemned the survivors to an endless peregrination – where 'endless' denotes both the lack of purpose and the lack of an end point, at least until death supervenes.[23]

---

[23] Cf. a similar existential situation in *Zone One*: 'There was no other reality apart from this: move on to the next human settlement, until you find the final one, and that's where you die' (*ZO* 257).

Just as with the wasteland, McCarthy's use of the chronotope of the road is intertwined with the critique of the apocalyptic understanding of American history. As Janis P. Stout underlines, 'From its beginnings, the American literary tradition has been characterized to a remarkable and peculiar degree, by narratives and images of journeys. It has been a literature of movement, of motion, its great icons the track through the forest and the superhighway' (1983: 3). The reason of the predominance of the journey motif in American literature, Stout argues, is that the nation's history itself has been 'pervasively concerned with journeys' (1983: 17). Yet the ur-journeys of American civilization, those of the 'discovery' and colonization of the New World, as well as those of the expansion to the West, guided by Manifest Destiny, were informed by apocalyptic beliefs. Thus, it is highly significant of *The Road*'s subversion of Apocalypse America that the text should feature a journey and, in particular, a non-teleological journey which avoids the West, the 'primary direction of significance' in both American history and literature (1983: 18). If in its inception America was conceived as the 'Western site of the millennium' (Robinson 1985: xi), the man and the child originally head south, a movement which indicates the failure of the apocalyptic utopian expectations embodied by the West and furthers the critique of the New World put forward through the image of the wasteland. Indeed if, as Wesley G. Morgan argues, the unspecified southern coast is the South Carolina Coast (2008: 45), the father and son's eastbound journey is an inversion of Manifest Destiny, similarly to that of *The Pesthouse*. Since no permanent shelter is available in the irrecoverable wasteland, *The Road*'s journey also subverts the 'home-founding journey … [,] one of the primary forms of American journey narrative, most directly based on history' (Stout 1983: 41), and on the utopian expectations of the Pilgrim, Puritan and pioneer settlers. Stout remarks how 'the home founding is a forward-looking form' and a 'future-centered' narrative pattern (1983: 42), elements which, in the novel's static temporality, the father and son's journey lacks.

The motif of the car, one of the icons of the many American literary and filmic road narratives, 'celebrates technology as a liberating force that can lead us into the future' (Laderman 2002: 4–5). However, this symbol of the apocalyptic myth of progress, and of the social and spatial mobility of capitalist America, appears as a form of prison in McCarthy's novel. People were burnt alive in their cars, possibly when the apocalypse hit. The only motor vehicle still in working order is the truck of the 'bad guys', which signifies the reversal of the utopian possibilities linked to the image of the car as, when 'foraging', the truck gives the cannibalistic group a dangerous advantage over the other survivors. As opposed to many contemporary road narratives, rather than travelling by car, *The Road*'s protagonists are walking, accompanied by a grocery cart.[24] The cart is suggestive of post-technological United States, signalling the future-past of temporal inversion as well as the critique of the myth of infinite progress and of the neoliberal order, for as a reminder of the 'excess and waste' of late-capitalist consumer culture, it 'represent[s] the system whose collapse has created such despair' (Kollin 2011: 160). The cart is also hardly conducive to the utopian potentialities of freedom and futurity which David Laderman (2002) associates with American 'driving visions'. Although it helps the father and the child to carry their meagre possessions, the cart risks attracting the attention of the 'bad guys' and slowing them down in case of attack. Furthermore, the cart often breaks and needs to be substituted – and for the man and the boy it is not always easy to find a new one – and, when the road becomes too strewn with debris, the vehicle is an impediment to their walking. The cart also brings to mind the homeless of the readers' world, an image which well resonates with the novel's emphasis on post-apocalyptic existential homelessness. Lastly, the cart, a residue from a dead civilization, is evidence that the survivors are reduced to living off the remains of a past America, from food to useful objects, and therefore foregrounds how the world they are living in is hardly a New World.

The Road's narrative structure reinforces the static temporality embodied by the chronotope of the road. The novel is not organized in traditional chapters but in often very short paragraphs separated by blank spaces on the page. This textual fragmentation breaks up the linear continuity of the apocalyptic model of history and narrative and of the image of the road, while underscoring the survivors' static temporality, as it suggests that the only thing left to the post-apocalyptic travellers is a precarious present – a temporal fragment – devoid of those 'long term goals' that the child anxiously asks his father about (*TR* 160–161). Indeed, the possibility of a future perspective is closed off by *The Road*'s circular plot: the father and son's journey is constituted by two main alternating patterns – the protagonists encountering the cannibalistic communities of the 'bad guys' and looking for food – and framed by the oneiric image of a cave.[25] Although the novel ends with the boy joining the new family, the conclusion does not break the circularity of the narrative but, rather, reinforces the critical temporality articulated by this structure. *The Road*'s plot ultimately suggests the

---

[24] For an analysis of the motif of walking in contemporary post-apocalyptic fiction, see Tate (2017: 83–101).
[25] Repeating patterns and a cyclical history are also key to the critical temporalities of Mitchell's *Cloud Atlas* and Jeanette Winterson's *The Stone Gods* (2007), discussed in the next chapter.

circularity of the protagonists' journey on the road, for in the post-apocalypse, it is as if the survivors are walking in circles – 'like rats on a wheel' (*TR* 273) – until they die, deprived as they are of the chance to ever reach a telos and better their condition.

The plot's cyclical repetition of two alternating patterns identifies the main events taking place on the road and the basic survival issues in the post-apocalyptic world: avoiding being killed by cannibalistic tribes, i.e. becoming food, and finding food, as the wasteland keeps the father and son on the verge of starvation. The two protagonists seem to have on their side a stroke of luck that always gets them through, no matter how desperate their situation seems to be. Thus, the man and his child go from managing to escape a close encounter with one of the 'bad guys', and a cellar full of prisoners who are being eaten, to finding shrivelled old apples and pure water in a derelict house, and a bunker full of food; from coming again face to face with an instance of cannibalism, this time of a human baby, to discovering another house and a boat with some provisions; and, finally, to retrieving everything a thief has stolen from them and surviving, once again, a dangerous encounter with other survivors. Yet 'good luck might be no such thing' (*TR* 230), as it does not really take the father and son anywhere – just like the road itself. Their condition never permanently improves; rather, the man and the child are simply safe, for the time being. In this sense, the alternating patterns, with the constant repetition of almost identical events, ultimately signal the survivors' static temporality, for they indicate that after the disaster there is nothing more to life than walking, while scavenging for food and attempting to escape the 'bad guys'. If typically, 'Conjuring an array of utopian connotations (most generally, "possibility" itself), the road secures us with direction and purpose' (Laderman 2002: 2), *The Road*'s cyclical repetition of narrative patterns undercuts the typical associations of the image of the road with teleological 'direction and purpose' and closes off the very possibility of possibility, as it signifies that no significant change or real future perspective are open for these travellers stuck in the precarious 'meantime' of the 'already dead' (Cazdyn 2012).

The opening and closing dreams of the cave emphasize the hopeless circularity of the journey. Darkness is central to these dreams, an element suggesting that the cave stands for the post-apocalyptic dim wasteland itself. However, signalling the motif of the fire carriers that punctuates the entire novel, in the father's dreams the novel's protagonists are carrying a source of light. The presence of this motif in *The Road*'s opening dream directly follows from the ending of McCarthy's previous novel, *No Country for Old Men* (2005), where

Sheriff Bell describes a dream of his father carrying fire in a horn (309). Bell reports his dream soon after having talked to his wife about Revelation and having asked her whether 'Revelations [sic] had anything to say about the shape things was takin [sic]' (McCarthy [2005] 2006: 304). Drawing on this episode, in which Bell turns to the final book of the Bible looking for the apocalyptic sense of an ending, *The Road*'s story of the fire carriers is the father's loving attempt at apocalyptic sense-making. Yet, similarly to the American Phoenix PR stunt in *Zone One*, this story is nothing more than that – a narrative.

The man concocts the story to distinguish him and his son, the 'good guys' who are carrying the fire, from the cannibalistic 'bad guys'. The fire, an image replete with Promethean echoes (Luttrull 2010), symbolizes the light of civilization, goodness and morality in a physically and morally dark world. This dualism resonates with the typical apocalyptic moral dualism of the elect versus the damned and with the rhetoric of American exceptionalism that underpins the War on Terror. However, 'The dichotomy "good guys" versus "bad guys" gets more and more diluted as the pilgrimage progresses' (Broncano 2014: 129), so much so that the boy anxiously keeps asking his father whether they are still the 'good guys', since in order to survive the man is forced to perform morally questionable acts – from killing one of the 'bad guys', to leaving another without clothes or shoes in the cold. The blurring of this distinction problematizes the simplistic sense-making structure of apocalyptic moral dualism and challenges the self-righteous policies this dualism legitimates, including the messianic innocence of post-9/11 politics. Not only is the goodness of one of McCarthy's 'good guys', the father, repeatedly questioned in the narrative, but their telos – that of carrying the fire of civilization, an image which resonates with the project of exporting American democracy to the supposedly less 'enlightened' countries behind the terrorist attacks – appears to be illusory at best.

The apocalyptic goal of the renewal of civilization attempts to give a sense of an ending to the father and son's journey, thus dispelling the hopeless lack of futurity which characterizes the survivors' static temporality. The father tells the boy that, because they are walking down the road to carry the fire, 'nothing bad is going to happen' (*TR* 83). And it is revealing that, when he is about to die, the man tries to encourage his son to go on by evoking the image of the fire once more: the boy 'ha[s] to carry the fire', a fire which is 'inside [him]', the 'best guy' (*TR* 279). A passage also connects the fire carriers motif to that of the grail as, soon before dying, the man sees the child 'kneel[ing] with the cup of water he'[s] fetched' and remarks that 'There [i]s light all about him' (*TR* 277). Here, the father appears to conceive of his son as a grail which will heal the wasteland through the fire of civilization and morality he embodies. However, in the rest of the novel the man often betrays scepticism about his own narrative, musing about the hopeless devastation, the irrecoverable end of nature and the unlikelihood of there being many people still alive.

And indeed, the circular narrative frame given by the two dreams of the cave draws attention to the lack of regeneration of the wasteland and the absence of a telos to the protagonists' journey on the road, notwithstanding the boy's fire. Said otherwise, the circular narrative frame emphasizes the failure of the apocalyptic narrative of the fire carriers as a *mise en abyme* of the critique of the sense-making function of apocalyptic logic portrayed throughout *The Road*. In the father's final vision, the candle the boy carries in the cave is just a 'fading light' (*TR* 280), which signifies that the child's goodness is merely a flickering fire in the brutal darkness of the post-apocalyptic world and that the grail he represents is not enough to ensure the healing of the wasteland and open up again the possibility of the future for the survivors. The image of the cave is indeed evoked in what is possibly the bleakest moment of the novel, when the protagonists find a dark cellar full of people locked up by the 'bad guys', who are eating the prisoners piece by piece. The protagonists are carrying a lighter, which is described as 'pitiful light' (*TR* 110), in stark contrast to the 'pitiless dark' (*TR* 187) of the post-apocalyptic world and its violence. However, the man and his child – the fire carriers – cannot save the prisoners without putting their own lives at risk and, in fleeing, the father tellingly drops the lighter. If, as the father states in his final vision, their journey on the road is 'measured ... solely by the light they carried with them' (*TR* 280), the 'fading' luminous trail left by their travelling in the encroaching darkness draws attention to the journey's futility. There is no way out of the post-apocalyptic wasteland, no real possible futurity for the survivors, not even for the 'good guys'. Hardly by chance, the man and the child's journey together ends in the post-apocalyptic cave, where it begins. This element restates the circularity, rather than the teleology, of their travelling and the static critical temporality embodied by the chronotope of the road.

A few pages after the final vision of the cave and the father's death, the boy is rescued by a family of seemingly 'good guys'. Yet the readers cannot help but wonder how long they will be safe, as the final paragraph also restates that the wasteland cannot 'be made right again' (*TR* 287). What this paragraph ultimately suggests is that the cycle of mere survival, at least until canned food is available, will simply start again for the new family, without any substantial improvement in their chances of ever knowing a more meaningful life. The journey on the road might have ended, but the hopeless patterns which characterize the journey have not, so that the teleology of the image of the road is yet again undercut. Just as the apocalypse of *The Road* is merely an end point, and not a telos bringing about a new utopian beginning, the hope for a renewal that the end of the road – namely, when the boy joins the new family – might initially appear to signify is contradicted by the final paragraph.

Endings are crucial to the apocalyptic model of history and narrative, and in his novel's ending McCarthy critiques the plenitude of meaning associated with the apocalyptic notion of end. On the one hand, *The Road*'s conclusion reinforces the subversion of the sense-making utopian teleology that shapes apocalyptic history. The opening of the final paragraph, 'Once there were brook trout in the streams in the mountains' (*TR* 286), emphasizes the motif of the wasteland by implicitly juxtaposing the concluding description of a bygone pre-apocalyptic era, in which nature was still thriving, to the post-apocalyptic ashen landscape of the rest of the text. The extinction of the trout is made all the more poignant by the fact that 'On their backs were vermiculate patterns that were maps of the world in its becoming. Maps and mazes. Of a thing which could not be put back. Not be made right again' (*TR* 287). What cannot 'be made right again' is 'the world in its becoming', an image that powerfully restates the motif of the irrecoverable wasteland, for which the extinct trout synecdochically stand. The reference to 'becoming' signifies the post-apocalyptic lack of futurity, thus reinforcing the idea of the wasteland as a chronotope for a static critical temporality. On the other hand, the very final word of *The Road* is 'mystery': 'In the deep glens where they [the trout] lived all things were older than man and they hummed of mystery' (*TR* 287). And, by leaving the conclusion open, 'mystery' arguably undercuts another apocalyptic conjunction of meaning and end, that of narrative itself. *The Road* ends, but 'mystery' invites an endless play of interpretation. As Sarah Dillon writes, *The Road*'s 'textual undecidability gives way to two mutually possible interpretations of the end of the novel. Either, the novel shifts genres at this moment [from horror to fantasy, in Dillon's reading] because the author is seduced by the consolation of fantasy, and/or the novel is self-consciously demonstrating the man's refusal unto the very last to confront the full horror of his situation' and, in this sense, the final pages, in which the boy is saved by the 'good guys', might be read as the father's dying fantasy (2018: 18). In this final undecidability, the novel is beyond the plenitude of meaning of the sense of an ending, which characterizes apocalyptic history and traditional narrative plots alike.

Just as in *The Road*, the contrast between America as we know it, with its apocalyptic self-identification as the culmination of history, and its post-apocalyptic dystopian future structures Crace's novel. Signalling this underlying contrast, according to archival material held at the Harry Ransom Center, 'This used to be America' (Crace [2007] 2008: 7) was supposed to be the first line of *The Pesthouse*.²⁶ Following an unspecified apocalypse, Crace's American future is a return to the past – an Old World, similarly to McCarthy's American future, rather than the New World of the apocalyptic imagination – combining medieval imagery with elements from the nation's pioneer past. Paralleling the critical temporality of temporal inversion, *The Pesthouse* reverses the myth of Manifest Destiny by depicting a country that is emptying as its post-apocalyptic pioneers attempt to emigrate eastwards hoping to reach wealthier countries across the ocean. The West, and by extension America, has lost its association with utopian expectations and historical teleology, so much so that going westward is to go 'against the tide of history' (*TP* 21). The very fact that the catastrophe appears to have hit only America suggests a negative form of American exceptionalism: rather than representing the conventional Apocalypse America, *The Pesthouse* gives us an anti-apocalyptic America.

As Crace writes in his notes for the novel, *The Pesthouse* represents 'A future landscape: but not a science fiction one – a future landscape in keeping with true history', as he mischievously gives America's future the contours of 'something that many of its citizens have always wanted and lacked – a medieval "past," an ancient European experience'.²⁷ In one of the narrative's many inversions, post-apocalyptic America comes to embody the 'decadence, decay, [and] death' typically associated with the Old World (Robinson 1985: 2) precisely because America's future is an 'ancient European experience'. America 'used to be the safest place on earth' (*TP* 7) but this past America, described in terms clearly reminiscent of the American Dream as a 'land of profusion'

---

²⁶ All further references to Crace's *The Pesthouse* as *TP*. For archival material that identifies 'This used to be America' as the original opening sentence see Jim Crace Papers, Harry Ransom Center, The University of Texas at Austin (henceforth HRC), 'Notebook 2003–4', box 11, folder 6. This original opening line went on to have a life of its own, with Amazon announcing, and selling, a phantom novel by Crace titled *Useless America*, complete with a customer's review (Jim Crace Papers, HRC, 'Useless America', box 16, folder 8). Crace explains: 'When Penguin [Viking Penguin held the original license, but *The Pesthouse* was ultimately published by Picador in the UK] contracted me to write the novel a few years ago, I had not yet decided on a title. But the first line of the book was going to be "This used to be America." It was convenient to use that as a working designation. Nobody would know or care except me, my agent and my editor. Now we are in the world of guesswork. When the book was "announced" all those years ago, someone at Penguin couldn't type, possibly, or someone at Amazon was hard of hearing. "Used to" became "Useless," an amusing error. But an error with a life of its own. The Amazon computer sucked the information in, fleshed it out, nurtured it, gave it provenance' (Crace 2006). *Useless America* was finally published as a signed, limited edition notebook by Doubleday, Crace's North American publisher (Jim Crace Papers, HRC, 'Useless America', box 16, folders 8 and 9).

²⁷ Jim Crace Papers, HRC, 'Notebook 2003–4', box 11, folder 6.

(*TP* 42), has given way to a country of 'famine and lawlessness', where there is no work and 'salvation [i]s in short supply' (*TP* 51, 86). *The Pesthouse*'s world is post-technological and post-scientific, devoid of government institutions, rife with diseases and superstitions, and insecure, so much so that Margaret and Franklin, the novel's protagonists, together with many others, are trying to flee the country. *The Pesthouse* is the story of this journey and, adding to the neo-medieval temporal inversion, carts and wagons, the icons of pioneer life, abound in this narrative where everybody is on the move.[28] Inverting the apocalyptic myth of Manifest Destiny, the post-apocalyptic pioneers move east, looking to board boats that will take them to the former Old World, which has now become the embodiment of the hopes once connected to the American New World. Across the ocean, people believe, are opportunities and fertile soil for everyone, and even a utopian Cockaigne where 'Hogs run through their woods ready-roasted with forks sticking out of them' (*TP* 106). In an 'ironi[c] revers[al] [of] the cultural imaginary of the American Dream' (Edwards 2009: 774), for the post-apocalyptic pioneers America is a 'nightmare [to be] left behind' (*TP* 199).

As Crace explains in the Amazon short 'Love, Hate & Kicking Ass' (2007), *The Pesthouse*'s aim is to untangle his love/hate relationship with America. On the one hand, his love for the literature, the wilderness and the informality, on the other, his dislike of America's global hegemony, both in terms of foreign policy and in terms of the world's cultural Americanization. *The Pesthouse*'s depiction of the future United States, Philip Tew observes, articulates 'an implied critique of America's new imperium with its hubristic sense of power and authority' (2006: 197). In particular, the future demise of the nation in this post-9/11 novel challenges the way in which, in the wake of the attacks, America sought to justify its 'new imperium' through the recourse to the old exceptionalist self-righteousness of apocalyptic logic. Crace's temporal inversion exposes just how fragile a narrative the nation's apocalyptic construction of history is. Echoes of old apocalyptic myths haunt Crace's future America but, re-contextualized in this superstitious world, they are even more clearly just that – myths. Among Margaret's 'lucky things' – all objects from the pre-apocalyptic 'best-forgotten' days – are some coins, which she anxiously fingers in the eponymous pesthouse while waiting for the 'flux', an often-lethal disease, to run its course. Margaret pauses to consider the coins' symbols – from the motto 'In God We Trust' to

---

[28] Crace extensively researched the pioneer era of American history and westward expansion, as evidenced by his notes on G. M. Candler's *The Way West: Transportation in the American West*; Frank McLynn's *Wagons West: The Epic Story of America's Overland Trails*; Parke S. Rouse Jr's *The Great Wagon Road: from Philadelphia to the South*; and Francis Parkman's *The Oregon Trail*. Jim Crace Papers, HRC, 'Notebook 2003–4', box 11, folder 6.

the eagle, from the heads of Founding Fathers and Presidents to the flaming torch of liberty – which come to signify the catastrophic end of America's apocalyptic beliefs.[29] On the one-cent coin, she traces the contours of the 'man who, storytellers said, was Abraham [Lincoln] and would come back to help America one day with his enormous promises' (*TP* 26–27). Lincoln's conflation with a messianic figure parallels the apocalyptic self-identification of the United States with a 'Redeemer Nation' (Gray 2007: 112) in American exceptionalism, Manifest Destiny and the post-9/11 operation 'Enduring Freedom', while the word 'enormous' already suggests a certain scepticism of Abraham's apocalyptic promises, and by extension America's. And indeed, rather than in America's salvation, people seem to believe in the prophecy that 'before the doors of Paradise could open there would have to be a blackened, hot and utter silence in America, which could be quenched only by the sea and would be survived only by the people of the boats' (*TP* 82–83). No longer Apocalypse America, the locus of apocalyptic expectations, in the novel's critical temporality America is the Old World that needs to be destroyed before the utopian renewal can take place in the New World across the ocean – a hope that, as we shall see, is itself misguided.

Yet Crace's world is a far cry from the desolate wasteland of *The Road*, for the landscape of *The Pesthouse* is lush and nature has mostly succeeded in obliterating America's technological past.[30] The tar of the Dreaming Highway, whose name encapsulates the dreams of emigration away from America as it takes the pioneers to the East Coast, has deteriorated with time and is covered in weeds. The few remaining machines and old buildings are described as 'rusting cadavers', 'rotting hulks and carcasses', 'smelling of decay and dust' (*TP* 119, 261, 205), in stark contrast, with their deathly and ugly appearance, to the lively beauty of the natural world.[31] Indeed, the characters react with awe and uneasiness to these remains, which they regard as 'the craziest work of men, or of something worse than men' (*TP* 261). The sect of the Finger Baptists, which

---

[29] Cf. a similar image in *The Mandibles*, where, upon the release of new, more cheap-looking and poorly-reproduced dollar bills, one of the characters reflects upon the past dollar bills and the meaning of their various symbols, concluding that the new bills make her 'feel robbed, personally insulted, and anxious for the United States, as if in compromising the integrity of its mere emblems of value the nation had devalued itself' (Shriver [2017] 2016: 306–307).

[30] For this reason, Edwards goes as far as identifying *The Pesthouse* as an example of 'pastoral post-apocalypticism' (2009: 770), though, as Deborah Lilley underlines, the novel 'challenges the familiar dynamic of pastoral's "backward glance" towards a simple past in contrast to a degraded present' (2018: 42).

[31] Crace makes extensive notes on the time it will take for objects from our present to decompose, from roads to concrete buildings and constructions in steel and glass. Jim Crace Papers, HRC, 'Notes and Research 2003–5', box 11, folders 7–8.

gives refuge to Margaret when Franklin is kidnapped by a gang of rustlers, even considers metal as 'the Devil's work[,] … the cause of greed and war' (*TP* 184). That is why every person seeking to enter the sect's quarters has to leave their metallic possessions outside, including patently harmless things like buttons and children's toys. The twenty Helpless Gentlemen at the head of the Baptist community do not use their hands at all. Hands, the means through which humankind builds tools and technologies, also do 'the Devil's work' and devotees have to help the Helpless Gentlemen in every task, from scratching to masturbating. The Finger Baptists' rules, aimed at preserving their world from metal, betray a lingering fear of the long-forgotten causes of the apocalypse. For there remain a few areas – the 'junkle', Crace's version of the wasteland – in which the technological past has left an enduring legacy of destruction: in them nothing grows because the land is poisoned.

In one of his notebooks, Crace writes that he wants to 'Establish [an] environmental/green ecological theme – that this is a poisoned landscape destroyed by industry, technology, science'.[32] *The Pesthouse*'s neo-medieval future subverts the utopian teleology of progress and foregrounds its illusoriness, as well as the catastrophic environmental risks of this apocalyptic ideology, which is central to the readers' world and, in particular, as Crace comments, to that 'hot seat of technological, and business development, which is America' (Lawless 2005). Similarly to the images of cars and the road itself in McCarthy's novel, *The Pesthouse*'s critique of unfettered progress is rendered through images of difficult or denied movement. The Dreaming Highway makes Margaret uneasy with its unnatural appearance: 'This was no escarpment provided by nature, unless nature had on this one occasion broken its own rules and failed to twist and bend, but had instead hurtled forward, all symmetry and parallels' (*TP* 110–111). Not only does the highway's linearity intrude upon the beauty of the natural landscape, imposing an artificial order on it, but the road's promise of a speedy advancement towards the couple's destination – the coast – is deceptive. For while the road originally assists Margaret and Franklin on their journey by providing an even surface that makes proceeding with their barrow easier, its openness exposes them to the band of rustlers that kidnap Franklin and interrupt their journey until the two manage to reunite. By the same token, on the 'dream-making coast where, surely, all the worst of the past could be forgotten by the emigrants', Margaret is shocked to see 'old-style ships', with their 'massive symmetry' that '[n]ature could not – would not want to – shape',

---

[32] Jim Crace Papers, HRC, 'Notebook, undated', box 50, folder 9.

staining the mud with 'unearthly' oily colours. These ships, as another woman wryly observes, 'didn't get them [the pre-apocalyptic people] very far' and Margaret is led to muse on whether 'America had once been populated by a race of fools' (*TP* 261–262). The stuck pre-apocalyptic ships, which synecdochically stand for 'the worst of the past' and the catastrophic halt of the dream of infinite progress, foreshadow Margaret's discovery that they cannot emigrate and, more broadly, the deceptive nature of the pioneers' apocalyptic expectations about the New World across the ocean. The image's environmental undertones, given by the contrast between nature and technology's poisonous effects and artificial symmetry, which connects back to the Dreaming Highway, also convey the foolishness of the apocalyptic dream of progress and its illusory imposition of order on the chaos of historical contingency.

As a reviewer observes, *The Pesthouse* 'excise[s] from history a nation that once proclaimed itself at the end of history' (Deb 2007). Not only does Crace's temporal inversion subvert Fukuyama's end of history thesis (1992) but *The Pesthouse*'s world appears to be beyond the very idea of history. The characters know there once was a different America for they see its traces, from highways and Margaret's lucky talismans to the 'junkle' and remains of cities. Local lore also tells fabulous stories of 'sky-high buildings' (*TP* 241), but it stays silent over why these do not exist anymore. The apocalypse happened a long time before the narrated events – according to an outline for the novel, *The Pesthouse* is set about two hundred years from the time of writing – and the memory of the catastrophe appears to be completely lost to the characters.[33] Tellingly, the remains of the past world hardly include any written records. There is only one instance in which Margaret and Franklin happen across an old text but they are unable to read it – and, indeed, this society appears to be wholly illiterate – signifying the spectre of the complete and irreversible destruction of the written archive, and thus of history and literature, that, as we shall discuss in the Conclusion, haunts the contemporary post-apocalyptic novel. If in *The Road* McCarthy at least mentions the unspecified apocalypse, in *The Pesthouse* Crace does not make any reference to the end which is the origin of the text's post-apocalyptic America. Contrary to what one might expect, it is not the apocalyptic catastrophe but a widespread impoverishment which is to blame for the narrative's mass migration. The Jim Crace Papers at the HRC are not particularly illuminating on the nature of the apocalypse either. In his notebooks, Crace clips articles about climate change, which contribute to emphasize the

---

[33] Jim Crace Papers, HRC, 'Notebook 2003–4', box 11, folder 6.

novel's environmental theme, but his notes also reveal that 'disaster or natural historical evolution' are equally possible causes of the dramatic change in America's fortunes, as are impact events, floods, volcanic eruptions and fires.[34] The absence of the apocalypse from *The Pesthouse*'s history arguably reinforces the novel's critique of apocalyptic logic.

It is not only that, as in *The Road*, *The Pesthouse*'s absent apocalyptic end cannot perform its sense-making function, but that, just like *The Island at the End of the World* considered in Chapter 1, *The Pesthouse* foregrounds the aporia of the end. Unlike the alleged eventfulness of 9/11, Crace's absent apocalypse is truly a radically unpredictable event that ruptures history and cannot be reduced to previous conceptual categories and to a linear and univocal trajectory of causes and effects. For as Derrida puts it when describing the 'absolute nuclear war', the apocalypse would be the 'trace of what is entirely other .... [the] ultimate and a-symbolic referent, unsymbolizable, even un-signifiable' (1984: 28). As part of the genre of eschatology (from *eschatos*: last, furthest, edge), the apocalyptic narrative is a discourse on a temporal edge, a temporal limit. But the apocalyptic temporal limit, encapsulated in the idea of a historical teleology, translates into an epistemic limit, an aporia. 'Apocalypse', Gomel writes, 'the catastrophic end of history to be followed by an eternal and immutable millennium, ... creates a humanly meaningful narrative of historical change. But apocalyptic narratives are peculiarly self-destructive because they deny what they pretend to explain: time, history and mortality. Apocalypse is time's bomb; a conspiracy against history' (2010: 120). Thus, the apocalyptic representational impasse – where 'impasse' emphasizes the idea of a 'non-passage', the etymological meaning of aporia – consists in the aporia of recounting an alterity which is non-temporal and, therefore, utterly non-narrative, since narratives are essentially temporal forms of representation. '[E]ven though apocalyptic narrative is a story with a beginning and a middle and an earthly setting', Quinby observes, 'it is a narrative that seeks to be nonnarrative [sic], to get beyond the strictures of time and space' (1994: xiv). It is this tension that *The Pesthouse*'s critical temporality foregrounds, drawing attention to how apocalyptic logic bases itself upon a construct that is beyond our epistemic and conceptual limits and ultimately unrepresentable.

Having abandoned its original opening, *The Pesthouse* instead begins with the catastrophic 'Everybody died at night' (*TP* 1). What is being referred here,

---

[34] Jim Crace Papers, HRC, 'Notebook 2003–4', box 11, folder 6; 'Notes and research, 2003–5', box 11, folders 7–8.

however, is not the unspecified event that brought about America's neo-medieval future but a landslide that, by releasing toxic gases from a lake, destroys the community of Ferrytown.[35] Crace writes in a note that the 'novel should be marked throughout by the tragedy of Ferrytown'.[36] Indeed, the landslide performs the function of the absent apocalypse in the narrative and draws attention to this absence, foregrounding the aporetic nature of the apocalyptic sense of an ending. Just as the absent apocalypse is the origin of the post-apocalyptic world of *The Pesthouse*, the landslide triggers the plot by bringing Margaret and Franklin together. In the disaster Margaret loses all her family and Franklin his brother – Jackson – so that, left alone, the two decide to head to the East Coast together. It is also significant that the landslide strikes the wealthy Ferrytown, which has made a fortune out of the emigrants' need to cross a river, exactly as the apocalypse seemingly wrecked only America, the locus of contemporary global capitalism. In parallel with the American Dream's rhetoric of upward mobility open to all, Ferrytown harks back to the old American capitalist ways by making a profit out of the supposed opportunities provided by the dream of emigration, while hiding the truth from the would-be emigrants, that is, that the journey to the coast becomes even more dangerous after the river crossing and that many are turned back once they manage to reach the ships. Apocalyptic expectations are once again exposed as deceptive and as propping up exploitative power structures. Gesturing to the unrepresentability of the apocalyptic end, the toxic gases hit the town when everybody is asleep, 'without a sound and almost without a shape' (*TP* 7), while their deathly effects are not described but are only hinted at through suspension dots (*TP* 6–7). Examining the corpses to find the causes of such widespread death, Margaret and Franklin cannot find any clues, for the bodies appear untouched, as is the village. The landslide remains invisible to them, unrepresented and unrepresentable, as *The Pesthouse*'s apocalypse is for the readers, thus subverting the unveiling at the core of the sense-making function of the end.

The narrative structure of *The Pesthouse*'s opening chapters, which deal with the catastrophe in Ferrytown, challenges teleology and the narrative drive for the sense of an ending, articulating a critical temporality that emphasizes the present and invites us to read for parallels, thus going beyond the aporia that structures apocalyptic history. The novel begins with an unnumbered section that stands out of the narrative's temporal sequence, represented by

---

[35] Ferrytown's catastrophe is inspired by a similar event at Lake Nyos, Cameroon, in 1986. Jim Crace Papers, HRC, 'Notebook 2003–4', box 11, folder 6.

[36] Jim Crace Papers, HRC, 'Notes and research, 2003–5', box 11, folder 8.

the numbered chapters, gesturing to the unrepresentable temporal liminality of the apocalyptic end. This section functions as the anchoring point for *The Pesthouse*'s first five chapters, as it recounts the moment around which the following chapters revolve, the moment the landslide hits Ferrytown. From the first numbered chapter up to the fifth, the narrative follows a similar structure: focussing on Franklin, or his brother, Jackson, or Margaret, each chapter begins a few hours before the disaster, backs further away from it thanks to analepses that provide background details on the main characters and on the post-apocalyptic world, and then moves forward to finish around the time the landslide hits. This structure, which, following Elizabeth Ermarth's lead, we can define as paratactic, 'moves forward by moving sideways[,] [e]mphasizing what is parallel and synchronically patterned rather than what is linear and progressive' (1992: 85), complicating the teleology of apocalyptic history and the narrative drive for the sense of an ending. In apocalyptic history the present has significance only insofar as it is part of a predetermined teleological pattern; in other words, in apocalyptic history the emphasis is always on 'what is linear and progressive'. By placing the focus on events that are happening at the same time, instead, the structure of the beginning of *The Pesthouse* articulates a critical temporality, for readers are encouraged to focus on the present and read for parallels, rather than for a retrospective patterning. Both the end of the landslide and the end of the absent apocalypse are, after all, hardly sense-making events. In this respect, it is not a coincidence that Margaret and Franklin do not succeed in their attempts to reconstruct retrospectively a meaningful order of events leading to the devastation they find in Ferrytown.

From the fifth chapter onwards, the novel moves to the days after the natural disaster, tracing the story of Margaret and Franklin's journey to the coast. Just like that of the father and son in *The Road*, the apocalyptic teleology of this journey is subverted. Having reached the coast, most people find out that they cannot board the ships, as these only accept strong men, single girls and rich people. *The Pesthouse* provides no revelation of a better world beyond America. Rather, what lies across the ocean, as imagined by the migrants, remains a utopia only in the etymological sense of nowhere – from the Greek '*ou*', not, and '*topos*', place – while a dystopian America closes on these people. Yet to Margaret and Franklin the impossibility of sailing away is not a defeat. The two, having adopted a little girl, deliberately go back westward to the eponymous pesthouse where they had first met. As Crace writes in a 2006 email, 'The idea was to take away the Myth of the Pioneer West and then to return it in the final pages, swept clean, still virginal and innocent like Margaret and Franklin. Those two unlikely heroes (representing the USA) can start over. (Maybe they'll get it right this time)'.[37] The pesthouse becomes the fulcrum of the novel's reinscription of Manifest Destiny and the utopian potential of the West and, by extension, America.

In the image of the pesthouse, what historically houses death and despair comes to house life and hope. Crace's pesthouse is inspired by an actual building from the eighteenth century on St. Helen's, on the Isles of Scilly, where ill people travelling to the British Isles were quarantined and left to die (Begley 2003).[38] But although at the beginning of the novel Margaret is quarantined in the pesthouse because of the flux, in the rest of the narrative the image of the pesthouse is not at all reminiscent of a dystopian forced confinement and mass death. Rather, it is a utopian place 'of greater safety', 'remedy and recovery' (*TP* 167, 306) and a recurrent dream for Franklin and for Margaret. After all, Margaret survives the flux, and it is this illness that prevents her from perishing with her family in the disaster in Ferrytown and that makes her meet Franklin. It is once again the flux, or at least the visible sign of it – namely, Margaret's shaven head – that saves her from the rustlers who kidnap Franklin. And on the way back west it is the young man's turn to be shaven, in order to pretend he has the flux, thus discouraging any marauder and ensuring the newly formed family a journey free from harm. The pesthouse, historically the epitome of danger, becomes 'the safest acre in America' (*TP* 306). In consonance with this reversal, America, which at the beginning '*used* to be the safest place on earth' (*TP* 7; emphasis mine), by the end of the novel regains its utopian status.

Significantly, when Franklin realizes that he does not want to leave America, he recognizes that 'His dream [i]s not the future but the past. Some land, a cabin and a family' (*TP* 249). Franklin is thinking of his own past back home, but what he describes is the nation's past as well. His name, with its illusion to Benjamin Franklin, is important in this respect, for it signifies Franklin's role as a post-apocalyptic Founding Father giving America a chance to go back to its apocalyptic roots, to Apocalypse America. In Crace's first drafts, Franklin and his brother Jackson are called Suffolk and Norfolk: 'Yes, Norfolk and Suffolk Lopez – North and South – named for their parents' two small home towns on the plains and known inevitably if not logically, because of their height, as the Poles'.[39] Crace then turns to 'good-old Yankee name[s]' (*TP* 179), with Jackson being a reference to the seventh president of the United States, in a move that

---

[37] Jim Crace Papers, HRC, 'Correspondence (email printouts) 2005–10', box 51, folder 2.
[38] Cf. also Jim Crace Papers, HRC, 'Research and photographs 2005', box 51, folder 1, for Crace's pictures of the pesthouse on St Helen's.
[39] Jim Crace Papers, HRC, 'Drafts', box 12.

parallels the shift from what was originally planned as an eastward-bound conclusion to one that sees the protagonists heading west again, back into the nation's past.

The novel's final passage emphasizes the connection between the couple's journey westward and the apocalyptic ideology of Manifest Destiny: 'They could imagine striking out to claim a piece of long-abandoned land and making home in some old place, some territory begging to be used. Going westward, they go free' (*TP* 309). The rhetoric of this sentence harks back to the expansion westward, when ideas of empty, 'long-abandoned' lands and a 'territory begging to be used' were interpreted as signs of the nation's Manifest Destiny and fuelled the violent colonization of lands that were, of course, not empty at all. More broadly, the novel's very final words, 'Going westward, they go free', which echo Henry David Thoreau's words 'Eastward I go only by force; but Westward I go free' in 'Walking' (1862), reinscribe the apocalyptic trope of America as a land of utopian possibilities and the teleology of apocalyptic history. On their way west, Margaret and Franklin 'no longer fe[el] defeated by America', as they had on their journey to the coast (*TP* 287). Rather, the 'land provision[s] them' (*TP* 289) and the couple is ready to uncover something of the old America, described at the beginning of *The Pesthouse* (*TP* 42) in words that closely follow those by Franklin's namesake depicting a country whose 'Encouragements … to Strangers, are a good Climate, fertile Soil, wholesome Air, and Water, plenty of Provisions and Fuel, good Pay for Labour, kind Neighbours, good Laws, Liberty, and a hearty Welcome' (Franklin 1783).

Let us pause for a moment, however, on the beginning of this final passage: 'They could imagine'. The apocalyptic hopes offered by the ending of *The Pesthouse* are the stuff of imagination, of narrative. Thus, the concluding page parallels Margaret and Franklin's American Dream with the emigrants' deceptive hopes of reaching the countries overseas – both are equally constructions. As Crace writes in 'Love, Hate & Kicking Ass' (2007), his original intention for the novel was to turn the myth and ideologies of America on their head entirely, ending of the novel included. And indeed, a note from 2003–2004 reads 'At the end of the novel, they reach the sea to make a boat of escape (to Europe, implied). A new world. East. East. East'.[40] But this intention, Crace writes, 'was defeated, in a way, by narrative itself', that is, by long-standing national narratives, which are all informed by the imaginary of the American West as representing 'Liberty, Opportunity, and

---

[40] Jim Crace Papers, HRC, 'Notebook 2003-4', box 11, folder 6.

Adventure' (2007: 8).[41] Reminding us of the power, as well as the fragility, of this mythology, the old coins with Lincoln and the American eagle make their reappearance at the novel's conclusion, as Margaret is reunited with her lucky charms, left in the pesthouse. If *The Pesthouse*'s critical temporality works to expose the sense of an ending as an aporetic construct and to deconstruct the apocalyptic ideologies at the core of the United States, the novel's ending is also careful to acknowledge the power of these narratives.

Written in a post-9/11 geopolitical situation in which apocalyptic logic resurfaces in the self-righteous exceptionalist politics underlying the War on Terror, the novels analysed in this chapter subvert America's profound reliance on the utopian teleology of apocalyptic myths by representing the end of the world order dominated by the United States. The texts' critical temporalities expose apocalyptic ideologies as fragile constructions complicit with the nation's oppressive power dynamics. The divided United States of *American War* challenge the discourse of American messianic innocence; the reverse evolution of *Future House of the Living God* deconstructs the image of the nation as the culmination of history; *Zone One* debunks the myth of America's endless reinvention; *The Road*'s wasteland negates the very possibility of futurity, including for the American 'good guys'; and *The Pesthouse* reverses Manifest Destiny to undercut the utopian expectations associated with the New World. At the heart of Apocalypse America lies the identification of the nation with the New World. It is to this apocalyptic trope, and specifically its role in the origins of the capitalist world-system responsible for the Anthropocene, that the next chapter turns.

---

[41] In his article on Amazon's phantom novel *Useless America*, Crace also comments: 'while I was writing *The Pesthouse* I became overly self-conscious about upsetting my American readers in this timid, post-9/11 climate. I pulled my punches a bit. There was the novel I wrote, and there was the more discourteous novel I might have written had I been more thick-skinned. *Useless America* would have been its perfect, blunt title. The Amazon computer knew that, of course, and must have simply completed the volume that I was too pusillanimous to attempt' (2006).

3

The New Worlds of the Anthropocene

An environmentally-devastated America has dissolved into city-states, and Manhattan is now controlled by the Manhattan Company. Its leader, James Stuart, sends a group of men to the Indian territory of Virginia to trade for resources and found the colony of Jamestown. The group's communications specialist, Johnny Rolfe, tasked with liaising with the native population, falls in love with Pocahontas, the daughter of the chief Powhatan. If this story is beginning to sound somewhat familiar, it is because Matthew Sharpe's *Jamestown* (2007) transposes the seventeenth-century founding of Jamestown, the first permanent English settlement in North America, to a near post-apocalyptic future. 'The future looks a lot like the past', a character in David Mitchell's *The Bone Clocks* (2014: 479) warns us, and indeed we have seen in previous chapters how the contemporary post-apocalyptic novel recurrently deploys the critical temporality of temporal inversion to undermine the modern apocalyptic construction of history as progress. But in cases like *Jamestown*, the future return to the past of temporal inversion is quite literal. If, to put it with the apt title of David Ketterer's study (1974), the traditional apocalyptic imagination is essentially about 'new worlds for old', *Jamestown*, as well as the two novels that are the focus of this chapter, Mitchell's *Cloud Atlas* (2004) and Jeanette Winterson's *The Stone Gods* (2007), complicate the teleological movement from old to new worlds through patterns of repetition. These link our colonial past to the ecological crises that bring about the novels' post-apocalyptic futures, foregrounding the profound imbrication of apocalyptic logic with colonialism embodied in the very idea of the colonial New World.

Scholarship often acknowledges the relationship between science fiction imagery and the discourse of colonialism. Exploring post-apocalyptic nuclear narratives, for instance, Paul Williams parallels 'The uncharted spaces lying in wait for European cartographers *and* the space of the world after nuclear war [for both] are positioned outside human civilization, either awaiting its imprint or the result of its self-destruction' (2011: 90; emphasis in original).[1] Yet it is not

---

[1] See also Rieder (2008) and Kerslake ([2007] 2010).

merely that the future new worlds of science fiction hark back to the imagery of the colonial New Worlds. Rather, the very idea of 'uncharted spaces lying in wait for European cartographers' and powers is informed by apocalyptic logic, as signalled by Marcel Theroux's *Far North* (2009).

The novel's protagonist, Makepeace, is the only survivor of a Quaker community who settled in Siberia to escape the ravages of climate change and 'because the land was empty and [they] wanted the freedom to create their world new' (Theroux 2009: 57). Complicating the possibility of an apocalyptic new world, Makepeace wryly comments:

> What an old story that is. You'd think people would be done believing in a fresh start by now .... But no, ... This time the bright new future was really just around the corner, and with god on our side and a collective determination to do good, we'd put a bunch of New Jerusalems right here in the frozen north. What hooey. (Theroux 2009: 57)

Makepeace's reflections capture the complex history that this chapter untangles. Her ancestors' dream of an 'empty' land, which affords the freedom to create a New Jerusalem on earth, is underwritten by an 'old story' indeed, namely, the colonial doctrines of *terra nullius* and *vacuum domicilium*. These constructed the land of the new worlds as empty and uncultivated, territories that could and should be conquered in order to be put to good use by the superior European powers, i.e. bring them profit (Fitzmaurice 2014). Such doctrines combined with the discourse of the 'civilizing mission', which legitimized colonialism through assumptions of racial, cultural and ethical superiority over the native population (Nayar 2010: 36–39). As Andrew Fitzmaurice maintains, the colonial occupation of lands conceived as empty aligned with the modern understanding of history in terms of progress, particularly economic progress, itself based on the exploitation of, and dominion over, nature and its resources (2014: 3–4). This idea is exemplified by the settlers' delusion in *Far North* that they can just 'put' their New Jerusalems in the 'frozen north', moulding nature according to their wishes. As Makepeace's reference to the New Jerusalem indicates, the convergence between colonial occupation and the ideology of progress derived energy from the apocalyptic imagination. It is because of this connection between colonial and apocalyptic logic that the new worlds of the contemporary post-apocalyptic novel are ideally placed to interrogate colonial discourse and its contemporary permutations and legacies, specifically, the networks of (neo)colonial power, capital, and conceptions of nature that lie at the heart of the Anthropocene and the post-apocalyptic scenarios analysed in the following pages.

I open this chapter by discussing the significance of the apocalyptic imagination in the colonial era and then turn to the notion of Anthropocene, a proposed geological epoch shaped by human activity. I add to current debates on this epoch by tracing the influence of apocalyptic logic on what Jason W. Moore terms the capitalist 'world-ecology', a formation 'joining the accumulation of capital, the pursuit of power, and the co-production of nature in dialectical unity' (2014: 287). I argue that, by outlining the imbrication of apocalyptic logic with colonialism, the critical temporalities of *Jamestown*, Lidia Yuknavitch's *The Book of Joan* (2017), *Cloud Atlas* and *The Stone Gods* emphasize, first, how the trope of a new world serves to justify oppressive power dynamics as part of a historical development deterministically tending towards betterment and, secondly, how the 'objectification of the apocalyptic millennial future' in the New World (Keller [1996] 2005: 141) leads to modernity's instrumentalist approach to nature, which risks culminating in the anthropogenic apocalypse of late capitalism represented in these fictions.

Avihu Zakai speaks of the 'Apocalypse of the New World', since 'Centuries of interpreting history in terms of sacred, ecclesiastical history conditioned Europeans to view the discovery of the New World in terms of the prevailing providential scheme and ideology of history, that is, according to Christian historiography' ([1992] 2002: 84). Columbus inaugurated this process, claiming 'God made me the messenger of the new heaven and the new earth of which he spoke in the Apocalypse of St. John after having spoken of it through the mouth of Isaiah; and he showed me the spot where to find it' (Zakai [1992] 2002: 85). As Keller argues, 'The biblical hope of a future new creation by God the Creator is [in these words] read as having been *already* fulfilled. The new creation therefore is available to "discovery." *Apokalyptein*, meaning etymologically "to unveil," that is, "to discover" in the sense of "to disclose," now functions as a self-fulfilling prophecy' (1994: 65; emphasis in original). In Columbus' perspective, and the perspective of the ensuing colonizers of the Americas, Revelation's future New Jerusalem became an actual physical space, the New World, awaiting the mastery of the self-proclaimed elect European powers.[2] An apocalyptic understanding of history thus fuelled the genocidal and exploitative colonial project.[3]

---

[2] For an in-depth analysis of the equation of the New Jerusalem with the Americas in early colonial texts see Beebee (2009).
[3] Zakai ([1992] 2002) explores at length the biblical interpretations and theological discourse used to prop up the colonial project. As Keller notes, there is a certain irony about the apocalyptic justification of colonialism, for 'the biblical apocalypse constitutes one long protest on the part of a colonized people against the world-colonizer, Rome as Whore of Babylon'. Yet, 'the Crusades, as an apocalyptically inspired movement against dark unchristian peoples, had in fact already accomplished [the] conversion of apocalypse into imperial aggression' that is central to the colonization of the New World ([1996] 2005: 162).

In line with the patriarchal nature of apocalyptic discourse explored in Chapter 1, the 'discovery' and acquisition of the New World was codified, from Columbus onwards, as 'male conquest at once of women and of feminized space' (Keller [1996] 2005: 154), the virgin land to be taken by the male explorer – after all, the New Jerusalem is itself codified as a bride in Revelation 21:2. And if the gendering of the New Jerusalem was reflected in the image of the New World, so was its 'typical urban uprootedness from its nonhuman habitat' (Keller [1996] 2005: 148). As Heather Davis and Zoe Todd argue, colonialism 'was always about changing the land, transforming the earth itself, including the creatures, the plants, the soil composition and the atmosphere' (2017: 770) in the name of the apocalyptically-inflected ideology of progress, the yearning for a perfect world, which disregarded the reality of a world that was neither new nor empty, and of profit.[4]

Tracing the nexus between the apocalyptic justifications of colonialism and the modern capitalist economy that emerged from the exploitation of the New World's resources, Keller notes how Columbus' 'eschatology render[ed] the planet endlessly available to cartography, to conquest, to commodification', for 'When the new heaven and earth lies "before" in space rather than in a numinous spacetime, human control of space and what lies "in" it gains force' ([1996] 2005: 153, 159). The crux of the matter is of course the word 'endlessly', for the finitude of planet's resources threatens the reliance of capitalist growth on an endless access to nature, where nature is understood to include flora, fauna and human bodies, especially those of the non-western other. This is what Moore terms 'Cheap Nature', a 'system of domination, appropriation and exploitation' (2017: 620), which originated with colonialism and is central to the current ecological crisis.[5]

As Moore explains, Cheap Nature does not simply involve techniques of acquisition and exploitation of the 'Four Cheaps of food, labor, energy and raw materials' (2017: 620); rather, Cheap Nature signifies an ontological and symbolic praxis based on the Nature/Society binary. At the beginning of capitalism in the

---

[4] Cf. also 'Colonialism, such as U.S. settler colonialism, can be understood as a system of domination that concerns how one society inflicts burdensome anthropogenic environmental change on another society' (Whyte 2016: 5).

[5] For an exploration of the impact of Columbus's 'discovery' and colonialism more broadly on the development and consolidation of a capitalist world-system, see also Anievas and Nişancıoğlu (2015), in particular Chapter 5. As Moore (2017: 595) underlines, the periodization that traces the genesis of capitalism back to the New World is at odds with the dominant periodization, which erases capitalism's early-modern roots in colonial and racist practices to focus on the trajectory from the Industrial Revolution onward. By the same token, as we shall see, Moore reads Crutzen and Stoermer's proposition of James Watt's invention of the steam engine as the start date of the Anthropocene (2000) as perpetuating this erasure.

'discovery' of the New World this praxis meant, first, 'the separation of humans from the rest of nature, and the domination of the latter by the former', an instrumentalist approach perfectly embodied by the modern 'era's cartographic, scientific and quantifying revolutions' (Moore 2018: 244). Second, this praxis involved 'the expulsion of many humans – probably the majority within the orbit of early capitalist power – from Humanity. Most women, most peoples of color, and virtually all Amerindian peoples were excluded from full, often even partial, membership in Humanity' (Moore 2017: 600). Both moves were aimed at reducing the cost of labour and at accumulating capital. This is a dynamic that continues today through carbon colonialism, namely, the way in which emissions trading and offsetting protects corporations' profits by effectively making a carbon dump out of the Global South, perpetuating the long history of land dispossession in these regions (Bachram 2004), as well as through globalization's neo-colonial exploitation of a racialized, and hence made disposable, workforce. Thus, via colonialism and its 'master metaphor of "dis-covery"' that constructs nature 'as the new and ultimate "other," the recipient of the messianic aggressions of Progress' (Keller [1996] 2005: 165), one finds the imprint of the apocalyptic conception of history upon the capitalist world-ecology and the Anthropocene's environmental risks. It is this imprint that the present chapter foregrounds by discussing novels whose plots trace the colonial roots of their anthropogenic post-apocalyptic futures.

If the Anthropocene is to date an informal geological time unit, the term has been widely adopted across disciplines and in the media, which is why I continue to deploy it while underlining its problematic aspects below. The Anthropocene Working Group recommended the formalization of this epoch to the 35th International Geological Congress in August 2016, suggesting the Great Acceleration of the mid-twentieth century as the Anthropocene's start date (University of Leicester Press Office 2016). The Great Acceleration names the sharp increase in human activities that leave an enduring imprint on the Earth System following World War Two, including 'a major expansion in human population, large changes in natural processes, and the development of novel materials from minerals to plastic to persistent organic pollutants and inorganic compounds [as well as] the global fallout from nuclear bomb tests' (Lewis and Maslin 2015: 176). In the Humanities, debates around the Anthropocene focus on the political and ethical implications of the name of the epoch, as well as on, and indeed often related to, when to pinpoint the epoch's beginning.

Moore, for instance, proposes the term 'Capitalocene', arguing that 'Global warming is not the accomplishment of an abstract humanity, the *Anthropos*.

Global warming is capital's crowning achievement. Global warming is *capitalogenic*' (2018: 237; emphasis in original). He traces the origins of the Capitalocene back to the dawn of capitalism in the 'discovery' of the New World, for dating the epoch back to the invention of the steam engine, as Crutzen and Stoermer do (2000), or to the Great Acceleration obscures the imperialist, racist, and patriarchal practices at the basis of capitalism.[6] For Moore, indeed, the concept of the Anthropocene is problematic, insofar as the implication of a homogenous humanity in its very name perpetuates the Nature/Society binary. As Françoise Vergès summarizes the matter in her call for acknowledging a racial Capitalocene grounded in colonial dynamics, 'The Anthropocene is a catchy term that makes for an easy story. *Easy, because it does not challenge the naturalized inequalities, alienation, and violence inscribed in modernity's strategic relations of power and production*' (2017; emphasis in original) – inequalities that extend to the fact that it is the Global South and Indigenous populations who are bearing, and will continue to bear, the brunt of the environmental crisis (Parenti 2011; Whyte 2016). Davis and Todd similarly note that 'in its reassertion of universality, [the Anthropocene] implicitly aligns itself with the colonial era', for it 'serves to re-invisibilize the power of Eurocentric narratives, again re-placing them as the neutral and global perspective' (2017: 763). Rather than dispensing with the name, however, they argue for making the link between the Anthropocene and colonial logic explicit by dating the dawn of the epoch back to colonialism. In doing so, Davis and Todd draw on Simon L. Lewis and Mark A. Maslin (2015: 174–175), who suggest the 'Orbis spike' as the geological marker for the beginning of the epoch, namely, the dip in atmospheric CO_2 corresponding to the genocide of the native population of the Americas, whose numbers dropped from 54 million people in 1492 to 6 million in 1650. In its name, from the Latin for 'world', the Orbis spike signals the violent global networks of power and capital that lie at the heart of the Anthropocene's world-ecology, from the colonial era to the present. It is the imbrication of these networks with apocalyptic logic that the critical temporalities articulated by the novels discussed in this chapter expose.

Critiques of the notion of the Anthropocene are, naturally, about the ways in which we construct time and history, and not merely in the sense of debating

---

[6] Other proposed names for the epoch include 'Chthulucene', which stresses the need to 'make kin' with other species (Haraway 2016), 'Necrocene' (McBrien 2016), which draws attention to the mass extinctions that dominate the era, 'Plantationocene', which refers to the plantation system's 'appropriation of land as if land was not there' (Latour et al. 2018: 592) and Christophe Bonneuil and Jean-Baptiste Fressoz's various coinages (2016), from 'Thermocene', which places the emphasis on energy and CO_2, to 'Phagocene', which foregrounds the development of consumer society.

the epoch's start date. Underlining the 'technological determinism' implied by analyses that have the Anthropocene begin with the Industrial Revolution and propose technological, rather than political, solutions to the epoch's environmental problems, Daniel Hartley (2015) writes:

> [I]nherent to the Anthropocene discourse is a conception of historical causality which is purely mechanical: a one-on-one billiard ball model of technological invention and historical effect, which is simply inadequate to explain actual *social* and *relational* modes of historical causation. [...] the Anthropocene can only ever think the past in its proleptic trajectory towards our present. Its specific narrative mode translates the time of initiative and praxis into the time of pure physical necessity. Moreover, precisely because of this, it can only explain *our own present* as part of the empty, homogeneous time of linear succession, which increasingly contracts as ecological catastrophe approaches. This implicit philosophy of historical temporality goes hand in hand with a Whig view of history as one endless story of human progress and enlightenment. (emphasis in original)

In his critique of this understanding of the Anthropocene's history, Hartley is gesturing towards what I have defined, throughout the book, as the apocalyptic model of history and narrative: time as a linear and homogeneous continuum in which the past is 'backshadowed' (Bernstein 1994; Morson 1994) as deterministically leading to the present, the present, in turn, has significance only insofar as it is part of a necessary teleological development, rather than being the locus of agency, and alternative trajectories, explanations and possibilities are erased.

Troubling this construction of the Anthropocene's history, Davis and Todd speak of the 'seismic shock of dispossession and violence' produced by colonialism, a seismic shock that 'kept rolling like a slinky – pressing and compacting in different ways in different places as colonialism spread', with its reverberations now finally reaching those countries that were responsible for the introduction of colonial and capitalist practices across the globe in the first place (2017: 771–772). Kyle Powys Whyte similarly argues that 'thinking about [contemporary] climate injustice against Indigenous peoples', namely the way in which Indigenous people face heightened climate risks, is 'less about envisioning a new future and more like the experience of *déjà vu*. This is because climate injustice is part of a cyclical history situated within the larger struggle of anthropogenic environmental change catalysed by colonialism, industrialism and capitalism' (2016: 16). Both images, that of the slinky's ongoing reverberations, compression and expansion and that of a cyclical history, resonate with the critical temporalities articulated by the narrative structures of

Mitchell's *Cloud Atlas* and Winterson's *The Stone Gods*, which warp the linearity of apocalyptic history through patterns of repetition that can be conceptualized as a concertina – *Cloud Atlas* – and as a cycle – *The Stone Gods* – and that serve to highlight the legacies of colonialism within our Anthropocene present.

Before discussing *Cloud Atlas* and *The Stone Gods*, however, let me return to *Jamestown* and introduce Yuknavitch's *The Book of Joan*, which we shall further consider in the Conclusion of this study. *Jamestown*'s critical temporality, with its duplication of colonial history, chimes with Whyte's idea of *déjà vu* when it comes to Indigenous populations' experience of climate injustice. Sharpe's choice of the Jamestown settlement is hardly coincidental. As Karen Ordahl Kupperman maintains, 'Jamestown has always occupied an equivocal position in American history' (2008: 1). On the one hand, 'These colonists planted the tiny seed from which would grow a powerful nation where all the world's people would mingle' (Kupperman 2008: 1). On the other, Jamestown is 'the creation story from hell', for 'The settlement's first years were marked by belligerent intrusions on the Chesapeake Algonquians [...] the colonists exploited the land and one another in the scramble for profits. Ultimately, they would institute slavery' (Kupperman 2008: 1). Just as in the novels analysed in Chapter 2, Sharpe's future, through the repetition of the colonial encounter with the native population in all its brutality, deconstructs America's exceptionalist mythology of a 'powerful nation where all the world's people would mingle'. Just as in the novels analysed in Chapter 1, however, this deconstruction is articulated through a parodic distance within the repetition that serves to subvert the apocalyptic core of colonialism from within.

Where, through the discourse of the civilizing mission, white colonization apocalyptically legitimizes its violent practices as the inevitable advance of progress, in Sharpe's novel, the civilized nature of the Manhattan Company's mission, Jamestown, and by extension white society itself, is frequently parodied. Johnny Rolfe opens the novel by explaining that they are travelling 'from civilization into its counterpart', to then immediately undermine this statement and the implied civilizing mission: 'if indeed civilization's what to call what we're fleeing, or exporting, or both' (Sharpe [2007] 2008: 4).[7] Indeed, Rolfe ironically questions the idea of history as an apocalyptic teleology of progress when, quipping on Hegel's philosophy, he describes history and the violence of the post-apocalyptic world as '*thesis, antithesis, steak knife, bread knife*' (J 3; emphasis in original). On the founding of Jamestown, Jack Smith comments: 'That they dared make *town* of this wet and sucking thing that vied with my foot

---

[7] All further references to Sharpe's *Jamestown* as *J*.

for my boot at every step bespoke the glorious and yearning bullshit of men's souls' (J 224; emphasis in original), a sentiment echoed by the native population, who look at the 'town' in utter disbelief. And if the civilizing mission functions by imposing the English language and customs on the Indigenous population, deemed inferior, in *Jamestown*, the Native Americans pretend not to speak English as an ironic homage to the past and a ruse, 'both necessary and hilarious, a hundred years' supply of laughs squeezed from one small, hard joke' (J 189). In fact, the supposed Native Americans, Pocahontas reveals, are not Native Americans at all – 'What Indians were on this land the Europeans' microbes killed; and who was left the Europeans' microbes' hosts killed; and who was left after that the bombs killed' (J 285) – a move that, if problematic in that the novel has people 'redfacing' with SPF 90, discloses just how apocalyptic, in the sense of end of the world, the history of colonization has been for the Indigenous population.[8] The 'natives' are people of all ethnicities who, post-'annihilation', decide to go back to the Chesapeake's way of life, as an antidote, one can surmise, to the capitalist system that has brought about the catastrophe.

In a world in which the trees are mostly dead, rain is acid, and animals and plants are poisoned with toxins as a consequence of the instrumentalist approach to nature underwriting the Anthropocene, the 'native' population refuses to own lands or animals. This peaceful coexistence with nature is yet again shattered by the arrival of white colonizers. The Manhattan Company, which recalls the seventeenth-century Virginia Company and encapsulates the colonialism-capitalism nexus, settles into native territory seeking to trade food and oil for 'protection and technological know-how' (J 131), a statement that echoes the benevolent rhetoric of the civilizing mission. Underscoring just how deceptive this rhetoric is, the natural resources acquired on native land will support the Manhattan Company's core business, advertising, and thus promote further exploitative missions to Virginia through the promise of '*food and ease and return to past lifestyles and values*', as well as accommodating natives who '*enjoy cultural and economic exchange with energetic and enterprising northerners*' so much that they give away barrels of oil as tokens of appreciation (J 141, 371; emphasis in original). This is the alluring promise of peak Cheap Nature, to go back to Moore's notion. Indeed, chiming with Cheap Nature as both resources and non-western labour, *Jamestown* closes on Johnny Rolfe mourning

---

[8] A post-apocalyptic sensibility indeed pervades Native American literature beyond the post-apocalyptic genre itself. As Erdrich (1985) puts it, 'to American Indians it is as if the unthinkable has already happened, and relatively recently. Many Native American cultures were annihilated more thoroughly than even a nuclear disaster might destroy ours, and others live on with the fallout of that destruction, effects as persistent as radiation – poverty, fetal alcohol syndrome, chronic despair'.

Pocahontas' death and conceiving of the electricity that powers his fridge as Pocahontas' life energy, which 'we [the colonizers] sucked all up in a tube [to] keep our ham sandwich cold' (*J* 407). This – rather crude – metaphor for the bodies of the colonized powering capitalist accumulation and white comfort frames a cycle of colonial exploitation that, the novel suggests, seems destined to repeat itself, at least until there are resources left. To put it with William Sanders' short story 'When This World Is All on Fire', 'better than five hundred years after Columbus, and here we are again with white people trying to settle on our land. [...] Seems like they're running out of places for people to be' ([2001] 2015: 186–187). Similarly to *Jamestown*, Sanders sets his short story in a world of climate breakdown, where most of the North American coastline is under water and the inland territories are reduced to a desert. It is this environmental devastation that has the world running out of places conducive to human habitation: 'when this world is all on fire/Where you gonna go?', asks the song which gives Sanders' short story its title. By drawing connections between their anthropogenic post-apocalyptic futures and the colonial past, Sharpe's and Sanders' critical temporalities expose how the apocalyptic dream of a new world on earth fuels practices that, in the name of capitalist progress, consume the world itself.

The Book of Joan is set at a moment in which this consumption has already taken place. In the contemporary post-apocalyptic novel's typical conflation of future and past, which troubles apocalyptic teleology and the myth of progress, Yuknavitch transposes into circa 2049 the medieval figures of the soldier and martyr Joan of Arc (in the novel Joan of Dirt, a name that signals her allegiance to the wasteland that Earth has become), the proto-feminist writer Christine de Pizan, author of *The Book of the City of Ladies*, and her poetic adversary, Jean de Meun (in the novel de Men), famous for his continuation of *Roman de la rose* in which he brutally satirized the vices of women. Future Earth is a scorched ball of dust, inhabited by a few bands of survivors reduced to living in underground caves. The elites have abandoned the planet for CIEL, a suborbital complex that precariously sustains itself by siphoning Earth's scarce remaining resources through 'skylines'. These are described as 'technological umbilical cords' (*BoJ* 6), the last, and engineered, maternal vestiges in a society that cannot reproduce anymore, since the radiations of a geocatastrophe have caused a devolution in Yuknavitch's future humans, who have no sexual organs. As seen in Chapter 2 with Louise Erdrich's *Future Home of the Living God* (2017), where fewer and fewer babies are born, and Cormac McCarthy's *The Road* (2006), where there are virtually no women, a failed maternal imagery mirrors the anthropogenic death of the ecosystem, traditionally conceived as Mother Nature, conveying humanity's no future.

As Christine de Pizan puts it, human beings are 'ravenous immoral consumers. Eaters of everything alive, as long as it sustained a story that [gives them] power over the struggling others' (*BoJ* 64). It is such an apocalyptic story – 'how we blind ourselves purposefully in the name of progress' (*BoJ* 106) – that has resulted in the depleted world of *The Book of Joan* and it is an analogous story – the apocalyptic new world – that is evoked on CIEL by its dictatorial leader, Jean de Men. Earth, Jean de Men tells his subjects, 'was but an early host for our future ascension', an old world that needs to be sucked dry and abandoned for a new world in space, where humankind can be re-created in a different image – 'his own', Christine de Pizan wryly comments, signalling how apocalyptic discourse serves power structures (*BoJ* 14). Undercutting the apocalyptic logic of the new world by exposing its dystopian and anthropogenic effects, eco-warrior Joan of Dirt, Jean de Men's enemy and the leader of the resistance on Earth, instead 'survey[s] [Earth's] territory differently from the way a discoverer would. This was the future city we had made. This viscous thickening wasteland' (*BoJ* 106). Gesturing to the colonialism-capitalism nexus that underwrites the Anthropocene, the territory Joan is surveying, and the location of the showdown between her and Jean de Men, is that of the Alberta Tar Sands, the embodiment of the capitalist 'drive to conquer, colonize, deplete' (*BoJ* 106) and its environmental risks. Here bitumen, a very viscous form of oil, is extracted and 'upgraded' by removing the sand, clay and water with which it is mixed and by adding hydrogen in a process that is even more energy-intensive and polluting than extracting and refining conventional oil (Avery 2013: 20–21). As ever, Indigenous populations are paying the price of capital's oil addiction. To allow the exploitation of the Alberta Tar Sands, First Nations people are being displaced and dispossessed of their lands, wetlands that have become a 'moonscape' (Avery 2013: 19), a reality evoked by the 'lunar landscape' of Yuknavitch's post-apocalyptic Earth (*BoJ* 64).

Significantly, CIEL's new world is populated by humans turned wholly white because of the geocatastrophe, or perhaps viruses. As Christine de Pizan muses, 'No one on Earth was ever literally white. But that construct kept race and class wars and myths alive. Up here we are truly, dully white', literalizing that construct and its power dynamics, for just like with the colonial new worlds, CIEL's white colonizers exploit Earth and its doomed survivors as 'raw material for the use of the living' (*BoJ* 83), in other words, Cheap Nature. But, in addition to depicting a new world that is just as devoid of a future as the old one – CIEL depends on a Cheap Nature that is not renewing and its inhabitants cannot reproduce – in an impetus that I shall define in the

Conclusion as anti-apocalyptic archive fever, *The Book of Joan* calls for new narratives beyond apocalyptic logic, where 'being human d[oes] not mean to discover, to conquer' (*BoJ* 227). Indeed, the novel ends with the destruction of CIEL and the colonizing drive it embodies.

Cloud Atlas and *The Stone Gods* bring to the fore the imbrication of apocalypticism, colonialism, capitalism and the Anthropocene by weaving transhistorical plots based on links and parallels between several narrative strands and epochs, rather than on the development of a single and teleological story-line. In their form, these fictions address the challenge of representing the 'hyperobject' (Morton 2013) of the Anthropocene, which, with its networks of responsibilities and effects, diffuse both temporally and spatially, 'demand[s] to think of human life at much broader scales of space and time' than that typically afforded by narratives (Clark 2015: 13). The novels' links and parallels serve to emphasize, first, how apocalyptic discourse continuously legitimizes oppressions in the name of a variously conceived utopian new world towards which history would tend, thus undermining the very idea of a *new* world and exposing its dangerous complicity with power. Secondly, these connections warp the linearity and determinism that the sense of an ending entails in narratives and apocalyptic history alike, thus underling the openness of the present and the power of narrative to help shape a future beyond the novels' eco-catastrophes.

Cloud Atlas consists of six narratives connected by a common theme, humankind's will to power, which Mitchell derives from Nietzsche (Mitchell 2005b), and by a metafictional device, whereby each story is featured in the one immediately following. The novel begins with the journal of Adam Ewing, a nineteenth-century American notary travelling across the Pacific and experiencing first-hand the damage inflicted by colonialism. This diary is found in Belgium in 1931 by the protagonist of the second narrative, Robert Frobisher, a young composer and amanuensis of invalid Vyvyan Ayrs. Robert's letters, which make up his narrative, are then read in the third story, set in the USA in the 1970s, by Luisa Rey. Luisa is a journalist who starts investigating the dangers of Seaboard Corporation's HYDRA Zero nuclear reactor, after the suspicious death of Rufus Sixsmith, the addressee of Robert's letters. A manuscript about her adventures is sent to Timothy Cavendish, a vanity publisher in contemporary Britain and the protagonist of the fourth narrative. Imprisoned in a nursing home, Timothy writes a memoir which is later made into a movie. This is then viewed by the protagonist of the fifth section, Sonmi-451, a clone living in a future dystopian hyper-capitalist Korea. Sonmi, finally, is transformed in the sixth chapter into the goddess of a Hawaiian post-apocalyptic community, where her orison – a device which recorded her testimony before she was executed for her rebellion against the regime of corpocracy – resurfaces.

The peculiarity of *Cloud Atlas* is that all the stories – with the exception of the sixth, situated in the middle – are interrupted in order to give way to the following one, and are then resumed in reverse order in the second half of the book. This structure is central to critical analyses of the book which draw on Robert's reflections on the cyclical trope of eternal return (Hicks 2016; Machinal 2011; Mezey 2011), on Timothy's image of the boomerang (Parker 2010), and on the matryoshka dolls brought up by Isaac Sachs, a scientist for Seaboard Corporation (Hopf 2011; McMorran 2011; Parker 2010), to conceptualize the development of the plot. While taking into consideration all of the above, I focus on an element which has hardly received critical attention: Timothy's image of the concertina, which captures the complexities of the book's critical temporality.[9] As Mitchell underlines, *Cloud Atlas*'s structure reflects the theme of the will to power, for 'each narrative is "eaten" by its successor and later "regurgitated" by the same' (2005). Yet, since the novel arguably depicts the will to power being legitimized by apocalyptic discourse, the structure mirrors the anti-apocalyptic content of the novel, with the centrality of the post-apocalyptic chapter signifying Mitchell's attempt to debunk the apocalyptic metanarrative. I argue that the concertina-like structure articulates a critical temporality as it resists a telic closure, warps the deterministic linearity of apocalyptic history and of the narrative sense of an ending, and links the various recurrences of the will to power in the novel, foregrounding the dystopian implications of apocalypticism, from colonialism to the future neo-colonial biopower of corporations and anthropogenic environmental crises.

By opening and closing with the same narrative, *Cloud Atlas* appears to rely on a cyclical temporality and plot. This idea is reinforced by repetitive patterns in the narratives, by the theme of reincarnation, for a comet-shaped birthmark accompanies one of the characters in each section – we shall return to the elements of patterns and reincarnation later in the chapter – and, more importantly, by the references to Nietzschean eternal recurrence. Robert helps Vyvyan write a symphony named 'Eternal Recurrence' and, just before committing suicide, the young composer is comforted by what he terms, with a fitting musical metaphor, 'Nietzsche's gramophone record. When it ends, the Old One plays it again, for an eternity of eternities' (*CA* 490). Yet the cyclical repetition of the same cannot

---

[9] To my knowledge, Patrick O'Donnell is the only critic who mentions 'The notion of time as elastic or as a concertina' as a way of capturing 'the experiences registered in the novel' (2015: 97). O'Donnell, however, does not connect the concertina to the novel's critique of apocalyptic logic.

account for *Cloud Atlas*'s plot. The very fact that the only passage in the novel explicitly expounding a cyclical conception of time is associated with Robert's desperate act suggests Mitchell's cautiousness about the theory. When hearing a song about the eternal recurrence, Timothy is horrified (*CA* 173). And the future Korean clones, which should by definition represent the return of the same, are instead as 'singular as snowflakes' (*CA* 191). The second half of *Cloud Atlas* goes back to the past, but it does so only in the sense of picking up the stories where they were interrupted, without any indication that time itself rewinds. The events of the first half are not reproduced; rather, the narratives are brought to their endings. Thus, the novel's conclusion does not really coincide with its beginning and there is no repetition of a cycle, unlike Winterson's *The Stone Gods*, where, as we shall see, one finds a destructive apocalypticism – the desire for utopian new beginnings that translates into the colonization of new worlds – leading humankind to a cyclical environmental demise.

It is Timothy who provides readers with two images that help us understand *Cloud Atlas*'s structure and critical temporality. In a first passage he declares that 'Time's Arrow bec[o]me[s] Time's Boomerang' (*CA* 149), which encapsulates how, in the first half of the text, the narratives follow a chronological order, from the nineteenth century to a distant post-apocalyptic future, to then boomerang back in the second half. The arrow embodies the sense of an ending which the structure of the novel complicates throughout. The names of the protagonists of the first and sixth story suggest a teleological development. Adam, reminiscent of the biblical progenitor of humankind, and Zachry trace with their initials an alphabetical progression that constructs a possible history of the Anthropocene, from the colonial antecedents of contemporary capitalism and its global patterns of exploitation to their anthropogenic cataclysmic end. The arrow, therefore, signifies a negative teleology, which subverts the utopianism at the core of the apocalyptic metanarrative. If modernity constructs history as progressive enlightenment, Mitchell, to draw on the name of the age of anthropogenic disasters in *The Bone Clocks*, depicts in the first half of *Cloud Atlas* a historical trajectory of 'Endarkenment'.[10]

---

[10] The apocalyptic tone devoid of any utopian element recurs in Mitchell's writings. The ninth chapter of *Ghostwritten* (1999) closes on a comet fast approaching Earth; the last words of *number9dream* (2001) refer to a major earthquake in Tokyo, a disaster made even more poignant in its devastation by the following empty chapter; *Black Swan Green* (2006), set during the Cold War, is pervaded by anxieties about a nuclear apocalypse. The only partial exception is *The Bone Clocks*, where, amidst the dystopian ecological collapse of the Endarkenment, Iceland, for which the niece and nephew of the protagonist Holly Sykes depart at the end of the book, appears to be a safe enough haven. However, it is in *Cloud Atlas* that the association of the dystopian post-apocalyptic section with the text's structure produces a fully articulated critique of apocalyptic logic.

In the typical trope of temporal inversion, after the 'Fall', the Hawaiian society depicted in 'Sloosha's Crossin' an' Ev'rythin' After' has reverted to an archaic way of life: the Valleysmen are herders and farmers, with very little technology. 'Time's Arrow bec[o]me[s] Time's Boomerang' also because, as suggested by Sonmi's hyper-capitalist and environmentally-devastated future, it is the apocalyptic ideology of progress that backfires, driving civilization to its own demise and to the dystopian future-past of temporal inversion. The post-apocalyptic chapter is a *mise en abyme*, for as Zachry's community returns to humankind's past, so does the text as a whole retrace its steps back to the beginning after 'Sloosha's Crossin''. Put differently, in the second half of the book temporal inversion's critique of apocalyptic teleology is made structural.

In articulating its critical temporality, *Cloud Atlas* also problematizes the arrow in terms of narrative teleology. On the one hand, the individual stories are abruptly broken off, and Mitchell emphasizes the extent to which our narrative practice is traditionally informed by the epistemic primacy of the end by replicating each interruption, and ensuing disappointment, at the diegetic level, thanks to characters who possess merely part of a journal, in Robert's case, or of a manuscript, in Timothy's, and so forth. All the textual disruptions climax in the chronological conclusion of *Cloud Atlas*. Not only is the apocalypse the interruption of what the apocalyptic metanarrative constructs as a progressive history, but the catastrophe is one of the gaps left between the stories. That in Zachry's post-apocalyptic language 'whole' is now spelt 'hole' emphasizes the void left by the cataclysm in the 'Hole World' (*CA* 284) and the fact that the text's history cannot be retrospectively made whole by this absent end.[11] The continuous deferral of closure in the first half of *Cloud Atlas* thus parallels the absence of a utopian resolution at the end of its history: like the final blank chapter of *number9dream*, the chronological conclusion of *Cloud Atlas* signifies devastation and textual incompleteness, not the meaningfulness of the sense of an ending.

On the other hand, the novel undermines foreshadowing, and hence, the deterministic inevitability which the conventional narrative structure dominated by the end imposes on events. Foreshadowing is crucial to the temporality of this type structure, where the present is 'the harbinger of an already determined future' (Bernstein 1994: 2). When we narrate history according to this apocalyptic narrative model, we subscribe to a teleological temporality which denies ethical value to the present and ignores the fundamental difference between

---

[11] Like Will Self with *The Book of Dave* (2006), discussed in Chapter 1, Mitchell acknowledges the influences of Russell Hoban's *Riddley Walker* (1980) on *Cloud Atlas*'s post-apocalyptic idiom (2005a).

conventional narratives and life: 'Unlike most art, life is genuinely eventful and set in open time, with loose ends and without closure' (Morson 1998: 600). *Cloud Atlas* rejects an understanding of history in terms of apocalyptic determinism and gives prominence to the individual's agency to shape the future, reflecting the openness and contingency of actual time, as opposed to the closure of time in conventional narrative structures.

In the first half of the novel, the chronological order of the narratives encourages us to read in the 'anticipation of retrospection' (Brooks 1984), looking for clues foreshadowing an ending that will integrate the various strands. Yet the shift from one era to the other remains unclear and Mitchell does not allow us to construct an unbroken causal and teleological sequence for the plot. The gaps in the fictional history traced by the arrow indicate Mitchell's wish to subvert the sense of an ending and keep spaces of possibility open in the structure. The boomerang of the second half of *Cloud Atlas* is even more effective in this respect. By situating 'Sloosha's Crossin'' in the middle of the book, Mitchell effaces it through the real ending, Adam's journal, and suggests that the temporal inversion of Zachry's society can still be averted in the readers' world. This notion of a future that is not predetermined is reinforced throughout the second half, for the stories are somewhat open-ended. Timothy's chapter features a double ending: the first is a cinematic 'THE END', contradicted in its closure by the words immediately above, 'Where all this will end, I do not know' (*CA* 401). This conclusion is followed by an epilogue in which Timothy looks forward to finding out Luisa's destiny. Hinting at an ongoing action, the other sections finish with the protagonist reading the following story, or in Sonmi's case, watching a movie about it. Even Robert's last letter before committing suicide contains a reference to Adam's journal, which he leaves to Rufus. The final chapter also closes in a suspended way, as Adam vows to pledge himself to Abolitionism once he is back in America.

Although the image of the boomerang captures some aspects of the critique of teleology, it does not account for another element of the novel's structure and critical temporality, the repetitive patterns that complicate both the teleological development of the plots and the apocalyptic metanarrative of progress, for they underscore the recurrence of an exploitative will to power in history legitimizing itself through the telos of a new world. These patterns, which straddle the different narrative strands and epochs, making tangible the diffused networks of responsibilities and effects constitutive of the hyperobject of the Anthropocene, can be conceptualized through Timothy's second temporal image: 'Time, no arrow, no boomerang, but a concertina' (*CA* 370). Made up of 'two hexagonal or square wooden endpieces, which carry the reeds and the buttons that control them, ... linked by folded cardboard bellows' (Montagu 2002), this musical instrument features a regular pattern, the series of zigs and zags of the folds, which can be compressed or expanded. Timothy's concertina-like perception of time occurs soon after he suffers a stroke, when he feels that everything is 'topsy-turvy' (*CA* 370) and that he has lost the ability to see his life-story as a linear sequence – as an arrow. However, the fact that Timothy's situation reminds him of Margo Roker, a comatose character in 'Half-Lives – The First Luisa Rey Mystery', which he was reading before the attack, suggests that the image of the concertina should be interpreted metafictionally, as setting out a protocol of reading. Instead of looking for chains of causality and for clues which may foreshadow the conclusion(s), the repetitive patterns of the bellows signal that we must pay attention to the interconnections between the six narratives. While the stories are sequential, to grasp the novel's critique of apocalyptic logic we should consider them as if they were running in parallel, each influencing our understanding of the other and, in turn, of our present anthropogenic predicament. The very title of the novel refers, on the one hand, to Zachry's notion that 'Souls cross ages like clouds cross skies' (*CA* 324), which emphasizes the links between the chapters, and, on the other, to Robert's final composition. The structure of this sextet is a clear allusion to the structure of *Cloud Atlas* itself (*CA* 463), an element gesturing to the importance of music in the theorization of the book.

The birthmark is one of the most important instances of the concertina-like narrative recurrences and provides us with an 'atlas' for finding a plot beyond the individual stories. Since characters often experience impossible analepses, it may be tempting to interpret the motif as indicating the reincarnation of the same soul throughout the centuries. Yet this possibility is metafictionally dismissed by Timothy as 'Far too hippie-druggy-new age' (*CA* 373). Furthermore, Timothy and Luisa, though they both have the birthmark, cannot be the same soul, for they were born around the same time – not to mention the fact that Luisa may just be a fictional character invented by Hilary V. Hush and, hence, not on the same ontological level as Timothy. The birthmark is instead a symbol, in the etymological sense of throwing something together (from the Greek '*syn*' and '*ballein*'), as it unifies the different strands of the novel. It embodies the concertina-like parallels between the narratives, pointing at how readers should interpret the book and replicating their experience at the diegetic level. Indeed, the source of the characters' 'uncanny moments of recognition' is not reincarnation but 'The act of reading' (Hopf 2011: 108). The birthmark signifies that the characters remember something they have read in what is for us another part of *Cloud Atlas* and we are encouraged to follow the motif and go beyond it, looking for other possible connections. The shape of the birthmark is revealing as well: the orbits of the comets make them recurrent phenomena, an element which corresponds to the repetitive patterns the device points to, while the tradition which sees these celestial bodies as omens of disaster hints at the apocalypse looming over the novel.

The birthmark engenders a sense of spatiotemporal compression and extension that can be pictured through the contraction and expansion of concertina folds and encapsulates the way in which the teleology of the apocalyptic model of narrative and history is warped and subverted in the book. Since in each section one of the characters is connected through the birthmark to the other stories, every instant in *Cloud Atlas* has the potential either to contract upon itself, back to past chapters, or to expand beyond itself, towards the future narratives. The concertina model of time indicates how the moments of *Cloud Atlas* do not yield to the arrow, namely, to the deterministic sense of an ending, but are 'elastic', with multiple 'ends … disappear[ing] into the past and the future' (*CA* 448) and into the other narratives, chiming with Davis and Todd's use of the image of the slinky to flesh out the reverberations of the impact of colonialism throughout the Anthropocene (2017).[12] As argued, Mitchell invites us to read for parallels – the repetitive patterns of the folds – and not for elements foreshadowing the end. The movements of expansion and contraction also explain the disorientation produced by the fact that, while Adam's sections are, in terms of their position, the frame of the novel, it is Zachry's chapter which contains all the others. Drawing on Isaac's '*model of time: an infinite matrioshka [sic] doll of painted moments*' (*CA* 409; emphasis in original), critics, and even Mitchell himself (2005b) often describe the embedding in *Cloud Atlas* as a Russian doll. However, this structure 'implies a process of framing, or mothering, in which each successive segment is contained within the previous segments[,] …. precisely the opposite of what actually happens', at least in the first half (McMorran 2011: 163). Folds, instead, by definition complicate the internal/external opposition, since what was once outside becomes inside, thus making the concertina a more accurate model of the novel's structure.

---

[12] Indeed, the concertina model of time, with its critique of the apocalyptic construction of narrative and history, should arguably be extended to Mitchell's '*Über*-book', for all of his novels are linked by recurrent characters and themes, in particular, that of predatory behaviour which, as we shall see, plays an important role in *Cloud Atlas*'s engagement with the colonial roots of the Anthropocene. As Joseph Metz maintains, the 'return, across multiple, otherwise unrelated novels, of characters in refracted and "redacted" form' signifies an 'attempt at constant rewrite and resignification, never wishing to commit to or accept a final version' so that the *Über*-book 'effectively evad[es] what Frank Kermode calls "the sense of an ending"' (2017: 123, 125).

In addition to the birthmark, the most notable recurrence in the narratives is that of the will to power. If we take the two endpieces of the musical instrument to stand for the beginning and the conclusion of *Cloud Atlas*, the concertina as a model of the novel's structure suggests that what goes on between these sections is not the repetition of the same, as in eternal recurrence, but repetition with difference. The pleated bellows are all identical, yet the flow of air generated by their expansion and contraction causes specific reeds to vibrate when the buttons are pressed. Thus the player, i.e. Mitchell, can produce different sounds, namely, various articulations of the will to power. Together with the structure, this pattern of predatory behaviour has been the protagonist of critical analyses (Dunlop 2011; Mezey 2011) that emphasize *Cloud Atlas*'s associations between will to power, colonialism, and global capital. What is missing from these analyses, however, is apocalyptic discourse, for arguably the predatory pattern makes tangible the dystopian implications of the modern and apocalyptic conception of history throughout the Anthropocene. Not only does the pattern warp the apocalyptic metanarrative of progress, showing that 'we share the predatory and cannibalistic impulses of earlier individuals' (Mezey 2011: 24), but what recurs in *Cloud Atlas* is the will to power as legitimized in all its greed and brutality by an apocalyptic understanding of history and its trope of the new world.

Cloud Atlas's structural critique of the determinism of apocalyptic and narrative teleology reinforces a content which debunks the end as a construct of the will to power, a threat to individual agency and freedom. In 'Half-lives', Isaac theorizes history as a dialectic between actual and virtual past (*CA* 408–409). His words recall Baudrillard's argument that, in our age of simulation, there is a *'precession of simulacra'*: representations come to precede what they represent, engendering 'a real without origin or reality; a hyperreal' (1994b: 1–3). Although Isaac does not seem to concur with Baudrillard in proclaiming the liquidation of the real *tout court* – after all, he still speaks of an actual past, though this is inaccessible – he does subscribe to a 'historiographical hyperreality', namely, that 'we know [historical reality] only in and by its representations' (Ankersmit 1994: 190–191). In Isaac's terms, the representations of the virtual past 'gro[w] ever "truer"' than the actual past, to the extent that this itself becomes a '*simulacrum of smoke, mirrors + shadows*' (*CA* 408–409; emphasis in original). In a truly postmodern fashion, what this theory foregrounds is that there is no history but only histories. *Cloud Atlas* emphasizes this point by featuring 'historical' narratives whose constructedness, consonantly with historiographic metafictions, is continuously underscored through Mitchell's play with different genres – from travelogue, to epistolary narrative, to thriller and memoir – and by the fact that 'each narrator becomes a fictitious character in the narrative that follows his or her own' (Machinal 2011: 131). But while *Cloud Atlas*'s virtual pasts flaunt their own textuality, historical simulacra, Isaac warns us, often partake in what Baudrillard terms a 'strategy of the real', for power seeks to 'restore the truth beneath the simulacrum' (1994b: 27), turning narratives into metanarratives. In the kind of backshadowing mechanism that we have seen at work in Ben's flood narrative in Sam Taylor's *The Island at the End of the World* (2009) analysed in Chapter 1, '*The present presses the virtual past into its own service, to lend credence to its mythologies + legitimacy to the imposition of will. Power seeks + is the right to "landscape" the virtual past*' (*CA* 408–409; emphasis in original).

Isaac notes that '*Symmetry demands an actual + virtual future*', that is, the will to power also 'landscapes' the virtual future as an act of self-legitimization, for consonantly with Baudrillard's precession of simulacra, '*the virtual future may influence the actual future*' (*CA* 409; emphasis in original). The concertina-like pattern of predatory behaviour exposes the apocalyptic metanarrative as a technology of power/knowledge which repeatedly 'landscapes' history as tending towards an ultimate state of perfection in order to justify oppressions and preserve the status quo. This is particularly evident in the opening and closing phase of the book's negative teleology, 'The Pacific Journal of Adam Ewing' and 'An Orison of Sonmi-451', where power fabricates narratives about an apocalyptic utopian telos – a new world – in order to legitimize the exploitations of nineteenth-century colonialism and a future corporate post-human slavery, as well as to conceal anthropogenic environmental disasters.

In a sermon reported in Adam's journal, preacher Horrox claims that '[i]t is Progress that leads Humanity up the ladder towards the God-Head' (*CA* 506). Horrox's 'Civilization's Ladder', however, is a racist order, where the race on the highest step, the Anglo-Saxon, rules over those on the lower. The sermon is not only a patent critique of the colonial discourse of the civilizing mission, but also of the apocalyptic roots of colonialism and the metanarrative of progress. The reference to the 'God-Head' suggests a teleology inherent in history and the preacher's final remarks are reminiscent of the utopian new world of the New Jerusalem, since catastrophic events are followed by the questionable eternal bliss of a 'glorious order … when all races shall know &, aye, embrace, their place in God's ladder of civilization' (*CA* 507). In Isaac's terms, Horrox's teleology is a way of apocalyptically 'landscaping' the future in order to justify colonialism, keep the native population submissive and conceal the fact that 'rapacity … powers [the white man's] Progress' (*CA* 509), colonial expansion and capital's violent acquisition of resources and labour. For Horrox's sermon, with its racist hierarchy, perfectly captures the colonial and capitalist praxis of Cheap Nature, in which entire populations are given only partial, if any, membership to humanity and are relegated to the realm of nature in order to be exploited. *Cloud Atlas* underscores that the will to power is often the ugly truth behind the simulacrum of progress and posits an exploitative apocalypticism at the heart of the history of the Anthropocene the novel depicts – a history that closely resembles our own up to Timothy's story.

In the recurring pattern of the concertina folds, the trope of the new world is also deployed to legitimize the neo-colonial oppression of the post-human other by the regime of 'An Orison', which constitutes Mitchell's extrapolation from present trends, signalling concerns over the rising power – especially biopower – of corporations under global capitalism, the system's staggering inequalities, as well as its environmental risks. As the neologism 'corpocracy' underlines, Nea So Copros, *Cloud Atlas*'s future Korea, is ruled by a disturbing conflation of state and corporate power, a conflation whose infancy the novel traces back to the beginning of neoliberalism in the 1970s through the depiction of Seaboard's abuses in 'Half-Lives'.[13] Echoing the Latin '*corpus*' (body), 'corpocracy' encapsulates the corporations' biopower, for the 'state Pyramid' (*CA* 342), a variation of Horrox's ladder, is based on a race deemed inferior and designed to perform menial jobs – again, Cheap Nature, this time produced through the creation of a post-humanity purposefully conceived as external to the realm of humanity itself. Like Horrox's Polynesians, who through the lenses of the discourse of the civilizing mission 'pa[y] for the benefits of Progress' (*CA* 510), the 'fabricants' are told that they are working to 'repay the Investment' which brought them into being, before being released at Xultation (*CA* 190). The fabricants thus represent the extreme development of the neoliberal subjectivity of the 'indebted man' (Lazzarato 2012), to which we shall return in Chapter 4.

Xultation is seemingly the new world of the subaltern and appears to conform to the liberationist reading of the apocalyptic paradigm, establishing a utopian teleology at the core of the clones' sense of time. In effect, recalling Isaac's reflections, Xultation is a simulacrum created by the will to power. The fabricants are repeatedly shown footage of their 'sisters' becoming 'consumers', that is, finally part of an ultra-neoliberal humanity in which everything, including the very essence of being human, is reduced to economic terms and metrics, and leaving for Hawaii, their materialistic New Jerusalem. These representations, though, do not make reference to an external reality; rather, they generate a

---

[13] For an argument that foregrounds corporations' domination over public life under neoliberalism, see Crouch (2011).

Baudrillardian hyperreal, and their medium – 3D film – emphasizes their power of simulation. The simulacrum of Xultation engenders a virtual future telos which affects the clones' actual future by keeping them submissive and depriving them of their agency. As in many of the novels analysed in this study, in *Cloud Atlas*'s critical temporality, apocalyptic discourse is exposed as what covers up, rather than as what reveals, oppressions, since Xultation is an end devoid of any utopian dimension.

In the Golden Ark which is supposed to take them to Hawaii, the fabricants are slaughtered to be fed to their own species and human beings (*CA* 357–360). The ark, a religious symbol of deliverance, becomes deadly and, to illustrate this anti-apocalyptic reversal in the nature of teleology, Mitchell draws attention to the inexorable linearity of the process which prepares the fabricants for their alleged journey. At first, Sonmi 'envie[s] their certainty about the future'. She then realizes that the very faith in a virtual utopian telos condemns the clones to an actual horrible death without leaving them any space for rebellion, a realization which foregrounds the dangers of apocalyptic determinism. Soon after Sonmi observes that 'the only direction [i]s onwards', Xultation is revealed to be a dystopian 'slaughterhouse production line' (*CA* 357–359). The repetitive actions of the latter expose the simulations of progress, a linear metanarrative concealing the iterated exploitations framed by the concertina folds, as well as capitalism's auto-cannibalistic loop. A production line, after all, is made of conveyor belt systems which continuously feed, so to speak, on themselves.

From 'The Pacific Journal' to 'An Orison' *Cloud Atlas*'s critical temporality traces a possible history of the Anthropocene in which the colonial construction of Cheap Nature culminates in the eco-apocalypse of consumer society. Nea So Copros is surrounded by the tangible result of overexploitation: 'deadlands' cover most areas of Sonmi's world and are inexorably advancing, with the mention of a 'Californian boat-people solution' (*CA* 224) already suggesting the collapse of the United States. Deadlands signal the end of Cheap Nature, for if capitalism historically solves its crises by 'extend[ing] the zone of appropriation faster than the zone of exploitation' (Moore 2014: 291), in 'An Orison' the world is shown to be literally 'running out of places for people to be', to return to the image of Sanders' short story ([2001] 2015: 187), and to exploit – a conjuncture which, in *The Stone Gods*, leads to space colonization.[14] Yet corpocracy conceals the impending eco-catastrophe and end of capitalism by 'landscaping' itself as

---

[14] According to Moore (2014), neoliberal capitalism is already at the end of Cheap Nature as a 'civilization strategy' precisely because of the exhaustion of the 'commodity frontiers' through which capital solves its cyclical crises.

the culmination of a progressive history: 'the most stable state Pyramid in the history of civilization' (*CA* 342). On the one hand, an apocalyptic conception of history serves, once more, to preserve the status quo and, by blinding people to the approaching end, deterministically condemns them. On the other, *Cloud Atlas*'s historical trajectory from colonialism to Nea So Copros' ultra-neoliberal capitalism indicates how it is the unquenchable will to power behind the apocalyptic 'landscaping' of progress which is driving this civilization – and our own, Mitchell's extrapolation indicates – towards environmental demise. As a character of the sixth story puts it, '*more gear, more food, faster speeds, longer lifes, easier lifes, more power, yay. Now the Hole World is big but it weren't big 'nuff for that hunger*' (*CA* 286; emphasis in original).

While Horrox's sermon and Xultation are exposed as simulacra of a virtual future the will to power fabricates according to the utopian teleology of the traditional apocalyptic paradigm, the two narratives are also part of a novel which 'landscapes' the anti-apocalyptic virtual futures of 'An Orison' and 'Sloosha's Crossin''. Through these sections, in which the end is a dystopian catastrophe caused by predatory apocalyptic logic, Mitchell seeks to debunk the apocalyptic metanarrative and positively shape the actual future, all the while respecting the latter's radical openness, in line with the novel's structural critique of the sense of an ending. As Luisa's neighbour, Javier, ponders, 'If you could *see* the future, like you can see the end of 16th Street from the top of Kilroy's department store, that means it's already there. If it's already there, that means it isn't a thing you can change' (*CA* 418; emphasis in original). Through its anti-deterministic structure, *Cloud Atlas* suggests that 'the end of 16th Street', be it a metaphor for the telos of apocalyptic history or for the chronological conclusion of the book, is not 'already there'. Rather, the novel's structural resistance to teleology exalts the individual's agency to inform the course of history and, therefore, avert the catastrophe in the readers' actual future. Since '*the answer* [to whether the future can be altered or not] *is not a function of metaphysics, but one, simply of power*' (*CA* 418; emphasis in original), the power of narrative to imagine anti-apocalyptic virtual futures and call the readers to action is what Mitchell, just like Yuknavitch in *The Book of Joan*, pits against the will to power and its apocalyptic simulacra. As Zachry points out, in a concertina-like parallel with Isaac's theory, 'pretendin' can bend bein'' (*CA* 297) – for the worst, as we have seen in Chapter 1 with *The Island at the End of the World*, but also for the best, as we shall further explore in the Conclusion.

Sonmi's testimony, archived in the orison (and we shall discuss the politics of Nea So Copros' archives in the Conclusion), can be seen as a symbol of the book as a whole and of *Cloud Atlas*'s critical temporality. Her narrative revolves around the dystopian dangers of apocalyptic determinism. Sonmi appears to embody the revolutionary and utopian possibilities of the apocalyptic paradigm, as she becomes the 'Messiah of the fabricants' (*CA* 346), the central actor in what is seemingly an uprising against corpocracy, preparing for a 'briter tomorrow' (*CA* 343). However, in this case too, the revolutionary and utopian possibilities of the trope of the new world are just predetermined simulacra produced by the will to power in order to pass even more coercive laws. Referring to the meaning of 'orison', though, Jonathan Boulter notes that the object functions 'as a prayer to the future' (2011: 135). From 'Sloosha's Crossin'' we know that, chronologically, Sonmi's prayer for a world beyond predatory apocalypticism is not enough to prevent the catastrophe from happening. Yet, thanks to the concertina structure, the effects of the fabricant's story are not written once and for all and it is as if her appeal is heard by the other characters, in particular by Adam, who pledges himself to Abolitionism. More importantly, her testimony 'confers upon [readers] a burden, the burden of responsibility' (Boulter 2011: 137). At the conclusion of 'Sloosha's Crossin'', Zachry's son invites readers to 'Sit down a beat or two' (*CA* 325) while Sonmi tells her story through the orison – a passage that embodies the anti-apocalyptic power of narrative. Mitchell here directly asks readers to reflect upon the fabricant's anti-apocalyptic appeal and to take responsibility for their own civilization, in order to avoid *Cloud Atlas*'s dire virtual futures. Indeed, the passage leads to the second half of the novel and, hence, encourages readers to 'believe', as Adam continues to repeat in the conclusion (*CA* 528), in the narrative boomerang, namely, in the possibility of a different history of the Anthropocene than one culminating in the apocalypse.

Adam's final words exalt the power of individual agency against determinism and the predatory anthropogenic civilization apocalypticism supports. '[A]ny ocean [is] but a multitude of drops' (*CA* 529), and thus any life, although a mere drop, can make a difference – a point that becomes all the more relevant in the current globalized context, to which the novel's transnational stories allude, where localized individual action may seem ineffective against decentered networks of power. After all, the image of the ocean, combined with the concertina structure, suggests that these individual acts of resistance can come together, transhistorically and transnationally, to amount for more than localized effects. To Adam, 'history admits no rules; only outcomes', that is, he rejects the way in which the apocalyptic metanarrative, by discerning a pattern in history, pre-empts any attempt to alter the course of events. The fundamental notion is, instead, that of belief, which narrative can inform. Since 'a purely predatory world *shall* consume itself', as the arrow of the Anthropocene's history in *Cloud Atlas*'s first half demonstrates, the key is not to believe that this 'entropy [is] written within our nature' and succumb to the passivity fostered by apocalyptic determinism. Rather, we must '*believe* that humanity may transcend tooth & claw, ... *believe* [that] diverse races & creeds can share this world ... *believe* leaders must be just, violence muzzled, power accountable & the riches of the Earth & its Oceans shared equitably' (*CA* 528; emphasis in original) – a repetition which is in stark contrast to the pattern of predatory behaviour and encourages the readers' active resistance to the pattern itself. The fact that 'The Pacific Journal' is set in the nineteenth century and thus that the world Adam wishes for has not come true, either in the novel's history or in the readers' world, only contributes to Mitchell's subversion of apocalyptic and narrative determinism. It is an instance of what Bernstein and Morson term 'sideshadowing' which draws 'attention to the unfulfilled or unrealised possibilities of the past [a]s a way of disrupting the affirmations of a triumphalist, unidirectional view of history' (Bernstein 1994: 3). By 'rel[ying] on a concept of time as a field of possibilities' (Morson 1998: 603), *Cloud Atlas*'s sideshadowing emphasizes the openness of futurity, contingency, and the ethical importance of the present moment as the locus of agency.

While *Cloud Atlas* sets out its protocol of reading through the device of the birthmark, which prompts readers to look for the concertina-like parallels between the narratives, Winterson's *The Stone Gods* does the same through the names of the main characters in its four parts. 'Planet Blue' is set in a futuristic civilization on Orbus, a dying planet which appears to have found its chance for a new beginning in the colonization of Planet Blue; 'Easter Island' takes place in the eighteenth century on the eponymous island soon after the arrival of Captain Cook, the explorer and cartographer, and at the time in which the very last tree on the island is cut; 'Post-3 War' develops in Tech City, run by MORE corporation, in a very near future after a nuclear war; and finally, 'Wreck City', the immediate sequel of the previous strand, is set in the eponymous Wreck City, where rebels and radioactive mutants live outside the boundaries of the power of MORE. Throughout the narratives the protagonist is Billie/y Crusoe, a woman in all the futuristic stories and a man in 'Easter Island' – and of course it is hardly a chance that, as signalled by Billie/y's surname, Winterson's hypotext is Daniel Defoe's *Robinson Crusoe* (1719), whose colonial logic she subverts.[15] Billie/y falls

---

[15] For an in-depth investigation of the relationship between *The Stone Gods* and *Robinson Crusoe* see Hicks (2016). Hicks, indeed, traces the echoes of Defoe's novel across many twenty-first-century post-apocalyptic novels.

in love with Spike/Spikkers, a female 'Robo *sapiens*' – namely, a robot capable of evolution – in the first, third and fourth chapter, and a male native of Easter Island in the second. The consistency in the names of the main characters gestures to the parallels between the epochs and narratives, parallels which culminate in the cyclical repetition of humankind's environmental catastrophic mistakes throughout different ages and planets, with the eponymous stone gods, in whose name Easter Island's entire ecosystem is destroyed, becoming the symbol of these mistakes.

Adding to Winterson's deconstruction of linear time in other novels (Jenzen 2009; Stowers 1995), *The Stone Gods'* cyclical critical temporality warps apocalyptic teleology and subverts its central dichotomy – the New Jerusalem versus the present world – by exposing alleged new worlds as already old, for they are co-opted, just as the previous ones, by an exploitative nexus of colonialism, capital and instrumentalist approaches to nature that will lead civilization to yet another demise. And while the cyclicality of the novel's history serves to exaggerate, and thus foreground, the determinism inherent in the apocalyptic model of history, what ultimately drives the book, just like *Cloud Atlas* and *The Book of Joan*, is the belief in the power of narrative to positively inform the actual future. As Winterson puts it, 'I am sure that when we challenge ourselves imaginatively, we then use that challenge in our lives. I want *The Stone Gods* to be a prompt, but most of all, a place of possibility' (Onega 2011: 275), those very possibilities that the sense of an ending closes off.

Similarly to 'An Orison', where late capitalism is running out of Cheap Nature to appropriate and exploit, the first narrative of *The Stone Gods* depicts a late capitalist world threatened by exhausted natural resources, a growing population and the unquenchable capitalist drive – or hunger, to go back to *Cloud Atlas* – for more. This hunger is embodied by the name of the corporation, MORE, which controls the Central Power and whose branch MORE-*Futures* ironically risks leading to decline and 'less' and the very absence of a future for humankind. In a culmination of the instrumentalist approach, MORE regiments nature in all its forms. People get 'fixed' at a certain age, that is, they prevent their bodies from getting old, and most are 'born outside the womb' (Winterson [2007] 2008: 77).[16] Orbus engineers all its food, for the little natural world that survives the encroaching desert is considered unsanitary. And, in an attempt to keep global warming in check, the planet has a 'weather shield' and permanent refrigeration in the polar regions (*TSG* 37). Yet, if MORE is 'running out of planet' on Orbus

---

[16] All further references to Winterson's *The Stone Gods* as *TSG*.

(*TSG* 4), it has found a new one in Planet Blue, which should allow capital to renew its reserves of Cheap Nature.

Recalling the American Phoenix PR stunt in Colson Whitehead's *Zone One* (2011) discussed in Chapter 2 as well as Jean de Men's propaganda in *The Book of Joan*, the obsessive repetition of the word 'new' in the descriptions of Planet Blue (*TSG* 3–8) hints at how the Central Power is deploying the apocalyptic motif of the New Jerusalem, 'a new heaven and a new earth' (Rev. 21:1), to prevent panic and rebellions in the face of the approaching environmental catastrophe. The end is coming for Orbus, but, to go back to Isaac's terminology in *Cloud Atlas*, it is apocalyptically 'landscaped' as a 'Chance of a lifetime – new start – brave new world – wipe the slate clean' (*TSG* 55). The expression 'brave new world' retains all the irony of Aldous Huxley's eponymous dystopia (1932), for just like *The Book of Joan*'s CIEL, Planet Blue will be an elitist state, under the aegis of MORE. The corporation's secret plan is to transport to the new world only those who can afford it, leaving the poor to die on the soon-to-be-uninhabitable Orbus, except those poor, that is, who will be deployed by MORE to work for the rich in this hierarchical society – Cheap Nature, again. This exclusionary dynamic parodies the apocalyptic dichotomy of the elect versus the damned, putting capital at the centre of MORE's secular Last Judgment. As in *Cloud Atlas*, the apocalyptic trope of the new world is exposed as an instrument of power structures, which deploy the simulacrum of a utopia towards which history would tend to keep the population submissive and legitimize the status quo.

When introducing the Planet Blue space mission to the population, the President of the Central Power draws attention to the connection with past colonial enterprises to the Indies and the Americas (*TSG* 6).[17] This parallel is further evoked by the name of the space-liner which will take people to Planet Blue, the Mayflower, and framed by one of the various textual refrains, whose role is to reflect, at the level of the narrative structure, the repetitions in the cyclical history traced by the novel: '*The new world – El Dorado, Atlantis, the Gold Coast, Newfoundland, Plymouth Rock, Rapanaui* [sic]*, Utopia, Planet Blue*' (*TSG* 8, 94, 150, 238; emphasis in original). Not only does the refrain signals that the new world is a recurrent dream for humankind, thus complicating the apocalyptic idea of a radical new beginning, but it underlines how this allegedly utopian trope is imbricated with the conquest, exploitation and devastation

---

[17] These references do not imply that Orbus is Earth – indeed, as we shall see, the existence of the dinosaurs on Planet Blue, as well as the presence of a radio signal sent by Spike at the beginning of the colonization of Planet Blue and discovered in 'Wreck City', suggest that Planet Blue is Earth – but, rather, emphasize the cyclical repetition of colonial violence, even across different planets.

of the Age of Discovery and colonialism. El Dorado, a mythical country full of gold, was the driving force behind many of the expeditions of the Spanish conquistadores to the New World. The Gold Coast, Newfoundland, and Rapa Nui – the latter being the indigenous name of Easter Island – were all colonies, while Plymouth Rock is the alleged site of arrival of the Mayflower pilgrims to what would become the United States. The island of Atlantis, finally, was an ancient colonial power, according to Plato's myth in *Timaeus*. However, given the presence of Utopia in the refrain, Winterson's reference could also be to the *New Atlantis* (1627), a utopian narrative by Francis Bacon, which, together with Thomas More's *Utopia* (1516), features expansionist ideological elements that reflect the historical beginnings of colonialism (Balasopoulos 2004). By tracing this connection between the new worlds of the colonial era and the new world of Planet Blue, Winterson's critical temporality signals that the conquest of this new world in space perpetuates the very imbrication of apocalyptic logic, colonialism and capitalism that is bringing the old world to an anthropogenic end.

As we have seen, Revelation's gendering of the New Jerusalem as the virgin bride is reflected in the codification of the New World as a feminized space, a virgin land awaiting the always male explorer. This codification, in turn, links back to the colonial and capitalist production of a Cheap Nature free to be exploited, for '"Nature" … encompasses the underside of rationalist dualisms that oppose reason to nature, mind to body, emotional female to rational male, human to animal, and so on' (Plumwood 2003: 52). The name of the Captain in charge of the mission to Planet Blue, Handsome, emphasizes the patriarchal motif of the conqueror, of women and lands. For his journeys, Handsome is promised by MORE 'a vast virgin country' and a 'princess' (*TSG* 58), Spike. To Handsome, the Robo *sapiens* is as much of a 'new-found land' to be conquered as Planet Blue (*TSG* 81), though both colonizing projects backfire. The presence of Cook's *Journals* on the spaceship amplifies Handsome's colonizing impulse and excerpts from the *Journals* are among the narrative's refrains (*TSG* 59; 112; 117; 193), a further element signalling the repetition of colonial dynamics across planet and epochs. Following Cook's footsteps, Handsome's first voyage to Planet Blue is aimed at a form of mapping, namely, at collecting data on the new world, so that MORE can plan what it euphemistically terms 'relocation'. For as Graham Huggan underlines, the 'key rhetorical strategies implemented in the production of the map, such as the reinscription, enclosure and hierarchization of space, … provide an analogue for the acquisition, management and reinforcement of colonial power' (1989: 115), and are at the core of the colonial and capitalist production of Cheap Nature. The novel thus exposes mapping as central to the colonial project and its instrumentalist approach to nature, as it already was the case with Cook's expeditions.

The colonization of Planet Blue begins, and indeed ends, with an ecocidal act that condenses the history of the Anthropocene the novels analysed in this chapter outline, from the colonial era to anthropogenic climate change. Handsome's spaceship deflects an asteroid and makes it collide with Planet Blue, thus provoking a dust storm aimed at blacking out the sun and killing the dinosaurs that represent the biggest obstacle to MORE's neoliberal brave new world. This act of dominance reproduces colonial dynamics that constructed the lands of the new worlds as 'unused, underused or empty – areas of rational deficit' (Plumwood 2003: 53): Planet Blue's resources can be exploited and its inhabitants mercilessly annihilated because they are conceived as 'area[s] of rational deficit', pure nature that needs to yield profit. The mission, however, fails, as the asteroid triggers an ice age that makes Planet Blue uninhabitable for humans in the immediate future. Tellingly, when Handsome understands his mistake, he wishes for yet another new chance, mirroring the cyclical history of humankind's desire for apocalyptic new worlds traced by *The Stone Gods*. Just as the apocalyptic emphasis placed on futurity leads to the disregard for the present, which is understood as merely part of a predetermined pattern, the promise of a utopian renewal embodied by a new world, Winterson suggests, may provide us with an excuse for not taking care of, and responsibility for, our world.

Planet Blue, in fact, 'isn't new at all but a memory of a new world', since humankind, after devastating a planet, has travelled to other worlds before, so that 'the universe is a memory of our mistakes' (*TSG* 105–106). In one of the exploratory journeys to Planet Blue, Handsome's crew discovers Planet White, a dead world once inhabited by a civilization whose CO_2 emissions 'caused irreversible warming' (*TSG* 68). 'The rest', Handsome explains, 'is history[, a history] looking more and more like ours' (*TSG* 68), where 'ours' obviously refers to Orbus, but Winterson's implication is that it could refer to Earth as well, as the novel's sections set on a Post-3 War Earth ravaged by climate change and nuclear war make clear. Orbus's name emphasizes the novel's cosmic cycle of self-destruction as, '*orbis*' in Latin means both world and circle, sphere. In a cyclical history there can be no true rupture with the past and, hence, no apocalyptic new beginning – and here is the key to the novel's critical temporality. As Kermode underlines, 'apocalyptic thought belongs to rectilinear rather than cyclical views of the world' ([1966] 2000: 5), since at the core of the sense of an ending lies the fact that the end and the ensuing renewal are unique events. It is this radical break from anything that happened before that *The Stone Gods* subverts through its cyclical apocalypses and new worlds. The slaughter of the dinosaurs on Planet Blue further warps a linear history, with its distinction between past and future and the teleological movement from old to new world, by suggesting that the futuristic-looking Orbus is the planet humankind colonizes and destroys before Earth, known as the Blue Planet due to its high percentage of water. Planet Blue is thus, quite literally, an old world – ours. As Hope Jennings argues, Winterson deconstructs the 'utopian desire for a complete break from history and thus a more "pure" beginning, which always requires a forgetting or repression of the material conditions (and mistakes) of the past' (2010: 133), a past that *The Stone Gods* foregrounds by exposing the colonial roots of the Anthropocene.

Even beyond space colonization, *The Stone Gods* signals how apocalyptic discourse and its new worlds underlie the capitalist world-ecology. Amidst the nuclear and environmental devastation of a Post-3 War Earth, MORE understands that capitalism needs to reinvent itself: from the 'MORE is MORE' of rampant consumerism and the 'economics of greed', to the 'economics of purpose', a renting economy in which consumers become 'modest and eco-conscious members of a new world order' (*TSG* 164–165). This 'new world order', however, is nothing else than the rehash of old colonial dynamics. As a character named Friday predicts, 'The West will race ahead – we are the new clean green machine, and the developing world will stay the way we wanted it to stay – raw materials and cheap labour' (*TSG* 197), in other words, neo-colonial Cheap Nature, at least until there are 'raw materials and cheap labour' to appropriate and exploit. Winterson's Friday, as opposed to Defoe's Friday in *Robinson Crusoe*, is not a 'savage' saved and educated by a white 'civilized' man but a former and disillusioned economist for the World Bank, which is also indicative of *The Stone Gods*' critique of colonialism, in that the World Bank is an organ responsible for imposing the neoliberal agenda on the Global South through structural adjustment programs that effectively represent forms of neo-colonialism (Harvey 2005: 27–29). As Whyte argues, 'lowering emissions [or other similar "green" strategies] without addressing colonialism can be highly problematic' (2016: 5, 12). MORE's role in this new world order of a green renting economy signals how, rather than targeting the ideological and material causes of anthropogenic environmental risks, sustainability 'is inherently nonantagonistic with regard to global economic development. After all, sustainability began life as sustainable development. "Development," in turn, meant and means greater integration into the global economy', so much so that sustainability becomes a 'vital and core concept of neoliberalisation itself' (Elliott 2016: 9). As Billie muses emphasizing the apocalyptic conception of history which drives capitalism and to which we shall return in Chapter 4, through the 'economics of purpose' capitalism is simply going 'forward into its destiny – complete control of everything and everyone, and with our consent. This is the new world' (*TSG* 167).

As signalled by one of the novel's refrains – 'Everything is imprinted for ever with what it once was' (*TSG* 105, 144, 246) – *The Stone Gods*' cyclical history, in which humankind seems doomed to repeat the same mistakes bringing about environmental apocalyptic catastrophes over and over again, exaggerates the determinism inherent in apocalyptic logic. Yet the novel stresses that 'this is a quantum Universe … neither random nor determined. It is potential at every second. All you can do is intervene' (*TSG* 75). Glossing Winterson's point that she 'use[s] both Nietzsche and Ouspensky and the idea of eternal return', Susana Onega argues:

> Although [P. D. Ouspensky] took for granted the fixity of eternal return, he postulated the existence of various possibilities of action presenting themselves through the life of an individual, at least potentially …. However, individuals will unconsciously follow the same predetermined path once and again unless they are capable of recognising the potential for self-willed, conscious change inherent in each moment of their lives. (2011: 278–279)

Thus, just as in *Cloud Atlas* the concertina-like structure connects the repetitions of the will to power as well as the individual acts of resistance to it, what cyclically returns in *The Stone Gods* are also acts of love that attempt to subvert the exploitative apocalypticism behind the cyclical anthropogenic catastrophes. As another textual refrain goes, 'Love is an intervention' (*TSG* 83, 217, 244), or to go back to Winterson's words, a 'place of possibility' against the deterministic temporality of apocalyptic discourse.

As ever with Winterson, love is a vehicle for transgression and the queering of hegemonic discourses. The love between Billie/y Crusoe and Spike/Spikkers challenges heteronormativity, in that the couples are in each narrative homosexual ones, and articulates a fluid conception of gender, for the characters move from female to male across the ages. Indeed, that Spike is a robot in three of the narratives problematizes the notion of gender *tout court*. Spike is the very embodiment of a place of possibility: Robo *sapiens* should be incapable of emotions because they are machines, yet Spike breaks the limits deterministically set to her evolution, develops a heart and begins to feel. Importantly in terms of my argument, the love between Billie/y Crusoe and Spike/Spikkers is queer also in terms of Winterson's project of 'queering temporality', which characterizes

Winterson's oeuvre throughout (Jenzen 2009). This love goes beyond the norm of linear apocalyptic time, for it effaces the boundaries between past, present and future, and constitutes an attempt at an intervention against apocalyptic determinism and the dystopian implications of apocalyptic logic more generally. As Abigail Rine points out, Billie/y Crusoe and Spike/Spikkers's love is a 'renewed form of relationality that … seeks mutuality and intimacy rather than appropriation and objectification' (2011: 79). Through this love, Winterson fleshes out the model of a relationship with the other, at once the beloved and the planet, that intervenes against the anthropogenic cycle of devastation by challenging the imbrication of the motif of the new world with the appropriation and objectification of colonial and patriarchal discourses.

The very name of Billie/y Crusoe, thanks to the obvious reference to Defoe's *Robinson Crusoe*, whose excerpts recur in the novel, embodies this subversion. Winterson's Crusoe, Fiona McCulloch remarks, is 'not a white colonizer, but, rather a lesbian explorer of new possibilities, who has a relationship with a Robo *sapiens* post-human. She rejects the phallocratic narrative of territorial control and embraces a symbiotic co-existence with others that exceeds cartographies of differences' (2012: 63). Indeed, Handsome's colonial and patriarchal paradigm of travel is contrasted with Billie's reluctant approach to the colonization of Planet Blue, which she wishes could sail away from Orbus's explorers. And, when describing her post-human lover, Billie queers the image of the map and an exploitative approach to the trope of the new world. Spike is 'unknown, uncharted, different in every way … another life-form, another planet, another chance' (*TSG* 90) but Billie, contrary to his namesake, to the male explorer Handsome and to MORE, does not wish to map, categorize, and define this new world. 'When I touch her, my fingers don't question what she is' (*TSG* 107), Billie says, overcoming her initial concerns about the boundaries between human and post-human. Waiting for the death which will soon be upon them because of the ice age triggered by the asteroid, Billie goes back to another recurrent motif in the novel, that of the weight of the new world. While the inhabitants of Orbus know that Planet Blue 'weighs a yatto-gram' (*TSG* 3), as they have extensively mapped their new world and collected data on it, Billie realizes that 'This new world that [she] found and lost [namely, Spike] weighs nothing at all' (*TSG* 112). Spike is unquantifiable and, therefore, cannot be subjected to an exploitative logic, as instead happens to Planet Blue. By the same token, to Spike, the love for Billie represents the way in which she could '*find a language of beginning*', a new world which would remain '*my free and wild place that I would never try to tame* …. [that] *would never be sold or exchanged*' (*TSG* 82; emphasis in original). The references to 'a language of beginning' and a 'wild place' reinforce the connection between the new world represented by the beloved and the new world of Planet Blue. Indeed, Winterson juxtaposes Spike's appeal for a relationship which would not fall prey to the same exploitative apocalyptic logic and would defy patriarchal paradigms, as it would not be aimed at taming and at commodifying the loved one, with Handsome's own 'language of beginning' for Planet Blue: 'If we can wipe [the dinosaurs] out, we can begin again' (*TSG* 82).

Even Billy, the protagonist of 'Easter Island', though he is a sailor on Cook's ship, and thus part of a mission aimed at territorial mastery and exploitation, joins the ranks of the many travellers of Winterson's oeuvre, who, Cath Stowers (1995) argues, subvert the patriarchal paradigm of travel thanks to journeys which defy mapping, for they are labyrinthine and non-teleological, bridging irreconcilable temporal dimensions and/or taking place in fantastic worlds. As Billy muses, 'there are at once two voyages to be made – the first of direction and course, and the second unpurposed [sic] and untried, and if that voyage can be mapped I do not know any man that has mapped it' (*TSG* 131). The latter non-teleological typology best defines Billy's voyage. On the one hand, Billy avows that he joined Cook not in order to contribute to the cartographic and colonizing purpose of the enterprise, but, rather, because he is in love with another sailor. This presence of homosexual bonds among the members of Cook's crew queers the patriarchal heteronormativity that underlies the masculine paradigm of travel, 'an Otherizing where "woman" is deeply implicated as the mysterious *object* to the male *subject*' (Stowers 1995: 140–141; emphasis in original), which corresponds to the feminization of the colonial New World. On the other hand, when he is left behind on Easter Island by mistake, Billy abandons the journey 'of direction and course', the journey of the map, once and for all and articulates his love for Spikkers in terms that clearly go against colonizing discourse: '*No flag, no territory, no fortress, no claim, but this love*' (*TSG* 242; emphasis in original).

In addition to love, narrative is *The Stone Gods*' other anti-apocalyptic intervention and, as in *Cloud Atlas*, the critique of the determinism of apocalyptic history is combined in Winterson's novel with the critique of the narrative sense of an ending. Narrative is considered old-fashioned and useless on Orbus and Post-3 War Earth, which gestures to the contemporary post-apocalyptic novel's anxiety over the survival of the literary archive. As Billie concisely puts it, 'Neither art nor love fits well' (*TSG* 169) in these utilitarian late capitalist societies, so that her 'love for writing [and reading] materials, in a world where writing has become defunct, [is another element that] marks her out as queer' (McCulloch 2012: 66). However, corroborating Spike's belief that poetry saved humankind 'Not once, but many times' (*TSG* 95), when London is bombed during the nuclear war, the books of the British Library literally save Billie's life, protecting her from the collapsing building. Through this powerful image, Winterson conveys the hope that her novel, as a place of possibility fostering narratives and understandings that challenge an exploitative apocalyptic logic, may call us to action and save us from the anthropogenic apocalypses she depicts.

The Stone Gods' faith in the anti-apocalyptic power of narrative, which in the Conclusion I shall explore as anti-apocalyptic archive fever, is embodied by the found manuscript, *The Stone Gods* itself, which the Billie of 'Post-3 War' finds on the tube. 'Wreck City' actually reveals that the author is none other than Billie, who wrote it as a 'message in a bottle. A signal' (*TSG* 241) to her fellow citizens of Tech City, in the hope of awakening their conscience. Reflecting the cyclicality of the history traced by the text and pointing at the message she wants her readers to understand, that of humankind's endless repetition of the same mistakes in the name of a new world, Billie leaves the manuscript on the Circle Line. The device of the found manuscript initially suggests that the cosmic cycle of self-destruction is just Billie's fantasy, aimed at critiquing human nature in the wake of a devastating Third World War. And yet, in 'Wreck City' Spike and Billie, on the run from MORE, end up at the Lovell Telescope, which picks up a repeating signal. At first, Spike does not know what to make of it: 'I think it is something very strange, very old, and at the same time in front of us' (*TSG* 222), she says – a sentence which underlines the problematization of the distinction between old and new world, past and future, at the core of the novel's critical temporality. Soon, however, Spike recognizes the signal as a Robo *sapiens*'s line of code, sent sixty-five million years before, when the dinosaurs became extinct. Thus, inside the fictional universe, the boundary between fact and fiction collapses in the typical postmodern fashion that recurs in Winterson's writings.[18] To further complicate this boundary, a manuscript of *The Stone Gods* was found on the London tube in 2007 before the novel's publication, left by

---

[18] Cf. for instance *Sexing the Cherry* (1989), set at the time of Charles I of England but featuring characters that time-travel to the present days, and Winterson's points around the constructedness of history in *Oranges Are Not the Only Fruit*: 'People like to separate storytelling which is not fact from history which is fact. They do this so they know what to believe and what not to believe', a belief imbricated with power structures, since 'Knowing what to believe had its advantages. It built an empire and kept people where they belonged, in the bright realm of the wallet ... Very often history is a means of denying the past. Denying the past is to refuse to recognise its integrity. To fit it, force it, to suck out the spirit until it looks the way you think it should' ([1985] 1991: 91, 92; ellipsis in original).

someone working at Penguin (Briggs 2007). As Winterson recalls, 'I thought: I'll just play with that and see if it will go in [the novel] .... And then of course it swung the whole second part of the book' (Mullen 2007) and its *mise en abyme*. Billie's manuscript remains apparently unread, for '[she] s[ees] it [is] still there ... round and round on the Circle Line. A repeating world' (*TSG* 241) – where the expression 'A repeating world' mirrors the words Handsome deploys to frame the cosmic cycle of self-destruction (*TSG* 59), hence suggesting that the people who ignore Billie's text take part in this cycle, as they choose to remain unaware of the dystopian implications of apocalypticism revealed by the narrative. Yet Winterson's novel finds its readers: us. Just as in the conclusion of 'Sloosha's Crossin'', readers become responsible for decoding the anti-apocalyptic signal of the text. As Billie metafictionally points out, the crux of the matter is that 'it's possible to be telling the truth even in the moment of invention' (*TSG* 145) and, hence, each of our fictions, although it remains just a story among a variety of possible other stories, can be an intervention.

The Stone Gods' structure contributes to making the novel a place of possibility against the determinism of the sense of an ending. Evoking the previously discussed difference between conventional narrative structures, with their sense of closed and predetermined time, and life, with its sense of open time and contingency, Billie muses: 'When I look back at my own life ... what is it that I recognize? Not the stories with a beginning, a middle and an end, but the stories that began again, the ones that twisted away, like a bend in the road', shaped by actions that inform the future (*TSG* 106). Significantly, Billie deploys the linear and teleological image of the road but twists it, reflecting *The Stone Gods*' critical temporality, for, as she goes on to observe, 'True stories', namely, those stories which seek to represent time as it is lived, 'are the ones that lie open at the border, allowing a crossing, a further frontier .... Like the universe, there is no end' (*TSG* 106). As Winterson puts it in *Lighthousekeeping* (2004), 'There's no such thing in all the world ... As an ending', since only a story that 'begins again [reflects] the story of life' (49–109). Connections and recurring patterns between *The Stone Gods*' narratives do reinforce the determinism of the cyclical repetition of humankind's mistakes throughout history, yet, at the level of the narrative structure, they also convey the idea of openness, as if the stories could never come to a definite close. Even though the first two chapters end with death, they suggest that this is not final, and that the lovers will meet again, which the following section promptly illustrates through a new version of the Billie/Spike couple. 'Post-3 War', instead, frames the openness of its conclusion through the image of the open gate, which leads Billie and Spike into Wreck City and the following chapter. In 'Wreck City' another image exemplifies Winterson's critique of the determinism of narrative and apocalyptic teleology, as well as her faith in the power of narrative. Leaving Spike her manuscript, 'shuffled as a pack of cards', Billie explains that 'The book isn't finished, …. The pages are loose – it can be written again' (*TSG* 241, 242). If history, as Winterson's production continuously indicates, is just a story, that outlined by *The Stone Gods* is symbolically made of loose pages that can be rewritten and shuffled in a different order, an image which emphasizes humankind's agency and the subversion of the narrative sense of an ending. As yet another refrain of *The Stone Gods* goes, 'Is this how it ends? It isn't ended yet' (*TSG* 107, 154, 241), that is, there is still time to write with our actions a different history of the Anthropocene.

Written at a time in which the environmental risks of our system of accumulation are becoming more and more apparent, *Jamestown*, *Far North*, *The Book of Joan*, *Cloud Atlas* and *The Stone Gods* trace a long history of the Anthropocene, from the colonial era to a post-apocalyptic future, and in doing so uncover the influence of apocalyptic discourse, via the trope of the new world, on this geological era. Through their patterns of repetition, which trouble the apocalyptic ideology of progress and the teleological movement from old to new world, these novels foreground an insidious nexus of apocalyptic logic, colonialism and capitalism that produces the idea of an endlessly available and exploitable Cheap Nature. Against the determinism of apocalyptic history, determinism that becomes particularly damaging if to the utopian teleology of the traditional apocalyptic paradigm we substitute the negative teleology of an approaching environmental catastrophe, *Cloud Atlas* and *The Stone Gods* articulate critical temporalities that warp the deterministic linearity of the sense of an ending, opening up spaces of possibility for agency. At the core of this chapter's discussion of the Anthropocene's new worlds lies the capitalist world-ecology. It is to the apocalyptic echoes of capitalism, in particular neoliberal capitalism, that the next chapter turns.

4

After the Neoliberal Future

Let us go back to the novel from which we started, Karen Thompson Walker's *The Age of Miracles* (2012), where the eponymous age of miracles is nothing else than our age of technological progress. 'We performed all sorts of miracles', Julia reminisces listing things like rockets, satellites, nanotechnology, cloning and transplants. 'At the time of the slowing', she continues, 'stem cell researchers were on the verge of healing paralysis – surely the lame soon would have walked. And yet, the unknown still outweighed the known. We never determined the cause of the slowing' (*AoM* 266). The inexplicable slowing quite literally slows down and puts an end to the age of miracles, puncturing its central belief, namely, the belief in a future organized and made knowable by steady progress, as encapsulated by the proleptic 'surely' above. Now let us compare these reflections with the description of the pre-apocalyptic life of the zombie hunter Kaitlyn in Colson Whitehead's *Zone One* (2011) as an 'implacable march through a series of imaginative and considered birthday parties ... each birthday party transcending the last and approaching a kind of birthday-party perfection that once accomplished would usher in an exquisite new age of bourgeois utopia' (*ZO* 46–47). This 'exquisite new age of bourgeois utopia', of course, never comes to pass. Kaitlyn's 'implacable march' is halted by an anti-apocalyptic culmination, the zombie horde, very much non-exquisite and bourgeois in its gore, which makes visible the repressed and unsaid of capital as typical of the genre of the zombie narrative.[1] As Mark Spitz realizes, 'it wasn't utopia that they had worked toward after all'. Rather, Kaitlyn, as the representative of the current socio-economic order, neoliberalism, which she continues to prop up even after the apocalypse with her unwavering faith in Buffalo's regulations, 'had summoned the plague: as she cut into the first slice of cake at her final, perfect birthday party, history had come to an end'

---

[1] On the connection between the figure of the zombie and capitalism see, for instance, Newitz (2006), Luckhurst (2015) and E. C. Williams (2011).

(ZO 47).² Just as in *The Age of Miracles*, progress and its teleology come to a standstill and the future does not shape up the way people thought it would, revealing all its indeterminacy and contingency. Indeed, there seems to be hardly any future at all for humankind in both texts. Mark Spitz's reference to the end of history is significant. In the typical reversal of a utopian teleology into a dystopian teleology that, throughout this book, I have identified as the prime critical temporality deployed to deconstruct the pervasive legacies of apocalyptic logic on our present and denounce their catastrophic risks, the end of history personified by Whitehead's zombies point to the central concern of this chapter: the spectre of no future that haunts the apocalyptically-inflected neoliberal end of history and its supposedly utopian completion of modernity's project.

Analysing texts set in a near future or even an alternate present/near past – Nathaniel Rich's *Odds Against Tomorrow* (2013), Walker's *The Age of Miracles*, Whitehead's *Zone One* and the focus of this chapter, Emily St. John Mandel's *Station Eleven* (2014) and Douglas Coupland's *Player One* (2010) – I interrogate the hegemonic temporality of our neoliberal moment, the utopian end of history in which the future is constructed as more of the same, but which the novels' critical temporalities expose as the site of an extended hopeless present, no future, no alternatives and an ongoing slow apocalypse. The title of this chapter thus frames not only how the post-apocalyptic fictions discussed take us beyond the collapse of the neoliberal order, but also how neoliberalism's utopian proclamations are undercut by a pervasive sense of no futurity, a temporality that produces the dystopian visions which are the subject of my book. I open the chapter by considering the apocalyptic echoes of neoliberalism, encapsulated by the notion of the end of history and the ways in which financial capitalism manages the openness and contingency of time through debt and instruments like derivatives in an attempt to deterministically ensure the reproduction of the current system of accumulation. I trace the cracks in this apocalyptic construction of the future as more of the same, from anthropogenic climate change to the 2007/2008 financial crash and the dystopian foreclosed possibilities of 'capitalist realism' (Fisher 2009) that underlie the neoliberal end of history and its supposedly utopian foreclosed possibilities. The chapter then turns to theorizations of the neoliberal present as stalled, devoid of alternatives and hence of genuine futurity, from Jameson's argument that our sense of time

---

² Cf. Hicks: 'Constantly citing reconstruction regulations, [Kaitlyn] is emblematic of the very system of neoliberal economic and social regulation from which the apocalypse might have freed them' (2016: 127).

under global capital shrinks to a series of fragmented presents to Franco 'Bifo' Berardi's 'slow cancellation of the future' (2011) and Cazdyn's 'chronic' present (2012), and to the exploration of the critical temporalities of the selected post-apocalyptic fictions through these lenses.

Neoliberalism is a notoriously slippery concept but its core tenet is the belief in the economic and political benefits of a self-regulating global market. Its policies – economic deregulation, privatization and cuts to public spending and welfare, as well as, more broadly, the relentless reduction of all aspects of life to economic values, which produces forms of subjectivity that internalize market imperatives, from entrepreneurs of the self to human capital and the indebted man (Brown 2015; Foucault [2008] 2010; Lazzarato 2012) – are therefore aimed at realizing this 'utopia' throughout the world. The apocalyptic echoes of the neoliberal teleological credo are foregrounded by Fukuyama's formulations (1992), which, as mentioned in Chapter 2, deploy the inherently apocalyptic notion of the end of history to argue that modernity tends towards liberal democracy and global capitalism as the culmination of humankind's ideological evolution. To Fukuyama, after the triumph of liberal capitalist democracy with the end of the Cold War, the future consists merely in the expansion of this political and economic system across the globe, that is, the future consists in just more of the same. Consonantly with apocalyptic determinism and its erasure of contingency, therefore, the future is already written and no other possibilities are given, as perfectly captured by Thatcher's claim that 'there is no alternative', aka TINA. Neoliberal discourse around TINA, Sharae Deckard points out, should be understood as a 'concerted effort to repress those imaginative possibilities [of a different futurity] in their cultural and political expressions, to eradicate the very prospect of alternative cognitions and social organizations, and to reorganize lifeworlds for the economic and political benefits of elites' (2017: 84). In other words, as already seen across many of the texts considered so far but in particular in Chapter 3, apocalyptic discourse is a tool for the preservation of the status quo.

In the neoliberal 'free market fundamentalism' (Harvey 2005: 29), where the term 'fundamentalism' unwittingly registers the religious foundations of this construction of history, the self-regulating free market is conceived as 'not only the most efficient way of organizing the economy but also the most peaceful', since with its global reach it will supposedly ensure a world free from conflicts (Gray 2007: 120). Thus, Lisa Duggan speaks of neoliberal capitalism as a 'secular faith' (2003: xiii) and Jean Comaroff and John L. Comaroff define it a messianic and millennial form of capitalism, that is, a 'capitalism that presents itself as a gospel of salvation' (2000: 292). This salvific pretence is at the core of what Naomi Klein (2008) identifies as 'disaster capitalism', which uses catastrophic events, from the War in Iraq to Hurricane Katrina, as opportunities to spread the neoliberal credo and profit from the imposition of its policies, reforming the world in its image. Notice in this sense the apocalyptic echoes of that 'neo', which promises a utopian new world order through the regeneration of liberal ideals, while in effect ensuring the restoration of class power (an old world, in short) and the conditions for global capital accumulation, so that 'The theoretical utopianism of neoliberal argument has ... primarily worked as a system of justification and legitimation for whatever needed to be done to achieve this goal' (Harvey 2005: 19). As ever, apocalyptic teleology serves to mask and justify power's oppressions, including the uneven development between Global North and Global South, which is not a mere phase in the implacable march towards the neoliberal convergence but a necessary requirement for the functioning of global capital itself.

But if there is still a widespread sense of TINA and neoliberal capital as end of history, namely, of what Mark Fisher terms 'capitalist realism', the 'sense that not only is capitalism the only viable political and economic system, but also that it is now impossible even to *imagine* a coherent alternative to it' (2009: 2; emphasis in original), the cracks in the neoliberal 'new' world order and its apocalyptic construction of the future are showing. For while, in an embodiment of apocalyptic determinism and the end of history, 'The late capitalist present [i]s necessarily staked on the capacity to realize and replicate itself by borrowing against the guaranteed promise of the future as the site of *more of the same*' (E. C. Williams 2011: 2; emphasis in original) – recall in this sense the name of the corporation in Jeanette Winterson's *The Stone Gods* (2007), MORE – my discussion of the Anthropocene in Chapter 3 makes clear that the future of neoliberalism will hardly entail more of the same. Indeed, environmental risks represent, in Fisher's terms, one of the ways in which a repressed Lacanian Real irrupts into the reality constructed by capitalist realism, a 'reality' based on the fantasy of endless deregulated growth at the end of history. Further irruptions of the Real consist in the proliferation of mental health issues and useless bureaucracy, both the consequence of a pervasive 'business ontology' (Fisher 2009: 18–20), which also shatter the neoliberal utopian teleology.

Similarly, the financial crisis that began in 2007 as a subprime mortgage crisis and that forms the background of texts like *Odds Against Tomorrow*, *Zone One* and *Station Eleven* punctures the fantasy of the neoliberal good life, based on the promises 'everyone a shareholder, everyone an owner, everyone an entrepreneur', uncovering an omnipresent debt economy which deprives people of 'the future, that is, of time, time as decision-making, choice, and possibility' (Lazzarato 2012: 8–9).³ For, Maurizio Lazzarato argues, the debt economy is an economy of time: granting credit is an activity exposed to contingency and the uncertainty of the future so that 'The system of debt must ... neutralize time, that is, the risk inherent to it' (2012: 45). Through the guilt and responsibility that constitute the subjectivity of the 'indebted man', neoliberalism produces the future as the time in which subjects will simply repay their debt or be punished for this breach of trust, and no other significant possibility or alternative is given (of course, the same does not apply to financial corporations, which were bailed out after the crisis). Thus, debt is one of the mechanisms through which neoliberalism, in a dynamic that reflects how the apocalyptic sense of an ending gives shape to time and provides a comforting narrative by deterministically closing off contingency, seeks to reduce the future to the mere 'reproduction of capitalist power relations' (Lazzarato 2012: 48) – again, capitalist realism, or, the end of history.

More broadly, Elena Esposito reminds us, financial markets, and specifically the market of derivatives, the financial instrument which played a key role in the crisis, are a 'great apparatus for the production of the future' (2011: 127). Derivatives are contracts that assign a price to future contingencies and, in doing so, seek to neutralize unforeseen circumstances, namely, the very possibility of possibility. What we encounter with derivatives are thus, again, techniques aimed at managing the openness of the future in order to ensure the reproduction of the current system of accumulation, since, notwithstanding the proclamations of the neoliberal end of history, this system is threatened by growing risks, and 'For risks to be reliably calculable, the future must look like the present' (Martin 2007: 4). As Esposito puts it, derivatives are 'the markets of the risk society' (2011: 115). And while the projections of derivatives do influence the future, financial markets still operate in a 'reality that is structured in relation to an always open future (a future that is always heralding risks)' (Esposito 2011: 118), an open future that violently asserts itself in the crisis.

Thus, in analyses of our neoliberal moment, the end of history is critiqued as a stalled present devoid of alternatives – except that, perhaps, of a final dystopian apocalyptic catastrophe – and hence of genuine futurity. Jameson, for instance, argues that our sense of time under global capital shrinks to a series of fragmented presents, which in turn 'blocks or forestalls any global vision

---

³ For an account of the financial crisis see, for instance, Engel and McCoy (2011) and Esposito (2011).

of the [future] as a radically transformed and different system' (1991: 285). The derivative is the perfect example of this temporality, for 'each derivative is a new present of time. It produces no future out of itself, only another and a different present. The world of finance capital is that perpetual present' (Jameson 2015: 123). In this perpetual present, what we are left with is an 'appearance of random changes that are mere stasis, a disorder after the end of history' (Jameson 1994: 20). The neoliberal end of history marks the end of the apocalyptic teleology that underlies Western modernity in that it ultimately signifies the failure of this teleology and its dystopian implications, rather than representing its utopian culmination as neoliberalism itself claims. To put it with Berardi, with the dawn and affirmation of neoliberalism, the 'myth of the future' as tending towards betterment, a myth 'rooted in modern capitalism, in the experience of expansion of the economy and knowledge', has slowly been eroded and its utopian imagination has been replaced by the dystopian imagination of our 'century with no future' (2011: 12; 18), as encapsulated by the flourishing of post-apocalyptic fictions that forms the subject of my study. Berardi traces this cancellation of the future back to factors like mental health issues that proliferate under neoliberal governmentality, technological acceleration that leads to the collapse of the future into the present, and the precarity of contemporary labour that produces short-termist horizons and temporal fragmentation, precluding any vision of the future, let alone of the future as radically different from the present.[4] By the same token, Cazdyn speaks of our present as existing in the temporal mode of 'the chronic', 'an undying present that remains forever sick … [and that] insists on maintaining the system and perpetually managing its constitutive crises, rather than confronting even a hint of the terminal, the system's (the body's, the planet's, capitalism's) own death' (2012: 5). It is this 'hint of the terminal' that the contemporary post-apocalyptic novel brings to the fore, for while the conception of a neoliberal end of history works to banish any thought of the end – things will continue as they are already, since this is the millennium – the end comes in these texts and it is of course anti-apocalyptic in its dystopian effects.

With the partial exception of *Station Eleven*, whose celebration of the pre-apocalyptic beauty and ending make the text's critique of capitalist realism ambiguous, the post-apocalyptic scenarios analysed in this chapter shatter

---

[4] These are points that recur in critiques of neoliberalism. In terms of mental health issues and precarity, Berardi's analysis is echoed, for instance, by Fisher (2009) and Lazzarato (2012), whereas Harvey (1989) and Virilio (2010) focus on what Harvey terms the 'time-space compression' produced by advancements in information technologies.

capital's attempts at producing the future as more of the same. The novels' critical temporalities foreground what lies behind the fantasy of the neoliberal end of history and its utopian foreclosed possibilities: the dystopian foreclosed possibilities of no future at all. *Odds Against Tomorrow*, *The Age of Miracles*, *Zone One*, *Station Eleven* and *Player One* expose the apocalyptic foundations of the neoliberal construction of the future, underlining how apocalyptic determinism manages the openness of futurity by producing the sense of no alternative at the core of capitalist realism, and play apocalyptic logic against itself by showing how this cancellation of alternatives risks leading to a catastrophe. These texts zoom in on the cracks in the neoliberal construction of time to explode the linearity of apocalyptic history, attempting to pry open spaces of possibility and agency beyond the neoliberal endless repetition of the same and the catastrophe lurking behind this repetition.[5] *Odds Against Tomorrow* exposes the nightmare of no future underwriting disaster capitalism's attempt to construct the future as more of the same even amidst proliferating risks; *The Age of Miracles*' slowing embodies Berardi's 'slow cancellation of the future' and the sense of a 'slow apocalypse' (McMurry 1996) already in progress in our present; and *Zone One*'s stragglers, zombies that are stuck in a moment of the pre-apocalyptic life, literalize the undying neoliberal present and the lack of alternatives of the end of history. Finally, both *Station Eleven* and *Player One*, the focus of this chapter, depict catastrophes of global capital – the former a global pandemic, the latter a peak oil apocalypse – as encapsulated by the image of their end-times airports, and rupture apocalyptic determinism and the foreclosed possibilities of the end of history through their alternate histories and narrative structures, though Coupland's novel is more explicit and effective in its critique.

Rich's *Odds Against Tomorrow* explicitly engages with 'the markets of the risk society' (Esposito 2011: 115), illustrating how financial capitalism seeks to deterministically ensure the end of history, that is, the endless reproduction of the present system, even amidst the proliferating risks produced by our way of living. Gesturing to the economic crash that forms the historical backdrop of the novel, Rich's protagonist, Mitchell Zukor, begins his career as a mathematical wizard at a financial company's Department of Equities, Assets, and Derivatives before becoming a futurist and risk analyst for FutureWorld. Here, his job consists in anticipating potential catastrophes and calculating their costs so

---

[5] For another project that seeks to counter the neoliberal temporality of a 'neutral timeless "now"' through literary analysis, see Brouillette, Nilges and Sauri (2017: xv). Their point that 'Far from suggesting that we replace theories of an omnipresent "end of history" with a traditional, single diachronic timeline, we argue for developing the inverse: a synchronic, multi-faceted and multi-temporal history' (xvi) chimes with my theorization of critical temporalities in this book.

that the corporations that are FutureWorld's clients can be indemnified against lawsuits if one of such catastrophes were to strike.[6] In Rich's all-too-real satire of disaster capitalism, the point of anticipating risks is not to prepare for disasters and save lives, but, rather, to protect the conditions for capital accumulation. As the head of FutureWorld remarks, 'Catastrophe is all ours. We're going to make a killing' (Rich 2013: 30), an uncanny echo of the subtitle of Anthony Loewenstein's book on disaster capitalism (2015), 'Making a Killing out of Catastrophe'.[7] Significantly, Mitchell has been an insatiable imaginer of worst case scenarios ever since his childhood and a fan of Revelation, for 'The Christians were excellent worst-case scenarists' (*OAT* 71). Apocalyptic discourse, even if in this case as mere imagination of disasters, is for Mitchell a means to make sense time and neutralize contingency, since, as opposed to his boss, who sees 'the wedges that risk offered' and seeks to profit from it, 'Mitchell's fear [of disaster] ... [is] real, hot viral' (*OAT* 25), and projecting disasters is his way to address this fear. However, once the novel's apocalypse takes place, namely, the hurricane Tammy, which completely floods New York, Mitchell needs to face the limitations of his risk analyses. 'I've spent a lifetime worrying about this moment, doing the calculations, taking the measurements, trying to render catastrophe in calculable, precise dimensions, and still I'm not prepared?', he ponders, 'But real catastrophe was like that ... It astounded expectations, was unlike anything that came before' (*OAT* 154). Against the apocalyptic determinism of the end of history, 'real catastrophe' violently reasserts contingency.

Disaster capitalism seeks to rearrange itself after Tammy. Banking on Mitchell's prophetic fame, a former FutureWorld colleague of his, Jane, founds a new risk analysis firm, Future Days, whose tagline, at Michell's suggestion, is 'the future is not quite what it used to be' (*OAT* 304). Even if this tagline nominally recognizes the openness of the future, neoliberal capital still fashions itself as the only game in town, as signalled by the minimal change in name from FutureWorld to Future Days. Mitchell, however, soon realizes that, with climate breakdown, 'No one would have to pay to hear about worst-case scenarios – they'd be living them, night and day' (*OAT* 195). His 'imagination ... has [indeed] become a casualty of Tammy. Now when he thought about the future, all he found was blankness. *There would be no long term*' (*OAT* 237; emphasis in original), an image of precarious, negated and unreadable futurity that shatters the neoliberal construction of the future as more of the same. Hardly by chance, *Odds Against*

---

[6] See David Watson for an analysis of the parallels between the temporal logic at work in Rich's FutureWorld and that at work in the financial instrument of the derivative (2016: 64–65).
[7] All further references to Rich's *Odds Against Tomorrow* as *OAT*.

Tomorrow ends with Jane, the head of Future Days and the representative of disaster capitalism, admitting to herself 'I am *scared*' and telling her driver 'We don't have a lot of time' (*OAT* 306; emphasis in original). *Odds Against Tomorrow*'s critical temporality suggests that lurking behind the attempts to ensure the endless reproduction of the present system is the fear of no future.

In this sense, Walker's slowing in *The Age of Miracles* can be read as the physical manifestation of what Berardi terms the '*slow* cancellation of the future' (2011: 13; emphasis mine). The slowing shatters the 'age of miracles', in which the future is understood as a linear development of the present. Instead, the catastrophe signals how in our neoliberal moment, behind the reality as constructed by capitalist realism and the utopian end of history, the future no longer fulfils the promises and expectations of the present and what we are left with is, to put it with Evan Calder Williams' diagnosis of the late capitalist sense of time, 'the nervous repetition of the defaulted present to plow forward into nothing' (2011: 3). The world of the slowing is the world of such a 'nervous repetition' of the neoliberal present in the face of an ongoing apocalypse that forecloses any possibility of a future. The government desperately clings to the capitalist logic of the market, as if, in a world of solar superstorms and lethal radiations, climate breakdown and alterations to oceanic currents, the future as more of the same was not a thing of the past. Clock time, that is, twenty-four-hour days, remains in place, even though the days are in fact growing longer and longer because of the slowing of Earth's rotation, and citizens are invited to carry on living as before because, as the President of the United States explains, 'The Market needs stability' (*AoM* 83). Not only does this delusional preservation of the status quo frame the passivity and the sense of lack of alternatives fostered by the apocalyptic determinism embodied by capitalist realism but also how, notwithstanding a growing understanding that the neoliberal system has no future, we face a 'slow entropic loss of energy and profit, coupled with the state's brutal refusal – and ways of demanding the same of its citizens and subjects – to acknowledge that the eternal present has become an eternal past' (E. C. Williams 2011: 4). And notice, of course, how Williams' point about the '*slow* entropic loss of energy and profit' chimes with Berardi's slow cancellation of the future and the slowing itself.

Indeed, *The Age of Miracles*, together with *Zone One* and *Player One*, depicts an apocalypse in progress, articulating the critical temporality of a catastrophic duration that illustrates how the neoliberal 'mode of accumulation predicated on global growth, related state forms and foreclosed political horizons – isn't likely to disappear before our eyes overnight. On the contrary, the character of the years to come will likely be that of the non-ending' (E. C. Williams 2011: 3).⁸ With their 'non-ending', or 'chronic' (Cazdyn 2012), mode, these novels' catastrophes gesture to Andrew McMurry's notion of an ongoing 'slow apocalypse' underlying global capital, that is, 'an accretion of systemically deleterious effects which, incredibly, have become indistinguishable from progress' (1996) and which, precisely because of their accretive rather than punctual nature, risk being unreadable qua apocalypse.⁹ The slowing, after all, begins as a 'quite invisible catastrophe' in that it evades the request for the sensational and the spectacular of our fast-paced news cycle: 'There was no footage to show on television, no burning buildings or broken bridges, no twisted metal or scorched earth, no houses sliding off slabs. No one was wounded. No one was dead' (*AoM* 12). And while the origins of *The Age of Miracles*' catastrophe remain unknown, the world of the novel, where greenhouses are the only way of growing food but the fuel that keeps them functioning is running out, and where the Global South lacks the financial resources to adapt to the drastic environmental change caused by the slowing, does evoke what life in the advanced Anthropocene might look like. Thus, the initial invisibility of the slowing gestures to Rob Nixon's theorization of climate change as slow violence which, in its dispersal across time and space, 'patiently dispense[s] [its] devastation while remaining outside our flickering attention spans – and outside the purview of a spectacle-driven corporate media' (2011: 6). From Walker's slowing, to Whitehead's stragglers, to Coupland's and Mandel's characters, stranded in airports, we encounter in this chapter images that invite us to pause and consider the signs around us of an ongoing slow apocalypse lurking behind the flashy proclamations of a neoliberal end of history and the fast pace of our ever-accelerating lives.

'The age demanded an image of its accelerated grimace' – these words, from Ezra Pound's 'Hugh Selwyn Mauberley' (1920), are the epigraph to the second part of *Zone One*. It is this image that Whitehead's novel provides through the 'stragglers', zombies that, as opposed to the more conventional hungry and violent 'skels', are stuck in a moment of the pre-apocalyptic life, endlessly repeating the

---

⁸ The anxiety around a 'non-ending', slow entropic collapse of the current system surfaces, too, in the pre-pandemic world of Margaret Atwood's *The Year of the Flood* (2009), where, to draw on a character's reflections, 'Everybody knew. Nobody admitted to knowing .... *We're using up the Earth. It's almost gone*. You can't live with such fears and keep on whistling. The waiting builds up in you like a tide. You start wanting it to be done with. You find yourself saying to the sky, *Just do it. Do your worst. Get it over with*' (*YoF* 284–285; emphasis in original). For an analysis of the *MaddAddam* trilogy in relation to neoliberalism, see Vials (2015).
⁹ Cf. E. C. Williams's similar description of the apocalypse of late capitalism as 'the story of a yawning duration, an accretion so slow and naturalized that we can no longer recognize it' (2011: 13).

same gesture in a parody of our age that reveals the stalled present at the core of the neoliberal frenzy of acceleration. That the contemporary is an age of acceleration has become commonplace. Critical analyses of our era speak of an ever-speeding up 'fast capitalism' (Agger [2004] 2016) and of a 'great acceleration' in which the world is getting faster and faster (Colvile 2016). These ideas are also captured by the trajectory from Coupland's first book, *Generation X* (1991), whose subtitle is 'Tales for an Accelerated Culture', to his latest books in which he speaks of the 'proceleration', that is, 'the acceleration of acceleration' (*PO* 237), of our 'extreme present' (Basar, Coupland and Obrist 2015). Coupland's reference to an 'extreme present' in which 'our sense of time is beginning to shrink' (Basar, Coupland and Obrist 2015: 25) is significant, for the contemporary frenzy of acceleration, related to developments in information technologies, is, to return to Jameson, a 'disorder after the end of history' masking a static present devoid of genuine futurity (1994: 20).[10] Like the slowing, the stragglers put a stop to this acceleration and expose lying behind it what Hollinger terms 'the endless endtimes of the future-present' (2006: 452).

As Mark Spitz puts it with a metafictional observation that frames the purpose of the figure of the zombie, 'The intent of the caricature ... is to capture the monstrous we overlook every day' (*ZO* 239), specifically, as Leif Sorensen maintains, 'the monstrous nature of late-capitalist modernity' (2014: 571). Hardly by chance, *Zone One* takes place in the financial district, with Mark Spitz sweeping corporate office after corporate office and foregrounding similarities between the offices' pre-apocalyptic and post-apocalyptic zombified inhabitants, like the skel who 'possessed the determination befitting a true denizen of Human Resources ... The plague's recalibration of its faculties only hon[ing] the underlying qualities' (*ZO* 17), or the zombies haunting the Wall Street area, as monstrous as the investment bankers of the pre-plague era (*ZO* 77). These similarities signal that 'The zombie apocalypse is indeed one that is happening "now" (usually in some near future moment), but in a way that ... ultimately identifies it with the very *ongoing* character of "our" capitalist present itself' (Cunningham and Warwick 2014: 178; emphasis in original). Apocalypse is played against itself, for *Zone One*'s zombie plague is deployed to *reveal* how the apocalyptic structures underlying the neoliberal end of

---

[10] Cf. Harvey who, when describing the phenomenon of 'time-space compression', writes that 'time horizons shorten to the point where the present is all there is' (1989: 240); Paul Virilio, who similarly theorizes the contraction of past, present and future into the 'omnipresent instant' of cybernetic communications (2010: 71); and Bernard Stiegler, who discusses the 'permanent *present* at the core of the temporal flux' generated by real-time devices (2011: 75; emphasis in original), which corresponds to the systemic short-termism of neoliberalism (2010).

history and its construction of the future as more of the same mask an already catastrophic, monstrous present.

Like *The Age of Miracles*, *Zone One* depicts an apocalypse in progress, which gestures to the ongoing slow apocalypse of climate change in the readers' world.[11] The significantly termed 'flood' of the zombies is paralleled to 'the news programs'' global warming simulations' and, in turn, global warming is described in terms reminiscent of Nixon's slow violence as 'That other, *less flamboyant*, more deliberate ruination altering the planet's climate' (ZO 243; 193; emphasis mine). But it is the stragglers that best capture the novel's critical temporality in relation to our neoliberal monstrous present, for they represent the end of history with a vengeance, a 'Comeuppance for a flatlined culture' stuck in 'robotic routine' (ZO 217).[12] Frozen in the neoliberal present's 'interminable loop of repeated gestures' (ZO 50), from photocopying documents to surfing the web and flipping burgers, the stragglers expose the failure of the utopian expectations at the core of Western modernity and the nightmare of a present which, far from the millennium of the end of history, is already zombified with its lack of alternatives and futurity but that nevertheless refuses to die. Hardly by chance, the figure of the zombie is often evoked in analyses of the persistence of neoliberal policies even after the economic crisis has made their failure apparent, as encapsulated by Colin Crouch's theorization of the 'strange non-death' of neoliberalism (2011).[13]

This 'non-death' continues past the apocalypse in *Zone One*. The American Phoenix, with its motto 'We Make Tomorrow!', is not only an attempt to revive American apocalyptic ideologies, as discussed in Chapter 2, but also to restart the corpse of neoliberalism, restoring its construction of the future as more of the same. This future includes a blend of the corporate and the state, for

---

[11] On the 'plot of pestilence', of which the zombie plague is a variation, Gomel writes that it is not so much a '"fiction of an end" as a fiction of an end indefinitely postponed. It may become antiapocalyptic [sic] in its refusal of the transition from the tribulation to the millennium' (2000: 412), an observation that compounds my argument about *Zone One*'s critique of traditional apocalyptic discourse.

[12] Hollinger reads Atwood's posthuman Crakers in the *MaddAddam* trilogy along similar lines: 'the Crakers personify the end of history with a vengeance. They live in a frozen and unchanging present moment, with no memory of a past and no anticipation of a future – "they don't count the days". In any event, there is no longer anything like a future to anticipate' (2006: 458).

[13] See also, for instance, Fisher (2013); Harvie and Milburn (2011); Quiggin (2010). Cf. also the phenomenon of 'zombie companies', on the rise after government bailouts post-crash, which 'refers to a company that is officially "alive" despite being financially dead' (Golub and Lane 2015: 47). Given *Zone One*'s setting in the financial district, Sollazzo maintains that 'On one reading, Whitehead's novel simply literalizes the financial "apocalypse"' and argues that 'It is no coincidence … that Mark Spitz's "Last Night" – the first night of the apocalypse – begins in an Atlantic City casino. The financial crisis, after all, was precipitated by a series of risky bets made by banks and other large financial institutions' (2017: 463, 464).

Buffalo, the post-apocalyptic government, is sponsored by corporations, which support the reconstruction effort with goods not in a spirit of solidarity in the face of the catastrophe, but 'in exchange for tax breaks once the reaper laid down his scythe' (ZO 39). These are quite literal 'zombie companies' (Golub and Lane 2015) – 'There were understandable difficulties in tracking down survivors in positions of authority' (ZO 39), Mark Spitz wryly comments – which, in an incarnation of disaster capitalism, will not stop picking at the carcass of the system like ravenous skels.[14] To put it with the words that Kaitlyn, as the representative of the neoliberal order, counters to Mark Spitz's, the American Phoenix seeks to 'unsee the monsters again' (ZO 239), undoing the critique of the system articulated by the zombies. *Zone One*, Sorensen notices, continuously parallels the stragglers and the survivors, suggesting that 'While stragglers are physically paralyzed in poses that no longer make sense, the survivors are stuck … imagining a future that will look like the preapocalyptic past' (2014: 578), that is, as the endless repetition of the readers' neoliberal present. The American Phoenix apocalyptically narrates the crisis as the chance to renew the system, recalling the process of creative destruction, namely, the idea that capitalism's periodic crises serve to renew the conditions of accumulation.[15] As we have seen in Chapter 2, however, Mark Spitz expresses his suspicion of the American Phoenix's futurity throughout the novel. Indeed, 'Against the late-capitalist fantasy of a future that consists of an endless reproduction of the present, Whitehead offers the shocking possibility of an absolute ending' (Sorensen 2014: 561), at least for humanity, while implying that this 'shocking possibility' of no future was there all along, for the socio-economic system 'had long carried its own plague' (ZO 121), its own ongoing slow apocalypse. Hardly by chance, the survivors' most diffuse disease, PASD, or Post-Apocalyptic Stress Disorder, sounds remarkably like 'past' (ZO 55, 252), denoting the idea of the pre-apocalyptic past as already existing in a 'chronic' mode (Cazdyn 2012).

It is important to note that the turning point that marks the final collapse of the American Phoenix's neoliberal project is a straggler snapping out of her endless present, and specifically, a straggler who used to be a fortune-teller. The neoliberal future projections, which include the American Phoenix's belief that stragglers remain stragglers, rather than turning into violent skels, appear as mere fortune-telling in the face of an ongoing catastrophic present, and the

---

[14] For an in-depth analysis of the 'corporate anxiety' that drives *Zone One*, see Sollazzo (2017).
[15] For a discussion of the notion of creative destruction in relation to the financial crisis and an unnoticed ongoing apocalypse within the contemporary moment, see Cunningham and Warwick (2013).

contingency and openness of the future – albeit the compromised openness of a terminal catastrophe – is reasserted against the foreclosed possibilities of the neoliberal end of history. In snapping out of her endless present, the fortune-teller straggler recuperates a moment of agency, rebelling against the neoliberal colonization of the future as more of the same. And if *Zone One* leaves little hope of a future for humanity, in emphasizing how the stragglers exist, frozen, in a 'moment of possibility' (*ZO* 159), Whitehead suggests that we, the stragglers of the neoliberal present, can still fight against its endless repetition and cancellation of futurity.

Both *Station Eleven* and *Player One*, to which the rest of this chapter is devoted, feature end-times airports that signify the global capitalist order coming to a halt, shattering the neoliberal end of history and its apocalyptic utopian teleology, as well as gesturing, through characters stranded in these loci of a hyper-mobile and connected era, to a present that offers no genuine futurity and, hence, way out. Both novels situate their catastrophes in the readers' past, thus conveying, just like *The Age of Miracles* and *Zone One*, the notion of an apocalypse already in progress and creating, against the determinism of the neoliberal end of history, alternate histories that draw attention to the unrealized possibilities of the past and to the present as the moment in which we act to shape the future. Yet, we shall see, *Player One* is more explicit in its critique of the current system, as it directly addresses the sense of no future that hovers over our late capitalist temporality through the notion of denarration, whereas in *Station Eleven* this critique is too implicit, with mere textual traces of the Real disrupting the reality constructed by neoliberalism, so that the novel ultimately remains firmly within capitalist realism.

Station Eleven continuously shifts between events happening pre-, during, and post- the Georgia Flu. The novel opens with Arthur Leander dying on stage while he is performing *King Lear* on Night One, the night the pandemic begins. Arthur and Shakespeare hold together the novel's different strands, for all the main characters are, in one way or another, connected to Arthur, while the focus of the post-apocalyptic sections, mostly set in Year Twenty, is the Travelling Symphony, which tours across the 49th parallel and what used to be Canada and the United States performing Shakespeare's plays. As the chair of the 2015 Arthur C. Clarke Award, Andrew M. Butler, puts it, *Station Eleven*, which won that year's award, is 'the story of a global apocalypse' and an 'elegy for the hyper-globalised present' (2015). I argue, indeed, that at the heart of the novel lies a constitutive ambiguity. On the one hand, the global apocalypse ruptures the teleological construction of the future as more of the same and the novel articulates a critique of global capital and its risks, albeit often through mere asides within the narrative. On the other hand, the elegiac celebration of the beauty of the bygone era ends up problematically reinforcing the notion of neoliberalism as the apocalyptic culmination of history, with *Station Eleven*'s conclusion encapsulating this issue through the suggestion that our system might be restored.

Signalling *Station Eleven*'s implicit engagement with global capitalism, Year One, the year of the Georgia Flu, is established within the novel through a cursory reference to the economic crisis: 'That was the year when 12 percent of the world's shipping fleet lay at anchor off the coast of Malaysia, container ships laid dormant by an economic collapse' (*SE* 28). This image, the acknowledgement section explains, is taken from Simon Parry's 2009 *Daily Mail* article 'Revealed: The Ghost Fleet of the Recession Anchored Just East of Singapore'. *Station Eleven*'s plot thus articulates an alternate history of the present world, a 'sideshadowing', to return to Bernstein's (1994) and Morson's (1998) notion discussed in my analysis of David Mitchell's *Cloud Atlas* (2004) in Chapter 3, that ruptures the apocalyptic determinism of the neoliberal end of history and its construction of the future as more of the same by drawing attention to unrealized histories and to the very notion of possibility, including the possibility of a total collapse of the system. This critique of apocalyptic teleology is embodied within the novel's narrative structure.

Mandel self-reflexively plays with apocalyptic determinism to subvert it by deploying foreshadowing as a narrative device that connects the various sections. Sentences like 'The Georgia Flu would arrive in a year', 'Civilization won't collapse for another fourteen years', 'A year before the Georgia Flu', 'Two weeks till the apocalypse', 'just before the old world ended', 'the Georgia Flu so close now' (*SE* 40, 71, 110, 201, 217, 328) punctuate the narrative. And, by opening with the end that is foreshadowed by these sentences, *Station Eleven* highlights not only how the temporal order of the apocalyptic sense of an ending can be imposed on the randomness of time solely retrospectively, but also how this order ultimately implies a future that is already written, against which the novel repeatedly emphasizes that there is no deterministic pattern to history. Miranda curtly rebukes Elizabeth (both are Arthur's ex-wives and the latter is the Prophet's mother) for her apocalyptic belief that everything happens because it was supposed to by saying 'I'd prefer not to think that I'm following a script' (*SE* 106). Stressing the role of contingency and chance in life, Arthur muses that his life seems like an 'improbable outcome, when [he] look[s] back at the sequence of events' (*SE* 157). Looking back to his past towards the end of his life, a retrospection that by definition should allow the sense of an ending to emerge, Clark, one of Arthur's friends, does not see any meaningful order but only 'a series of photographs and disconnected short films' (*SE* 279). The apocalypse itself, in contrast to what the prophet Tyler believes, does not bring about any revelation of a deterministic sense-making pattern to history. Rather, Clark describes the period of contagion as a 'choreography of luck' and 'coincidence[s]', which are constructed as 'miracles' only retrospectively (*SE* 223, 224). Actual, rather than fictional time, *Station Eleven*'s critical temporality suggests, consists in a 'number of loose ends' (*SE* 27) and possibilities that resist apocalyptic teleology, something which the very idea of alternate history amplifies.

To return to the image that underpins *Station Eleven*'s alternate history, the 'Ghost Fleet of the Recession' (Parry 2009), Miranda reflects on how the ships were 'ordered in a moment when it seemed the demand would only ever grow, built over the following three years while the economy imploded, unneeded now that no one was spending any money' (*SE* 217). Thus, Andrew Hoberek writes, 'one might suggest that Mandel's book describes an apocalypse that already happened in 2008–2009: it is a novel not about a post-apocalyptic future but a post-apocalyptic present', for 'the ships embody the breakdown of capitalism's fundamental premise of eternal growth' (2015) and of the neoliberal apocalyptic construction of the future as more of the same. More accurately, by situating its pandemic in the immediate aftermath of the financial crash, *Station Eleven*'s critical temporality gestures not to a post-apocalyptic present but to the neoliberal end of history as the site of an ongoing slow apocalypse of the socio-economic system, since as Hoberek also points out, 'What has collapsed (*or rather failed to collapse*) in this earlier event is capitalism' (2015; emphasis mine). Similarly to *Zone One*, *Station Eleven*, through the reference, albeit in passing, to the 'remnant' ghostly fleet, which the local fishermen fear for its supernatural and otherworldly presence (*SE* 28, 217), points to the 'strange non-death' of neoliberalism (Crouch 2011).

The current socio-economic conjuncture is described through a gothic vocabulary capturing a system that, notwithstanding its evident shortcomings, refuses to let go. When the apocalypse comes and reduces the former world to ghostly traces, it merely amplifies what was already true, conveying the sense of an apocalypse in progress in our present and of the spectre of no future haunting the neoliberal end of history. The corporate world is 'full of ghosts', a character muses before the Georgia Flu, a 'horror show' populated by 'sleepwalkers', trapped in the endless repetition of the neoliberal present with no alternatives (*SE* 163). The occasional moments of happiness that puncture a life entirely defined by work are, in fact, a mere distraction, as indicated by the 'iPhone zombies' lost in their screens (*SE* 160) – a portrayal that not only parallels Whitehead's stragglers but also, we shall see, Coupland's notion of denarration. And if nothing ever jolts these ghosts and zombies awake and makes them realize they are sleepwalking through the endless lists of tasks that constitute life under neoliberal capital in the Global North, the apocalypse appears, at least initially, to serve precisely this purpose, putting neoliberalism, already 'dormant' as indicated by the description of the fleet, down for a lasting sleep. Hardly by chance, characters in the post-apocalypse look back to the meaninglessness of their corporate lives and jargon with utter disbelief.

The Georgia Flu is, indeed, a catastrophe of global capital. As Mark West writes, 'What has come to an end [in *Station Eleven*] is the globalized world' (2018: 7), which is implicated in the apocalypse itself, for, Tate emphasizes, 'One of the reasons that the world dies so quickly in *Station Eleven* is because of its relentless mobility and the ordinary miracle of air travel: people travel across the globe in hours and the virus, horribly resistant to treatment, goes with them', spreading from Georgia to the rest of the globe (2017: 133). Tate's mention of the 'ordinary miracle of air travel' echoes a point made by Clark about the pre-apocalyptic 'taken-for-granted miracles' of travels and communications, which the novel invites us to marvel at anew (*SE* 233). Indeed, in *Station Eleven*, flight becomes the main signifier of our globalized neoliberal world, so much so that a character in the post-flu years keeps looking for planes in the sky as long-awaited signs that 'There was still a civilization somewhere' (*SE* 134). This conflation between civilization and the current system, to which I shall return in the analysis of the post-apocalyptic Museum of Civilization, housed significantly in the Severn City Airport, indicates how the novel ends up reinforcing capitalist realism's deterministic sense of no alternative notwithstanding its tracing of an alternate history post-economic crash and its critique of life under global capital. Framing the post-apocalypse as an alternate history characterized by 'the end of air travel' (*SE* 35), *Station Eleven* denaturalizes flight and by extension the globalized neoliberal world, implicitly gesturing to its risks and rupturing the triumphalism of the end of history, but also, more fundamentally and more problematically, celebrating its miraculous beauty and mourning its loss.

In addition to facilitating the pandemic, air travel, with its greenhouse gas emissions, is a major contributor to the other slow apocalypse of the current system, climate change, whose implicit presence, similarly to the economic crisis, we can detect in Mandel's novel. 'The fevered summers of this century, this impossible heat' (*SE* 138), *Station Eleven*'s narrative voice muses in one of the post-apocalyptic sections, gesturing to the lasting impact of human activity on the climate, even after the pandemic has drastically abated the world's overpopulation. Performing a symptomatic reading of the novel, Eve also notices how 'with its micro-storm clouds gathering within' the snow globe, an object to which I return later and which connects pre- and post-apocalyptic sections, having been given to Kirsten on Night One by Arthur, is 'one of the metadata traces … of the hyperobject of global warming' (2018: 17). That the world of the comic *Station Eleven*, penned by Miranda and whose title signals its nature of *mise en abyme* text, has been flooded by the failure of its systems represents a further 'moment of textual slippage' gesturing to the Anthropocene (Eve 2018: 20) and to the complicity of the late capitalist system in the environmental slow apocalypse.[16] Yet, as Eve emphasizes, the post-Flu world exists in a 'space in which air travel is no longer possible and in which there seems to be no way of continuing to extract the hydrocarbons that, when burned, would contribute to the ongoing radical change to the constitution of Earth's climate' (2018: 17), at least until the final pages' revelation of a functioning electric grid.[17] In other words, 'the inevitability of the hyperobject known as global warming [appears to have been] stopped', though, significantly, not 'by politics or collective action, but by the flu' (Eve 2018: 17), that is, paradoxically, by air travel itself, whose ambiguous role in contributing to both destroying and saving the world reflects *Station Eleven*'s constitutive ambiguity towards the neoliberal system and its apocalyptic temporality.

For while *Station Eleven* features symptoms of the Real of climate change and the economic crisis disrupting the reality of capitalist realism, the novel repeatedly emphasizes the beauty of the pre-apocalyptic world and its 'miracles', reinforcing the apocalyptic construction of neoliberalism as the culmination of modernity. In Mandel's novel, air travel, and by extension the pre-apocalyptic system of global capital for which it stands, is aestheticized by the survivors in

---

[16] Together with Tyler's Bible, discussed in Chapter 1, and the Shakespearean plays performed by the Travelling Symphony, the copies of the comic *Station Eleven* carefully preserved in the post-apocalypse by Kirsten and Tyler constitute some of the texts of *Station Eleven*'s post-apocalyptic archive, to which we shall return to in the Conclusion. In addition to flooding, the comic's world has suffered another apocalypse: the space station's artificial sky was damaged during a war with the aliens that have taken control of the Earth so that Station Eleven has been in a state of perpetual twilight for fifteen years – a state which parallels the lack of electricity in *Station Eleven*'s post-apocalyptic world. For a more in-depth analysis of the comic as a *mise en abyme* text, see Leggatt (2018).

[17] As West puts it, *Station Eleven*'s post-apocalyptic sections 'register not just the end of its characters' world but the end of th[e] "Age of Man"', namely, the Anthropocene (2018: 7). Indeed, tracing the beginning of the era back to the Age of Discovery, as I do in Chapter 3, West develops an astute reading of the presence of Shakespeare in the novel as bookending the Anthropocene.

a way that masks its dark underside. I use the word 'dark' hardly by chance, for Mandel returns time and again to the interplay between light and darkness in her elegiac descriptions of the pre-Flu world. In parallel with the stranded fleet, which strikes Miranda with the unexpected 'beauty' of its illumination at night (*SE* 29), Kirsten's memories of flying are about the 'beauty' of seeing 'clusters and pinpoints of light in the darkness' from a plane's window at night (*SE* 135), a description echoed in Mandel's 'incomplete list' of what is lost in the disaster: 'No more towns glimpsed from the sky through airplane windows, points of glimmering light' (*SE* 31). Just like the fleet's 'blaze of light' obliterates the night's darkness, with the beauty of this view distracting Miranda from considering further the implications of the economic crisis – indeed, West notes how Miranda's reflections on the 'casual' use of the word 'collapse' in relation to the economic crisis (*SE* 217) end up 'addressing the economic collapse of 2007–2008 only to disguise it by minimizing its effect in relation to a much larger collapse', the Flu (2018: 2) – 'the beauty of flight' (*SE* 247), conveyed through the spectacle of the 'dazzling power' of electricity (*SE* 31), prevents characters from seeing the environmental risks inherent in our hyper-connected world and contributes to the apocalyptic image of this world as modernity's telos.

Nowhere is *Station Eleven*'s constitutive ambiguity between critique and celebration of neoliberal capitalism clearer than through an analysis of the Severn City Airport, where Clark and other survivors were stranded on Day One of the Georgia Flu and then settled. Famously defined by Marc Augé as 'non-places', namely, 'spaces of circulation, consumption and communication' produced by 'supermodernity' ([1995] 2008: viii), airports are the ideal space to interrogate our globalized world. The location of the airport in the fictional Severn City, somewhere in the American Midwest near Lake Michigan, is another textual trace of the novel's implicit critique of neoliberalism, given that the region is typically considered flyover country, rather than a destination per se. Indeed, *Station Eleven*'s end-times airport amplifies the post-apocalyptic breakdown of the neoliberal utopian teleology, the sense of characters left stranded by the very derailment of the system, rather than simply by the now 'dormant' planes (*SE* 31) – notice the same adjective deployed to describe the fleet in Malaysia, similarly left stranded by the financial collapse. Severn City is not the destination characters were sold, neither in terms of the flights that were rerouted there when the pandemic broke out, nor in terms of the neoliberal construction of the future. Yet 'It is telling', Matthew Leggatt notes, 'that in *Station Eleven* those characters who choose to live in the Severn City Airport reside in the Departures lounge rather than Arrivals. They are forever waiting for a way out, for their connecting flight, or for the resumption of the old world now long departed' (2018: 16).[18] Even if stuck outside of the neoliberal teleology, these characters embody the sense of lack of alternatives fostered by the apocalyptic determinism at the core of capitalist realism, for they cannot imagine any genuine futurity if not the resumption of this teleology. Just like the people of the Undersea in the comic *Station Eleven*, they 'clin[g] to the hope that the world they remembered could be restored' (*SE* 213), a hope captured by the Airport's Museum of Civilization.

Set up by Clark to commemorate the bygone era of global capital, the Museum hosts everyday objects of our society, such as a laptop, an iPhone, a credit card and the already mentioned snow globe. These are elevated by the catastrophe to the status of artworks, 'beautiful objects' (*SE* 255). Once again, however, beauty masks the underside of neoliberal capital. Notice, in this sense, Clark's musings on the snow globe. His tracing of the production process of this object conceals, and indeed aestheticizes, workers' exploitation and alienation, as well as the inequalities of the global free market:

> Consider the mind that invented those miniature storms of snow, the factory worker who turned sheets of plastic into white flakes of snow, the hand that drew the plan for the miniature Severn City with its church steeple and city hall, the assembly-line worker who watched the globe glide past on a conveyer belt somewhere in China. Consider the white gloves on the hands of the woman who inserted the snow globes into boxes, to be packed into larger boxes, crates, shipping containers. Consider the card games played belowdecks in the evenings on the ship carrying the containers across the ocean, a hand stubbing out a cigarette in an overflowing ashtray, a haze of blue smoke in dim light, the cadences of a half dozen languages united by common profanities ... (*SE* 255)

As West points out, Clark's reflection 'addresses but rather miscasts the globalized trade networks' in that it 'fetishizes the "beautiful objects" at the expense of the workers who make them, workers who are dehumanized into assemblies of working parts (note the emphasis on their hands)' (2018: 19, 20). Indeed, the passage's beautiful writing and imagery sublimates and glosses over a production process that relies heavily on the exploitation of cheap labour from the Global South, something Mandel merely hints at through the mention of workers 'somewhere in China' and 'the cadences of a half dozen languages'.

In this sense, it is important to return to that conflation between civilization and the current system encapsulated by the singular 'civilization' of the Museum's

---

[18] My reading is, however, very different from Leggatt (2018), who argues that *Station Eleven* ultimately critiques this nostalgia for the old world.

name. This conflation not only signals how in the characters' mind there is no other possible civilization – again, capitalist realism – but also reinforces the myth of neoliberalism as the pinnacle of modernity and the apocalyptic teleology of a progressively unified world in which all difference is erased under the global free market. Hardly by chance, schooling in the Severn City Airport insists on transports and communications that create a hyper-connected world in which borders are essentially meaningless: children are told about the Internet, 'how it was everywhere and connected everything, how it was us. They [are] shown maps and globes, the lines of the borders that the Internet had transcended' (*SE* 262). This utopian narrative about the pre-apocalyptic past obscures the material labour that props up the hyper-connected globalized world and the inequalities between the Global North and South that lie beneath its seemingly seamless unity. *Station Eleven*'s problematic celebration of the pre-apocalyptic system and the reinstatement of its underlying apocalyptic structures reaches its culmination in the novel's ending.

While the American Phoenix's attempt to resuscitate the corpse of neoliberalism and its construction of the future as the endless reproduction of the present fails in *Zone One*, in *Station Eleven* the concluding discovery of a town with a functioning electrical grid suggests that the pre-apocalyptic system could slowly be restored. That this possibility is announced within the plot by the return of electricity is significant. As discussed, the power of electricity captures the novel's elegiac celebration of the beauty of the pre-apocalyptic world, so much so that electricity's myriad applications populate Mandel's 'incomplete list' of what is no more after the Georgia Flu (*SE* 31–32). And since neoliberalism is imbricated with an apocalyptic conception of history, it is no surprise that echoes of apocalyptic logic, and specifically of modernity, whose apocalyptic culmination neoliberalism should represent, resurface within the novel's final paragraph. As Clark looks at the ghostly remains of the global capitalist order – the planes stuck on the tarmac at the Severn City Airport – the narrator reports: 'He has no expectation of seeing an airplane rise again in his lifetime, but is it possible that somewhere there are ships setting out? … If nothing else, it's pleasant to consider the possibility. He likes the thought of ships moving over the water, towards another world just out of sight' (*SE* 332–333). The sense of possibility – compounded by the paragraph's accumulation of questions and speculations – chimes with *Station Eleven*'s alternate history and structural critique of the deterministic sense of an ending. Yet, the apocalyptic image of 'another world' reached by 'vessels' 'steered by sailors armed with maps and knowledge of the stars, driven by need or perhaps simply by curiosity' (*SE* 332) is redolent of the era of colonial modernity and of the maritime networks of commerce and exploitation that predate the global networks facilitated by air travel and that lie at the origins of today's environmental risks.[19] The beauty of the newly found electric grid (*SE* 311), indeed, obscures how the final return of electricity 'seems likely to imply the burning of fossil fuels', and thus that humankind will soon be 'back onto the destructive path taken by the pre-flu world; existing within the hyperobject of global warming' (Eve 2018: 20), which, as discussed in Chapter 3, originated with the apocalyptically-inflected modern 'discovery' of the New World. If *Station Eleven*, as typical of the contemporary post-apocalyptic novel, eschews the traditional apocalyptic movement from destruction to utopian renewal – what we have in the novel's ending is not a radical new world, but merely the slow 'awakening' of the old world (*SE* 332) – the novel is too complicit with the current system and its underlying apocalyptic structures, and ends up reinforcing the capitalist realist sense of no alternative to neoliberalism.

Coupland's engagement with the current system of accumulation in *Player One* is signified by the nature of the catastrophe itself, which, just like *Station Eleven*, is a catastrophe of global capital. In a peak oil apocalypse scenario, the price of oil quickly escalates, bringing to an end 'petromodernity', that is, an era and economy 'based in the cheap energy systems long made possible by petroleum' (LeMenager 2012: 60).[20] That this apocalypse unravels in an airport is all the more indicative of the novel's concern with the global networks of mobility, commerce and exploitation afforded by fossil fuels. I argue that *Player One*'s critical temporality signals the foreclosed possibilities haunting the neoliberal end of history not only through the collapse of petromodernity and its airport setting but also through the emphasis on 'denarration'. Denarration, *Player One*'s glossary explains, is 'The process whereby one's life stops feeling like a story' (*PO* 222), a process which, in turn, reflects the sense of a static present devoid of genuine futurity that characterizes life under global capital.[21] Denarration thus represents an irruption of the Real in the reality constructed by capitalist realism, for it points to the existential fragmentation and the erasure of the long-term lying behind neoliberalism's apocalyptically-inflected utopian claims. I show how *Player One* parodies an earlier post-apocalyptic novel by Coupland, *Girlfriend in a Coma* (1998), whose response to denarration is the

---

[19] Cf. Smith (2016) for an analysis of *Station Eleven*'s colonial echoes.
[20] LeMenager's notion of petromodernity chimes with Moore's Cheap Nature (2017), discussed in Chapter 3.
[21] The glossary, or 'Future Legend', of the book is reminiscent of the neologisms and definitions written on the margins of Coupland's first novel, *Generation X*.

recourse to an apocalyptic model of narrative and history, the same model which is at the core of the neoliberal crisis of futurity.

As typical of Coupland's fictions, which 'take place principally in the same year that they were written or published' (Tate 2007: 83), an element consonant with the loss of futurity and short-termist horizons the novelist registers in contemporary Western society, *Player One* is set in the cocktail lounge of the Toronto Airport Camelot Hotel during five hours on a day in August 2010, with each hour corresponding to a chapter in the novel. Just like *Station Eleven*, therefore, *Player One* articulates an alternate history of the present, which shatters the neoliberal utopian teleology by foregrounding how, rather than the apocalyptic culmination of modernity, neoliberalism represents its dystopian end. In an image that frames oil as the fuel of petromodernity's history, Rick, one of the novel's protagonists, reminisces about working at a gas station when he was a teenager and pretending that the pump's increasing numbers represent not money but time. 'He watched Western history begin at Year Zero-Zero-Zero-One and clip upwards and upwards', Rick remembers, until he reached a 'magic little piece of time a few numbers past $19.94 [1994 being the year of this memory] when he felt as if he were in the future' (*PO* 102; emphasis in original). That Rick is reminded of these moments after the peak oil apocalypse is telling. The forward march of the neoliberal teleology – represented by the pump's numbers – which constructs the future as more of the same thanks to its reliance on fossil fuels, stops when the apocalypse occurs in the second hour of the narrative and this future hardly seems 'magic' to Rick. The pre-apocalyptic world, fuelled by cheap oil, has disappeared forever: oil quickly goes from US$250 to US$900 a barrel and is then no longer on sale, power is cut, planes are grounded, borders are sealed, the media and the Internet go silent. The post-apocalyptic 'new world' – notice the apocalyptic trope and the subversion of the utopian teleology it traditionally embodies – 'exists within a state of permanent power failure. A perpetual Lagos, a never-ending Darfur' (*PO* 174). If this is the end of history, it is definitely not the utopian end of history promised by neoliberalism. Just as in *The Age of Miracles* and *Zone One*, the future does not shape up the way Rick thought it would during his gasoline-fuelled meditations as a teenager.

Significantly, and again as typical of Coupland's oeuvre in which we can identify a 'strategy of repetition and simulation that the novelist has deployed throughout his work, with key motifs and narrative conceits self-consciously cut, pasted and reworked' (Tate 2007: 13), the association of oil with the slow cancellation of the future under neoliberalism is not new in his fiction. In *Generation X*, Dag remembers a moment at a gas station in which his father invites him to smell spilled gasoline: 'Close your eyes and inhale. So *clean*. It smells like the *future*' (Coupland [1991] 1996: 107; emphasis in original). Just like with Rick's gasoline memory, Dag's memory, Liam Connell argues, 'is one of ironic failure. His father encourages him to imagine a promise of futurity that has already begun to end' (2017: 22) thanks to the advent of neoliberalism. As Connell notes, the memory is importantly located in 1974, when 'the oil-shock was about to bring such pre-lapsarian Keynesianism to an abrupt end' (2017: 22), and is thus directly linked to 'the end of History since [the oil shock] was a consequence of the ending of the Bretton Woods system' (2017: 21) and the beginning of neoliberalism. Indeed, the father's optimism and belief in the future stands in sharp contrast to Dag's and his generation's 'futurelessness' and 'presentism' (Connell 2017: 22) encapsulated by the 'McJobs' of the Gen-Xers, 'A low-pay, low-prestige, low-dignity, low-benefit, *no-future* job' (Coupland [1991] 1996: 6; emphasis mine). Dag underlining that the gasoline of this memory is leaded also gestures to the health and environmental hazards embodied by fossil fuels, ironically undermining the father's claim that gasoline smells 'so *clean*' and indicating the environmental undertones of the connection between oil and neoliberal negated futurity that *Player One* teases out through the catastrophic end of petromodernity. The term 'Anthropocene' features in *Player One*'s glossary in an entry that foregrounds the 'vast increases in anthropogenic emissions of greenhouse gases' (*PO* 217) directly linked to the burning of fossil fuels. For this reason, Karen, another of *Player One*'s protagonists, muses that the end of cheap oil might be a blessing in disguise: 'She once heard that the best thing for the planet world be for everyone to stay in one place for five years: no more transience, no more geographical cures, no more petro-holidays' (*PO* 94). Even before the apocalypse, the spectre of dwindling resources and climate change haunts the characters (*PO* 111, 175) signifying the sense of a slow apocalypse already in progress in our present and the Anthropocene's no future, which threatens the neoliberal end of history.

Both Dag's and Rick's gasoline memories signal a 'longing for a period of timefulness that contrasts with the presentism of the neoliberal era' (Connell 2017: 21), a longing that is key to Coupland's writings more broadly thanks to the focus on denarration. Denarration is a primary feature of contemporary life according to Coupland and a theme so pervasive in his works that in *JPod*, when the characters self-reflexively talk about the novelist himself, they frame his books through this phenomenon (Coupland [2006] 2007: 315). To Coupland, time is, together with free will, a characteristic that is unique to human beings –

'Time/Will Uniqueness', as *Player One*'s glossary puts it (*PO* 243) – but it is also something which we are imprisoned in and a pain only stories can alleviate. Narrative is our way to make sense of time passing, an element which echoes Ricoeur's argument that 'time becomes human time to the extent that it is organized after the manner of a narrative' (1984: 3). As Karen sums up, '*Our curse as humans is that we are trapped in time; our curse is that we are forced to interpret life as a sequence of events – a story – and when we can't figure out what our particular story is, we feel lost somehow*' (*PO* 5; emphasis in original).²² Coupland writes of a 'Narrative drive': 'The belief that a life without a story is a life not worth living – quite common, and ironically accompanied by the fact that most people cannot ascribe a story to their lives' (*PO* 232–233) in the neoliberal age.

The neoliberal end of history is, indeed, the age of denarration's crisis of futurity and hopeless extended present. Chiming with diagnoses of late capitalist temporality that speak of the contraction of time into the instant of cybernetic communications (Harvey 1989; Stiegler's 2011; Virilio 2010), Coupland writes that technological developments, especially in information technologies, denarrate lives. 'By rewiring our brains on the Internet, we've tampered with the old-fashioned organic perception of time … [Time] is simply moving more quickly' (Basar, Coupland, Obrist 2015: 28–29) and, in this situation of 'pro-acceleration', 'our sense of time is beginning to shrink' to a series of fragmented presents so that our lives, rather than meaningful sequences or stories, 'are becoming a lineup of tasks' in which 'The future is a practical joke that [we] have yet to acknowledge as such' (Basar, Coupland, Obrist 2015: 24, 25, 64). As Bertis, *Player One*'s prophet/sniper discussed in Chapter 1, yells in one of his rants, rather than by a sense of futurity, people are driven – and distracted from the pervasive sense of being denarrated – by the 'sputtering engine of the most banal form of capitalism …. Work, work, work: No moral. No plot. No *eureka!* Just production schedules and *days*. You might as well all be living inside a photocopier' (*PO* 136; emphasis in original), an image that recalls Mandel's sleepwalkers and the endless repetitions of the neoliberal present embodied by Whitehead's stragglers. Hardly by chance, a recurrent fantasy for *Player One*'s characters is that of making time stop, so as to recuperate a moment of agency to shape the future beyond the foreclosed possibilities of these endless denarrated

---

²² Tate underlines how 'The idea of the human "animal" with its idiosyncratic need to locate itself in time is frequently, perhaps obsessively, returned to in [Coupland's] novels' (2007: 51). Cf., for instance, exactly the same sentence in *Life after God* (Coupland [1994] 2002: 181–182) and a very similar one in *Polaroids from the Dead* (Coupland 1996: 179). These repetitions signal the already mentioned continuous rewriting that characterizes Coupland's oeuvre.

repetitions (*PO* 20, 106, 182). Coupland's denarration is, therefore, a critical temporality that exposes the lack of futurity lying behind the triumphalism of the end of history and the failure of apocalyptic sense-making teleology.

Player One's end-times airport is the ideal setting to explore denarration. Not only does the post-apocalyptic airport, with its grounded planes, show the collapse of the global fluxes that prop up neoliberalism and shatter the late capitalist construction of the future as more of the same but, as 'present tense crystallized into aluminum, concrete, and bad lighting' (*PO* 71), airports reflect the contraction to the denarrated present of neoliberal temporality. Augé's notion of 'non-place' ([1995] 2008) is very much on Coupland's mind: 'An airport isn't even a real place', Luke, another of *Player One*'s main characters, considers, 'It's a pit stop, an in-between area, a "nowhere"' (*PO* 71). Indeed, Augé's definition of 'non-place' as a 'space which cannot be defined as relational, or historical, or concerned with identity' ([1995] 2008: 63) chimes with *Polaroids from the Dead*'s definition of being denarrated as being with 'no religion, no family connections, no ideology, no sense of class location, no politics and no sense of history', 'all components [which were previously] essential for the forging of identity' (Coupland 1996: 180). To put it with Bertis, airports 'dissolve what few itty-bitty molecules of individuality you possess. After a plane trip, you need to rebuild your ego, to shore up your sense of being unique' (*PO* 135); in other words, you need to try to reconstruct your life-story. Stuck in an airport, one of the loci of global capital and denarration, *Player One*'s characters are confronted with the no future both of our economic system and of our individual lives.

The peak oil apocalypse simply amplifies the lack of genuine futurity that hovers over the sense of time of *Player One*'s protagonists. The novel opens with two references to time: 'Karen likes crossword puzzles because they make time pass quickly. Karen makes quilts ... because she savours the way quilting slows down time' (*PO* 1). While seemingly contradictory in their temporal effects, both activities denote a wish to escape a temporal sequence – a life – that appears utterly devoid of eventfulness and meaning, in a word, of a story. Hoping that her life might finally turn into a story, Karen has in fact flown to Toronto to go on her first date with Warren, whom – Coupland never one to refrain from irony – she has met in a peak oil apocalypse chat room. However, she soon realizes this hope is illusory and that the encounter with Warren is going to be just a dot that 'won't connect with any other dots to form a line with any beauty or meaning' (*PO* 47–48). Even before the apocalypse, Rick, an ex-alcoholic, hardly feels the faith in the future that characterized his younger self looking at the gas pump's progressing numbers. More than as a story, he sees his life as a cautionary tale

(*PO* 16) and, in a desperate attempt to renarrate his life, Rick invests all his savings in Leslie Freemont's preposterous 'Power Dynamics Seminar System', whose apocalyptic rhetoric of radical change, discussed in Chapter 1, seeks to create a sense of futurity through self-reinvention chiming with the neoliberal push for individuals to be entrepreneurs of the self. Having lost his faith and the meaning this afforded, pastor Luke robs his congregation, hoping that the money will fill the emptiness of his denarrated existence. While Rachel, an extremely beautiful young girl affected by several anomalies in her limbic system, does not seem to be preoccupied by denarration – 'Calling [life] a story changes nothing. It's just a sequence' (*PO* 87) – she is looking for a partner, in order to have a child and prove to the world, and specifically her father, 'her value as a human being' (*PO* 33). Leaving aside for the moment the fifth protagonist, Player One, Rachel's video game avatar, all these characters wish for change, eventfulness, futurity and meaning to the temporal sequence, which their life in the extended hopeless present of neoliberal capital does not afford.

Unsurprisingly, given the way in which apocalyptic logic deploys the narrative sense of an ending to impose order and meaning on time, *Player One*'s apocalypse appears at first to provide a renarration, and with it a sense of futurity. After the catastrophe, Karen feels that '*[her] life is a strand of magic moments strung together, a succession of mysteries revealed*' (*PO* 92; emphasis in original), where the reference to a revelation links back to the sense-making function of the traditional apocalyptic paradigm, the way in which this transforms time from *chronos*, '"passing time" or "waiting time" – that which, according to Revelation, "shall be no more" –' to *kairos*, 'the season, a point in time filled with significance, charged with a meaning derived from its relation to the end' (Kermode [1966] 2000: 47). Tellingly, Karen immediately associates this renarration to the end of work as *chronos* – 'No more afternoons in which time feels stillborn' spent in the office in which she works as a secretary (*PO* 94) – signalling how work under neoliberalism is just filler, and not particularly effective at that, to a denarrated existence. Similarly, to Rick the apocalypse is '*the end of some aspect of [his] life, but it's also a beginning – the beginning of some unknown secret that will reveal itself to [him] soon*' (*PO* 103; emphasis in original). And yet, news from the violent post-apocalyptic world outside the airport soon make Karen wish for a pill that could erase the catastrophe (*PO* 175), while the fact that Bertis later echoes Rick's thoughts word for word in his crazed and manipulative preaching (*PO* 134) undermines the latter's apocalyptic belief in the sense-making function of the end. Indeed, the revelation that both Karen's and Rick's sentences allude to is never provided in *Player One*, in stark contrast to the earlier post-apocalyptic novel by Coupland this text rewrites, *Girlfriend in a Coma*, whose recourse to traditional apocalyptic logic as a solution to denarration *Player One* parodies, deconstructing the apocalyptic structures underlying the neoliberal end of history and its crisis of futurity.[23]

Set in Vancouver between 1979 and about a year after the end of the world in 1997, *Girlfriend in a Coma* is rooted in the years in which neoliberalism takes over, and investigates the phenomenon of denarration and its slow cancellation of the future through the image of the coma. Karen's coma, the titular girlfriend (notice the parallel with the name of one of *Player One*'s protagonists, which signals *Player One*'s rewriting of the earlier text), lasts from 1979 to 1997, and is followed by the 'Sleep' apocalypse, the coma of the entire world with the exception of Karen's group of friends. Karen's function in *Girlfriend in a Coma* is to testify to the widespread sense of denarration and to the betrayal of the utopian expectations of Western modernity under neoliberalism. If Karen's boyfriend, Richard (notice again the name), considers that 'An overriding principle of our lives was that infinite freedom creates a society of unique, fascinating individuals' (Coupland 1998: 59), the reality of neoliberalism's 'freedom', Karen discovers upon waking up, is loneliness, alienation and *ennui*.[24] Similarly to Rick's gasoline meditations in *Player One*, in 1979, Karen thought that 'in the future the world would – *evolve* …. that we would make the world cleaner and safer and smarter, and that people would become smarter and wiser and kinder as a result of all the changes' (*GiaC* 213; emphasis in original). But, like Walker's slowing, Karen's post-coma observations reflect Berardi's theorization of the neoliberal era as the era in which the future is cancelled and no longer fulfils the promises and expectations of the past.[25] People do not 'believ[e] in the future', Karen notices, but merely 'expec[t] the end' (*GiaC* 215). As Hollinger writes, the coma is an apt 'metaphor for the distractions of contemporary existence', for while '*Girlfriend*'s characters do gradually develop an awareness of how blank and meaningless their lives have become, such awareness only leaves them paralyzed, devoid of both energy and agency' (2002: 172). When the coma apocalypse hits, an apocalypse tellingly

---

[23] One could extend Tate's observations about Coupland's 'strategy of repetition' (2007: 13) to argue that the writer at times revisits earlier novels in their entirety. *Generation A* (2009), *JPod* and *Player One* can be considered, respectively, as the *Generation X*, *Microserfs* (1995) and *Girlfriend in a Coma* of the 2000s. The fact that Coupland's narratives are generally set in the same year they are written or published is not extraneous to this compulsion to rewrite, for his very specifically temporally-located fictions constantly need updating.

[24] All further references to Coupland's *Girlfriend in a Coma* as *GiaC*.

[25] Cf. Hollinger, who points out that 'Reading the novel is like reading a fictional affirmation of Fredric Jameson's observation that contemporary Western culture can be defined, in part, through its loss of the sense of a viable future, concomitant with its loss of a sense of history' (2002: 166).

described as 'time vanish[ing]' (*GiaC* 263), it merely amplifies the sense that the neoliberal world is already frozen in a comatose extended present.

Yet, in accordance with the traditional apocalyptic paradigm, after about a year, the comatose post-apocalyptic world gives way to the revelation of a metaphysical truth that makes sense of history and renarrates the lives of Karen's friends. As Jared, the novel's ghost and the vehicle of this revelation, explains, 'The sweet and effortless nodule of freedom we all shared – it was a fine idea. It was, in its own unglamorous way, the goal of all human history – the wars, the genius, the madness, the beauty and the grief – it was all to reach ever farther and farther and farther and, well, *farther*' (*GiaC* 264; emphasis in original). Jared's revelation that 'Progress is real. Destiny is real' (*GiaC* 264) teleologically renarrates history, re-establishing the modern faith in progress and giving a sense of futurity back to the characters beyond the stasis of the neoliberal end of history: '*You* are the future, and the eternity, and the everything. You're indeed what comes *next*' (*GiaC* 280; emphasis in original). Thanks to Jared's ghostly intercession, the apocalypse is erased and time rewinds. Except for Karen who, as the Christ figure of this salvation history (Hollinger 2002: 168), sacrifices herself and returns into her coma for the redemption of her friends and of the entire world, the group is granted another opportunity, on the condition that they keep looking for the truth and 'testify' to its existence to others, so that a 'radical new world' can finally take place (*GiaC* 270, 281).

Jared's rhetoric is patently informed by traditional apocalyptic logic and it is this renarration of history through the recourse to the very logic that underlies the no future of the neoliberal end of history that *Player One* parodies by lifting sentences and concepts from the earlier novel. Bertis' sermon to Rick (*PO* 187–189) entirely consists of themes and sentences recycled from portions of Jared's concluding tirade (*GIAC* 269–271), where Bertis' patent craziness serves to parodically deconstruct Jared's apocalyptic rhetoric of change and its renarrating potential. While, by inviting his friends to 'Go clear the land for a new culture – bring your axes, scythes and guns' (*GiaC* 270–271), Jared 'uses a deliberate metaphor of the manifest destiny of religiously inspired colonial expansion', implicitly signifying that, like 'any revolution based on some unitary version of truth[, Jared's] will have to be forced violently on the rest of humanity' (Greenberg 2010: 30), Bertis's use of Jared's words, combined with the sniper's killings, foregrounds the intrinsic violence of Jared's apocalyptic renarration and the complicity of apocalyptic logic with oppressive power structures. Further undermining Jared's apocalyptic rhetoric, Leslie Freemont's mantra – '*Are you ready to change, to join, to become part of What's Next?*' (*PO* 5; emphasis in original) – and his slogans about '*Making choices and changing who you* are' (*PO* 15; emphasis in original) are a replica of Jared's call for action to his friends (*GiaC* 252, 268, 271–272). And if Leslie Freemont's toast to 'everyone on earth who's been eager, no, *desperate* for even the smallest sign that there exists something finer, larger, and more miraculous about our inner selves than we could ever have supposed' (*PO* 62; emphasis in original) recalls Richard's final inspired thoughts and his wish to '*shock and captivate [these people] into new ways of thinking*' (*GiaC* 279; emphasis in original), it is clear that in *Player One* these 'new ways of thinking' bring about neither a renarration nor the utopian renewal foreseen by Jared, but only more profits for the self-help guru, gesturing to the self-referentiality of apocalyptic logic discussed in Chapter 1. Where Jared explains that returning to life after the Sleep is erased will feel 'as if you've died and were reincarnated but you stay inside your own body' (*GiaC* 268), through its parodic rewriting of *Girlfriend in a Coma*, *Player One* exposes the 'near universal' desire for an 'instant reincarnation' (*PO* 228) as the other side of the debilitated agency which ensues from the neoliberal crisis of futurity encapsulated by denarration. After all, in *Girlfriend in a Coma*, the chance to bring about the new world is supernaturally and deterministically granted, and thus hardly something that fosters human agency. The wish for instant reincarnation, an apocalyptic clean slate from which to begin anew, is a form of escapism, rather than engagement with the present, that reflects the sense of lack of alternatives at the core of capitalist realism fostered by apocalyptic determinism.

Player One's critique of an apocalyptic solution to denarration's crisis of futurity is reflected in the novel's structure, which underlines how a sense of an ending to history and individual lives is just a narrative construct, and a deterministic one at that. The first four sections of each chapter/hour are narrated in the third person and, in each section, the narrative is limited to the perspective of a different character/focalizer, Karen, Rick, Luke and Rachel. The last section of each chapter/hour is instead narrated in the first person by Player One, Rachel's electronic double, who has a 'complete overview both of the world and of time' (*PO* 35), and indeed reports the other characters' inner thoughts as well as anticipating events that are yet to happen. As *Player One*'s final section makes clear when Rachel is shot by Bertis and her perspective merges with that of her double, *Player One*'s perspective is that of eternity. With her omniscience, Player One embodies the epistemically privileged position of after the end to deconstruct it from within, foregrounding the temporal aporia at the core of apocalyptic logic already discussed in my analysis of Sam Taylor's *The Island at the End of the World* (2009) and Jim Crace's *The Pesthouse* (2007) in Chapters

1 and 2. By drawing attention to the constructedness of her narrative through her frequent addresses to the readers when introducing her prolepses, Player One conveys the constructedness of the apocalyptic model of history's reliance on the sense of an ending which is, to put it with Karen, 'false linearity imposed on chaos' (*PO* 5), for the avatar's perspective from after the end is of course unavailable to human beings. Player One's prolepses foreground how the end is already deterministically in place in narratives, indicating how, if the sense of an ending gives order and meaning to the historical sequence, it does so at the expense of falsifying the openness of time as it is lived.

Similarly to the first five chapters of *The Pesthouse* analysed in Chapter 2, the structure of the first four sections of each of *Player One*'s chapters/hours is paratactic, namely, it subverts the apocalyptic conception of history and narrative by '[e]mphasizing what is parallel and synchronically patterned rather than what is linear and progressive' (Ermarth 1992: 85). Inviting readers to look for parallels between events happening at the same time instead than for the sense of an ending, these sections articulate a critical temporality that foregrounds the present as the locus of an agency that shapes the future, rather than as part of a predetermined teleological sequence which effectively denies futurity, as seen in the extended present of the neoliberal end of history. As Rachel/Player One reminds the readers, 'Non-linear stories? Multiple endings? No loading times? It's called life on earth' (*PO* 211). *Player One* suggests that a renarration of our denarrated lives, and thus a sense of genuine futurity beyond the repetitions of the endless neoliberal present, can be achieved not by going back to apocalyptic logic as in *Girlfriend in a Coma*, for apocalyptic structures underlie the neoliberal end of history, but by stressing the constructedness of the sense of an ending and the openness of time as lived against apocalyptic determinism.

To draw on Jameson's revision of his famous claim that 'it is easier to imagine the end of the world than to imagine the end of capitalism', the fictions analysed in this chapter 'attempt to imagine capitalism by way of imagining the end of the world' (2003: 76) precisely, I argue, because of the apocalyptic structures underlying neoliberal capital. Addressing these structures, the critical temporalities of *Odds Against Tomorrow, The Age of Miracles, Zone One, Station Eleven* and *Player One* subvert the utopian end of history by exposing the neoliberal present as static and devoid of genuine futurity. Shattering the neoliberal construction of the future as more of the same, these novels all covey the sense of an ongoing slow apocalypse in our present, from financial risks to climate change, as perfectly embodied by Walker's slowing. Both *Station Eleven* and *Player One*, the focus of this chapter, capture the collapse of the current globalized and hyper-connected system of accumulation through characters stuck in end-times airports, and rupture the apocalyptic determinism of the neoliberal end of history through their alternate histories and narrative structures. Coupland's engagement with narrativity as our way of making sense of time leads us to this study's Conclusion, which considers the power of narrative as a central concern in the contemporary post-apocalyptic novel.

Conclusion: The Post-Apocalyptic Archive

This book has started with texts that deconstruct the biblical origins of apocalyptic discourse and then moved to fictions that expose the wide-ranging influence of the apocalyptic understanding of history on Western modernity and our present, from American ideologies, such as Manifest Destiny and American exceptionalism, which continue to underwrite post-9/11 politics, to the colonial origins of capitalism and its anthropogenic effects, and to the neoliberal end of history. Through the notion of critical temporality, I have traced the ways in which the contemporary post-apocalyptic novel subverts the utopian teleology at the core of apocalyptic history, emphasizing its determinism, complicity with oppressive power structures and implication in the escalating contemporary risks. As the apocalyptic model of history is essentially a model of narrative based on the sense of an ending, the structures of the fictions in question, I have argued, undermine the sense of an ending, foregrounding its constructedness and preserving spaces for agency beyond its determinism. At the core of the contemporary post-apocalyptic novel lies, therefore, the faith in the transformative power of narrative, even in a post-catastrophic world in which the very survival of literature is endangered. This faith is perfectly encapsulated by the *mise en abyme* manuscript in Jeanette Winterson's *The Stone Gods* (2007), which Billie pens after a nuclear war to warn people against the environmental risks intrinsic in humankind's recursive longing for an apocalyptic new world, notwithstanding the waning influence of literary culture and writings more broadly in her society.

As Derrida writes, literature is constituted by 'a project of stockpiling, of building up an objective archive' but an apocalypse – Derrida is here considering nuclear war – presents us with the 'possibility of an irreversible destruction, leaving no traces, of the juridico-literary archive' (1984: 26). In this Conclusion, I turn to images of archived narratives in the contemporary post-apocalyptic novel, such as libraries and diaries, to draw together the main threads of my book: narrative, history, power and agency. I focus on Lidia Yuknavitch's *The*

Book of Joan (2017), where the archive is the human body thanks to the future storytelling form of skin grafting. The emphasis on the continuous relevance of narrative notwithstanding the possibility of a catastrophic destruction of archives serves to legitimize the contemporary post-apocalyptic novel itself. And, with their selective preservation of texts, records and memories, post-apocalyptic archives encapsulate the nexus between narrative, history and power deconstructed by the contemporary post-apocalyptic novel's critical temporalities, inviting us to be wary of the apocalyptic articulation of history. Drawing on Derrida's notion of 'archive fever' (1995), I identify an anti-apocalyptic archive fever in the contemporary post-apocalyptic novel, that is, the desire to preserve and foster narratives, such as Winterson's *mise en abyme* manuscript, that will contribute to shape a future beyond the apocalyptic sense of an ending and its power structures.

As readers of the contemporary post-apocalyptic novel, we are not only reading imagined futures but our present as imagined past, archived more or less successfully. Hollinger notes a 'striking symmetry' between the logic of the archive and 'science fiction's (SF) [and by extension, post-apocalyptic fiction's] own temporal logic as a future-oriented genre. Each requires an imaginative commitment to a future that recasts the present as the past' (2013: 242). Emily St. John Mandel's *Station Eleven* (2014) is a particularly good example of our present as imagined archived past. Alongside the Museum of Civilization, housing objects from the pre-pandemic times, the novel typifies a post-apocalyptic archive fever – the impulse to preserve the pre-apocalyptic world before it is lost forever – through Kirsten's collection of gossip magazines, over which she pores looking for her past (*SE* 40), namely, scoops about Arthur, the actor with whom she was on stage when the pandemic began, as well as the character of François Diallo, archivist and librarian, who is creating an 'oral history' (*SE* 108) of the collapse and the post-apocalypse, and whose interviews with Kirsten constitute some of *Station Eleven*'s sections. Thanks to the presence of a number of narrative forms in the post-apocalyptic future – the Shakespearean plays performed by the Travelling Symphony, the titular comic *Station Eleven*, interviews, scraps of tabloids, as well as the maxim 'Survival is insufficient' from *Star Trek Voyager* – *Station Eleven* 'defends the pleasures and imaginative possibilities of popular culture' (Tate 2017: 135). Conversely, images of destroyed archives indicate how the contemporary post-apocalyptic novel is haunted by the nightmare of our culture's impermanence and insignificance, especially in the face of an apocalypse that irrevocably alters societal structures. Consider, for instance, the total lack of written records about the pre-apocalyptic past in Jim Crace's *The Pesthouse* (2007); the charred ruins of a library in Cormac McCarthy's *The Road* (2006), where 'Shelves tipped over' indicate 'rage at the lies arranged in their thousands row on row' (*TR* 187); another library in Doris Lessing's *The Story of General Dann and Mara's Daughter, Griot and the Snow Dog* (2005), precariously preserved thousands of years into a new Ice Age thanks to long-lost technology only to be destroyed as soon as it comes into contact with air; and the image of the survivors of Colson Whitehead's *Zone One* (2011) burning 'the novels devoted to the codes of the dead world' for heat (*ZO* 195). The apocalypse risks undermining the *raison d'être* of literary works, including the post-apocalyptic fictions in question: conveying a meaningful story and message to the readers, even beyond the author's lifespan.

Art, Johnny Rolfe fears in Matthew Sharpe's *Jamestown* (2007), belongs to pre-apocalyptic times, 'when Earth produced a seemingly limitless supply of food and fuel' (*J* 396) and people, at least in the Global North, did not have to worry constantly over mere survival. Thus, at the beginning of each of the diary entries that constitute his sections in the novel, Rolfe questions the point of writing a diary – one's own personal archive. 'To whoever is out there, if anyone is out there' reads his very first entry, for instance, or, as he writes later on, 'To You, to whom I tell this, if indeed there is a You to tell, an I to do the telling, a This to tell about, and a Telling to bring You, I, and This together in the mystic wedding of communication' (*J* 3, 45). And yet he does continue to write, just as Cedar does in Louise Erdrich's *Future Home of the Living God* (2017), though she 'fear[s] that we are heading into a lightless future devoid of the written word' and that her unborn baby, to whom she addresses her diary, might never be able to read it (*FHLG* 31). By the same token, the man in *The Road* still tells his child 'old stories of courage and justice' (*TR* 41), the people of Ifrik in *The Story of General Dann and Mara's Daughter, Griot and the Snow Dog* build a new archive to attempt preserving and collating the remaining knowledge of pre-apocalyptic times, and *Zone One*'s the Quiet Storm 'wr[ites] her way into the future' by inventing a new alphabet and art form, consisting in cars meticulously arranged to form a message (*ZO* 233). In continuing to write their diaries notwithstanding their doubts, Rolfe and Cedar join a long history of characters in dystopian novels who find solace from their hopeless situations in recording their story, even if they worry this will never find an audience because of the impermanence and power structures of the post-apocalyptic archive.

Consider, for example, Winston Smith in George Orwell's *Nineteen Eighty-Four* (1949), whose rebellion against the Big Brother and the Party begins in earnest when he starts writing his diary, even though he is painfully aware that both he and the diary will be annihilated, and 'How could you appeal to the future when not a trace of you, not even an anonymous word scribbled on a piece of paper, could physically survive?' (Orwell [1949]2008: 29). Or, consider Offred in Margaret Atwood's *The Handmaid's Tale* (1985), who is driven to tell her story by the desire for a sense of control and communion with others she lacks under Gilead's oppressive patriarchy: 'If it's a story I'm telling, then I have control over the ending …. But if it's a story, even in my head, I must be telling it to someone. You don't tell a story only to yourself. There's always someone else. Even when there is no one' (Atwood [1985] 1996: 49). Like Rolfe and Cedar, Winston and Offred testify to the relevance and power of narrative in situations of total disenfranchisement, notwithstanding their anxieties over the lack of an addressee for their story. And of course, even if within the fictional universe their message might go unheard because of the volatility of the post-apocalyptic archive and power's manipulations of it, all of these characters find their audience outside the fictional universe: us. As emphasized by the closing image of 'Sloosha's Crossin'' in David Mitchell's *Cloud Atlas* (2004), where the narrator directly invites the readers to 'Sit down a beat or two. Hold out your hands. Look' (*CA* 325) and take in Sonmi-451's story, preserved in the orison, the readers are the ultimate addressees of the post-apocalyptic archive. This, after all, is about imagining our present as the past of the fictional future, thus literalizing the temporal dynamics at work in science fiction and future-oriented writings more broadly, which 'enac[t] and enabl[e] a structurally unique "method" for apprehending the present as history' (Jameson 2005: 288), specifically, as I have argued in this book, for apprehending the apocalyptic structures that underlie today's risks.

Importantly, Winston's, Offred's and Sonmi's attempts at articulating a story of their own are situated in worlds where totalitarian regimes exercise a strict control over history, manipulating archives to their own ends. Drawing on the etymology of the word 'archive', from the Greek "*arkhē*", which 'names at once the *commencement* and the *commandment*', Derrida notes that 'the meaning of "archive," its only meaning, comes to it from the Greek "arkheion": initially a house, a domicile, an address, the residence of the superior magistrates, the *archons*, those who commanded' (1995: 9; emphasis in original). Therefore, 'the question of a politics of the archive' is inherent in the very meaning of the word, so much so that this question runs through the whole of the field and in truth determines politics from top to bottom as res publica. There is no political power without control of the archive, if not of memory. Effective democratization can always be measured by this essential criterion: the participation in and the access to the archive, its constitution, and its interpretation. A contrario, the breaches of democracy can be measured by what a recent and in so many ways remarkable work entitles Forbidden Archives. (Derrida 1995: 10–11; emphasis in original)

Forbidden archives abound in the contemporary post-apocalyptic novel, signifying the nexus of power and the archive. Consider, for instance, the Department of Historical Integrity in Thomas Mullen's *The Revisionists* (2011), whose role is hardly to preserve the integrity of the archive but, rather, to erase historical records and even individual memories, rewriting history according to power's wishes; Dave's Second Book in Will Self's *The Book of Dave* (2006), whose existence is kept secret by the PCO and the Dävidic dynasty; Ben's hidden library in Sam Taylor's *The Island at the End of the World* (2009), which goes far beyond the Bible, the book of fairy tales and the Shakespearean plays the man allows his children to read; and Nea So Copros' security archives in *Cloud Atlas*, which contain not only historical records about the pre-corporate state past but also movies, for the state 'outlaws *any* historical discourse' (*CA* 243; emphasis in original).

In this context, as Theo Finigan maintains in his analysis of the archives of *Nineteen Eighty-Four* and *The Handmaid's Tale*, Derrida's notion of 'archive fever' (1995) comes not only to denote the drive to preserve records and stories, countering the possibility of loss and forgetting constitutive of the concept of the archive and indeed of human finitude itself, but 'might also signify an ethically informed passion for the "right" archive. In other words, ... the possibility that the archive could function as the means of a historiographic corrective that would counter the totalitarian manipulation of history' (Finigan 2011: 435–436). Importantly, power's public archives in *The Revisionists*, *The Book of Dave*, *The Island at the End of the World* and *Cloud Atlas* all articulate an apocalyptic history in which the post-apocalyptic present is constructed and legitimized as the culmination of history. It is this apocalyptic history that, in what might be termed an anti-apocalyptic archive fever, the novels' forbidden archives subvert through records and memories that undermine power's apocalyptic self-legitimation, as well as through the transformative potential of narrative itself. In *The Island at the End of the World*, for instance, Alice is alerted to the possibility that her father is lying about the catastrophic flood by reading Shakespeare's descriptions of the ever-moving sea, which contrasts to the static body of water she sees surrounding her presumed island. Equally, Sonmi's awakening to the injustices of her existence is informed by the forbidden narratives she consumes, which include texts by Orwell and Huxley in a metafictional commentary on the significance of dystopian fiction (*CA* 220).

For questions about the politics of the archive are inherently about time not only in the sense that the archive can construct a version of history that legitimizes those in power but also in the sense that, to put it with the Party's slogan in *Nineteen Eighty-Four*, 'who controls the past, … controls the future' (Orwell [1949]2008: 37). After all, as Derrida emphasizes, 'the idea of the archive', with its preservation of knowledge and memory for posterity, depends on 'the very concept of the future' (Derrida 1995: 24). To return to Isaac's theories in *Cloud Atlas*, power 'landscapes' virtual pasts and futures in order to shape the actual future, seeking to ensure its continuous existence. Thus, just as power's manipulations of the archive are not merely about constructing the past but also the future, the contemporary post-apocalyptic novel's anti-apocalyptic archive fever is about preserving and fostering narratives that counter power's deterministic apocalyptic history and support the readers' agency to shape the future, as perfectly encapsulated by Yuknavitch's *The Book of Joan*.

Like the medieval writer who is the inspiration for her character, Christine de Pizan wages her war against her opponent Jean de Men and his apocalyptic power through narrative, specifically, the new form of storytelling that is skin grafting, of which she is one of the foremost artists. On CIEL, bodies have become archives of stories, 'graft upon graft, deep as third-degree burns, healed in white-on-white curls and protrusions and ridges' that profoundly alter human morphology – the more altered and grafted, the richer the person (*BoJ* 17). The narrative Christine wants to embody, however, is a far cry from the romantic and erotic grafts that, in a society lusting after sexual encounters people can no longer enjoy given bodily devolution, have made the fortune of CIEL's tyrannical leader Jean de Men. Firmly believing that 'Two things have always ruptured up and through hegemony: art and bodies', Christine de Pizan wants to 'tease a story from within so-called history. To use [her] body and art to do it' (*BoJ* 97, 10). The forbidden story she wants to retrieve from power's 'so-called history' is Joan's. Charged with treason and terrorism against the state because of her defence of Earth from CIEL's abuses, Joan was supposedly burnt at the stake, her execution televised, and the bare mention of her name, let alone the telling of her story beyond 'the endlessly represented image and story of her "official" death' (*BoJ* 19), made a crime. The execution is, however, one of Jean de Men's fabrications to prop up his apocalyptic narrative about CIEL as the utopian new world. Joan actually managed to escape, and emphasizing power's meddling with events to legitimize itself, Yuknavitch's novel features excerpts from Joan's interrogation that show her questioners repeatedly striking Joan's answers from the record. To Jean de Men's manipulations and erasures of the archive, Christine de Pizan counteracts her own bodily archive of narratives, made even more effective by their medium: 'Not sacred scrolls. Not military ideologies or debatable intellectual history. Just the only thing we had left, and thus the gap between representation and living, collapsed' (*BoJ* 22). Christine becomes the eponymous book of Joan, living and breathing her message, conveying the importance of narratives to human agency.

Where our reality is constituted by a web of narratives, as discussed in Chapter 1, Christine becomes the embodiment of an anti-apocalyptic archive fever, that is, the passion for narratives that counter apocalyptic logic and do not consume the planet and others in their self-righteous teleology and hunger for power. As Donna Haraway reminds us many times throughout *Staying with the Trouble: Making Kin in the Chthulucene*, 'It matters what stories tell stories' (2016: 35). Chiming with Douglas Coupland's emphasis on the centrality of narratives to our identity considered in Chapter 4, Yuknavitch writes that 'To have a story [is] to have a self' and that stories 'give shape to action' (*BoJ* 128, 163). That is why Christine de Pizan writes Joan's story on other bodies as well, creating a 'resistance movement of flesh' against Jean de Men's, and humanity's, apocalyptic narratives of progress and new worlds that, as explored in Chapter 3, serve to embellish an anthropogenic and genocidal 'drive to conquer, colonize, deplete' (*BoJ* 90, 106). In her writing back to the oppressive ideologies that the apocalyptic conception of history facilitates, Christine calls for different 'fictions [from the ones] we consistently chose that forced our own undoing', fictions capable of shaping an equally different future from the environmentally depleted one she inhabits (*BoJ* 108). While she begins by idealizing Joan as a hero, Christine soon realizes that heroism is a concept 'Bound to a story that is not only man-made, but man-centered' and that Joan's body demands a different story. As an 'engenderine', a 'kind of human-matter interface' – notice the resonance with Haraway's invitation to 'make kin' with other species in what she terms the Chthulucene to undercut the anthropocentrism of the Anthropocene – Joan's body is 'of the earth', tethered to the planet's 'energy and matter' (*BoJ* 94, 190, 99). Therefore, Christine muses, 'The story born of her actual body will be burned into mine not to mythologize her or raise her above anyone or anything but to radically resist that impulse. Not toward any higher truth other than we are matter', interconnected with, rather than above, the rest of the planet, and indeed, universe (*BoJ* 100). Christine 'join[s] Joan in rejecting messiahs' (*BoJ* 100), Joan included, and thus apocalyptic narratives that legitimize those in power as the rightful interpreters and agents of the telos of history. That Joan's story is archived in what used to be a female body but is now 'without gender, mostly' (*BoJ* 9) is also telling. Christine's body provides a much-needed corrective to the patriarchal origins of the archive, what Derrida terms the 'patriarchive' (1995: 11), for the archons, the guardians of the law and of the archive, were of course men. Christine's grafts, indeed, stand against Jean de Men's patriarchal narratives and power – as signalled by his name (of men), de Men's grafts prop up a heteronormativity that sees women as living only to satisfy men, reproduce and then be discarded – which align with the patriarchal nature of apocalyptic discourse discussed in Chapter 1.

Christine's anti-apocalyptic archive fever succeeds in inciting a rebellion against Jean de Men. The book closes with the destruction of CIEL and Joan's voluntary death on Earth, where her engenderine energy will regenerate the wasteland humankind made of the planet with its reliance on apocalyptic narratives. Hardly by chance, given the imbrication of apocalyptic history with a narrative form shaped by the sense of an ending, *The Book of Joan* rejects the sense of an ending for its own plot. The novel closes on a sense of openness – to other narratives, of the text itself and of futurity. The regeneration of the planet that will follow Joan's death is not the utopian rebirth of apocalyptic logic but 'Some story we don't know yet untied from all the ones that have come before', 'A different story, leading whoever is left toward something we've not yet imagined' (*BoJ* 258, 260). In accord with Christine's anti-apocalyptic archive fever, Joan's final letter to her beloved Leone stresses that we are not bound to 'the shape of beginnings and endings', for 'Earth carried other meanings than the ones we used to make culture' (*BoJ* 264), thus foregrounding the limitations of the conventional model of narrative, with its emphasis on closure, and the importance of narratives that conceptualize an open present and future beyond the determinism and power structures embedded in the sense of an ending of apocalyptic history.

Like the contemporary post-apocalyptic novel itself, the archive asks 'a question of the future, the question of the future itself, the question of a response, of a promise and of a responsibility for tomorrow' (Derrida 1995: 27). The archives of the contemporary post-apocalyptic novel, therefore, compound these fictions' critical temporalities, that is, the critique of the apocalyptic conception of history that underlies today's risks and power structures as well as of the deterministic and teleological narrative structure that supports this model of history. In posing its 'question of the future', the post-apocalyptic archive is characterized by an anti-apocalyptic archive fever, in that it calls for narratives which will help bring about a future beyond the nexus of apocalyptic history and power, opening up alternative possibilities to the foreclosed possibilities of apocalyptic logic, whose disastrous effects are becoming more and more evident in our world. To put it with one of *The Book of Joan*'s epigraphs, the archives of the contemporary post-apocalyptic novel warn us to 'be careful what stories "count"' for they will shape our actions and, thus, our future.

Bibliography

Abrams, M. H. (1984), 'Apocalypse: Theme and Variations', in C. A. Patrides and Joseph Wittreich (eds), *The Apocalypse in English Renaissance Thought and Literature: Patterns, Antecedents, and Repercussions*, 342–68, Manchester: Manchester University Press.

Adams, Tim (2019), 'Ian McEwan: "Who's Going to Write the Algorithm for the Little White Lie?"' *Guardian*, 14 April. Available online: https://www.theguardian.com/books/2019/apr/14/ian-mcewan-interview-machines-like-me-artificial-intelligence (accessed 4 May 2019).

Agger, Ben ([2004] 2016), *Speeding Up Fast Capitalism: Internet Culture, Work, Families, Food, Bodies*, London: Routledge.

Anievas, Alexander and Kerem Nişancıoğlu (2015), *How the West Came to Rule: The Geopolitical Origins of Capitalism*, London: Pluto Press.

Ankersmit, F. R. (1994), *History and Tropology: The Rise and Fall of Metaphor*, Berkeley: University of California Press.

Atwood, Margaret ([1985] 1996), *The Handmaid's Tale*, London: Vintage.

Atwood, Margaret ([2003] 2009), *Oryx and Crake*, London: Virago.

Atwood, Margaret ([2009] 2010), *The Year of the Flood*, London: Virago.

Atwood, Margaret and Louise Erdrich (2017), 'Inside the Dystopian Visions of Margaret Atwood and Louise Erdrich', *Elle*, 14 November. Available online: http://www.elle.com/culture/books/a13530871/future-home-of-the-living-god-louise-erdrich-interview/ (accessed 9 July 2018).

Augé, Marc ([1995] 2008), *Non-Places: An Introduction to Supermodernity*, London: Verso.

Avery, Samuel (2013), *The Pipeline and the Paradigm: Keystone XL, Tar Sands, and the Battle to Defuse the Carbon Bomb*, Washington: Ruka Press.

Bachram, Heidi (2004), 'Climate Fraud and Carbon Colonialism: The New Trade in Greenhouse Gases', *Capitalism, Nature Socialism* 15 (4): 1–16.

Badiou, Alain (2005), *Being and Event*, London: Continuum.

Baker, Brian (2014), *Science Fiction: A Reader's Guide to Essential Criticism*, London: Palgrave.

Bakhtin, Mikhail M. (1981), 'Forms of Time and of the Chronotope in the Novel: Notes toward a Historical Poetics', in Michael Holquist (ed), *The Dialogic Imagination: Four Essays by M. M. Bakhtin*, 84–258, Austin: University of Texas Press.

Balasopoulos, Antonis (2004), 'Unworldly Worldliness: America and the Trajectories of Utopian Expansionism', *Utopian Studies* 15 (2): 3–35.

Balée, Susan (2007), 'Jim Crace's Violent Verities: *The Pesthouse* by Jim Crace; *The Road* by Cormac McCarthy', *The Hudson Review* 60 (3): 517–24; 526–27.

Barnes, Julian ([1989] 1990), *A History of the World in 10½ Chapters*, London: Picador.

Basar, Shumon, Douglas Coupland and Hans Ulrich Obrist (2015), *The Age of Earthquakes: A Guide to the Extreme Present*, London: Penguin.

Baudrillard, Jean (1994a), *The Illusion of the End*, Cambridge: Polity.

Baudrillard, Jean (1994b), *Simulacra and Simulation*, Ann Arbor: University of Michigan Press.

Baudrillard, Jean (2003), *The Spirit of Terrorism and Other Essays*, London: Verso.

Beck, John (2009), *Dirty Wars: Landscape, Power, and Waste in Western American Literature*, Lincoln: University of Nebraska Press.

Beck, Ulrich (1992), *Risk Society: Towards a New Modernity*, London: Sage.

Beck, Ulrich (2006), 'Living in the World Risk Society', *Economy and Society* 35 (3): 329–45.

Beebee, Thomas O. (2009), *Millennial Literatures of the Americas: 1492–2002*, Oxford: Oxford University Press.

Begley, Adam (2003), 'Jim Crace, The Art of Fiction No. 179', *Paris Review* 167. Available online: https://www.theparisreview.org/interviews/122/jim-crace-the-art-of-fiction-no-179-jim-crace (accessed 28 May 2012).

Berardi, Franco 'Bifo' (2011), *After the Future*, Chico: AK Press.

Berger, James (1999), *After the End: Representations of Post-Apocalypse*, Minneapolis: University of Minnesota Press.

Bernstein, Michael André (1994), *Foregone Conclusions: Against Apocalyptic History*, Berkeley: University of California Press.

Bishop, Kyle William (2015), *How Zombies Conquered Popular Culture: The Multifarious Walking Dead in the 21st Century*, Jefferson: MacFarland.

Blackmore, Tim (2009), 'Life of War, Death of the Rest: The Shining Path of Cormac McCarthy's Thermonuclear America', *Bulletin of Science, Technology & Society* 29: 18–36.

Bonneuil, Christophe and Jean-Baptiste Fressoz (2016), *The Shock of the Anthropocene: The Earth, History and Us*, London: Verso.

Boulter, Jonathan (2011), *Melancholy and the Archive: Trauma, Memory, and History in the Contemporary Novel*, London: Continuum.

Boxall, Peter (2013), *Twenty-First-Century Fiction: A Critical Introduction*, Cambridge: Cambridge University Press.

Bracke, Astrid (2017), *Climate Crisis and the 21st-Century British Novel*, London: Bloomsbury.

Briggs, Caroline (2007), 'Winterson's Novel "Left at Station"', *BBC News*, 8 March. Available online: http://news.bbc.co.uk/2/hi/entertainment/6430775.stm (accessed 23 August 2018).

Bromley, David G. and J. Gordon Melton eds (2009), *Cults, Religion, and Violence*, Cambridge: Cambridge University Press.

Broncano, Manuel (2014), *Religion in Cormac McCarthy's Fiction: Apocryphal Borderlands*, New York: Routledge.

Brooks, Peter (1984), *Reading for the Plot: Design and Intention in Narrative*, Cambridge: Harvard University Press.

Brouillette, Sarah, Mathias Nilges and Emilio Sauri eds (2017), *Literature and the Global Contemporary*, Cham: Palgrave Macmillan.

Brown, Wendy (2015), *Undoing the Demos: Neoliberalism's Stealth Revolution*, New York: Zone Books.

Buell, Frederick (2013), 'Post-Apocalypse: A New U.S. Cultural Dominant', *Frame* 26 (1): 9–30.

Bush, George W. (2001a), 'Remarks at Prayer Service', *Washington Post*, 14 September. Available online: http://www.washingtonpost.com/wp-srv/nation/specials/attacked/transcripts/bushtext_091401.html?noredirect=on (accessed 9 January 2018).

Bush, George W. (2001b), 'President Bush Addresses the Nation', *Washington Post*, 20 September. Available online: http://www.washingtonpost.com/wp-srv/nation/specials/attacked/transcripts/bushaddress_092001.html (accessed 9 January 2018).

Bush, George W. (2002), 'Graduation Speech at West Point'. Available online: https://georgewbush-whitehouse.archives.gov/news/releases/2002/06/20020601-3.html (accessed 24 November 2014).

Butler, Andrew M. (2015), '2015 Winner, The Arthur C. Clarke Award'. Available online: https://www.clarkeaward.com/2015-winner/ (accessed 9 August 2018).

Cazdyn, Eric (2012), *The Already Dead: The New Time of Politics, Culture, and Illness*, Durham and London: Duke University Press.

Carruthers, Jo and Andrew Tate eds (2010), *Spiritual Identities: Literature and the Post-Secular Imagination*, Oxford: Peter Lang.

Cameron, Claire (2014), '*Station Eleven* Offers Suspense and Science Fiction, but It Is Undoubtedly a Literary Work', *Globe and Mail*, 12 September. Available online: https://www.theglobeandmail.com/arts/books-and-media/book-reviews/station-eleven-offers-suspense-and-science-fiction-but-it-is-undoubtedly-a-literary-work/article20577909/ (accessed 4 May 2019).

Canavan, Gerry (2008), 'Look on My Works, Ye Mighty, and Despair'. Available online: https://gerrycanavan.wordpress.com/2008/01/21/look-on-my-works-ye-mighty-and-despair/ (accessed 8 June 2018).

Cant, John (2008), *Cormac McCarthy and the Myth of American Exceptionalism*, New York: Routledge.

Chabon, Michael (2007), 'After the Apocalypse', *New York Review of Books*, 15 February. Available online: https://www.nybooks.com/articles/2007/02/15/after-the-apocalypse/ (accessed 4 May 2019),

Chapman, Jennie (2013), *Plotting Apocalypse: Reading, Agency, and Identity in the Left Behind Series*, Jackson: University of Mississippi Press.

Clark, Timothy (2015), *Ecocriticism on the Edge: The Anthropocene as a Threshold Concept*, London: Bloomsbury.

Cohn, Norman (1996), *Noah's Flood: The Genesis Story in Western Thought*, New Haven: Yale University Press.

Colebrook, Claire (2015), 'Counter-Apocalyptic, Counter-Sex: 9/11 as Event and *The Year of the Flood*,' in Peter Childs, Claire Colebrook, and Sebastian Groes (eds), *Women's Fiction and Post-9/11 Context*, 1–16, London: Lexington.
Colvile, Robert (2016), *The Great Acceleration: How the World Is Getting Faster, Faster*, London: Bloomsbury.
Comaroff, Jean and John L. Comaroff (2000), 'Millennial Capitalism: First Thoughts on a Second Coming', *Public Culture* 12 (2): 291–343.
Connell, Liam (2017), *Precarious Labour and the Contemporary Novel*, Cham: Palgrave Macmillan.
Cooper, Lydia (2011), 'Cormac McCarthy's *The Road* as Apocalyptic Grail Narrative', *Studies in the Novel* 43 (2): 218–36.
Coupland, Douglas ([1991] 1996), *Generation X: Tales for an Accelerated Culture*, London: Abacus.
Coupland, Douglas ([1994] 2002), *Life after God*, London: Scribner.
Coupland, Douglas (1996), *Polaroids from the Dead*, London: Flamingo.
Coupland, Douglas (1998), *Girlfriend in a Coma*, London: Flamingo.
Coupland, Douglas ([2006] 2007), *JPod*, London: Bloomsbury.
Coupland, Douglas ([2010] 2011), *Player One*, London: Windmill.
Crace, Jim (2006), 'A New Kind of Ghost Writer', *Guardian*, 28 October. Available online: https://www.theguardian.com/commentisfree/2006/oct/28/comment.bookscomment (accessed 2 May 2018).
Crace, Jim (2007), 'Love, Hate & Kicking Ass', Amazon Shorts.
Crace, Jim ([2007] 2008), *The Pesthouse*, London: Picador.
Crouch, Colin (2011), *The Strange Non-Death of Neoliberalism*, Cambridge: Polity.
Crutzen, Paul and Eugene Stoermer (2000), 'The Anthropocene', *Global Change Newsletter*, 41: 17–18.
Cunningham, David and Alexandra Warwick (2013), 'Unnoticed Apocalypse', *City* 17 (4): 433–48.
Cunningham, David and Alexandra Warwick (2014), 'The Ambassadors of Nil: Notes on the Zombie Apocalypse', in Monica Germanà and Aris Mousoutzanis (eds), *Apocalyptic Discourse in Contemporary Culture: Postmillennial Perspectives on the End of the World*, 175–89, London: Routledge.
Currie, Mark ([2007] 2010), *About Time: Narrative, Fiction and the Philosophy of Time*, Edinburgh: Edinburgh University Press.
Curtis, Claire P. (2010), *Postapocalyptic Fiction and the Social Contract: 'We'll Not Go Home Again'*, Lanham: Lexington.
Davis, Heather and Zoe Todd (2017), 'On the Importance of a Date, or Decolonizing the Anthropocene', *ACME: An International Journal for Critical Geographies* 16 (4): 761–80.
Deleuze, Gilles (2004), *Desert Islands and Other Texts 1953–1974*, Los Angeles: Semiotext(e).
De Boever, Arne (2012), *States of Exception in the Contemporary Novel: Martel, Eugenides, Coetzee, Sebald*, London: Bloomsbury.

Deb, Siddhartha (2007), 'Manifest Destiny in Reverse', *Telegraph*, 18 March. Available online: https://www.telegraph.co.uk/culture/books/3663695/Manifest-destiny-in-reverse.html (accessed 2 May 2018).

Deckard, Sharae (2017), 'Capitalism's Long Spiral: Periodicity, Temporality and the Global Contemporary in World Literature', in Sarah Brouillette, Mathias Nilges and Emilio Sauri (eds), *Literature and the Global Contemporary*, 83–102, Cham: Palgrave Macmillan.

DeLillo, Don (2007), *Falling Man*, New York: Scribner.

DeLillo, Don (2016), *Zero K*, New York: Scribner.

Department of Justice (2001), 'The USA PATRIOT Act: Preserving Life and Liberty'. Available online: https://www.justice.gov/archive/ll/highlights.htm (accessed 20 September 2018).

Derrida, Jacques (1984), 'No Apocalypse, Not Now (Full Speed Ahead, Seven Missiles, Seven Missives)', *Diacritics* 14 (2): 20–31.

Derrida, Jacques (1992), 'Of an Apocalyptic Tone Newly Adopted in Philosophy', in Harold Coward and Toby Foshay (eds), *Derrida and Negative Theology*, 25–71, Albany: State University of New York Press.

Derrida, Jacques (1993), *Aporias*, Stanford: Stanford University Press.

Derrida, Jacques (1995), 'Archive Fever: A Freudian Impression', *Diacritics* 25 (2): 9–63.

Dillon, Sarah (2018), 'The Horror of the Anthropocene', *C21: Journal of Twenty-First Century Writings* 6 (1): 1–25.

Doran, Robert and René Girard (2008), 'Apocalyptic Thinking after 9/11: An Interview with René Girard', *SubStance* 37 (1): 20–32.

Duggan, Lisa (2003), *The Twilight of Equality?: Neoliberalism, Cultural Politics, and the Attack on Democracy*, Boston: Beacon.

Dunlop, Nicholas (2011), 'Speculative Fiction as Postcolonial Critique in *Ghostwritten* and *Cloud Atlas*', in Sarah Dillon (ed), *David Mitchell: Critical Essays*, 201–23, Canterbury: Gylphi.

Edwards, Caroline (2009), 'Microtopias: The Post-Apocalyptic Communities of Jim Crace's *The Pesthouse*', *Textual Practice* 23 (5): 763–86.

Edwards, Caroline (2012), 'Rethinking the Arcadian Revenge: Metachronous Times in the Fiction of Sam Taylor', *Modern Fiction Studies* 58 (3): 477–502.

El Akkad, Omar (2017a), *American War*, London: Picador.

El Akkad, Omar (2017b), 'Omar El Akkad on Writing *American War*'. Available online: https://www.panmacmillan.com/blogs/picador/omar-el-akkad-on-writing-american-war (accessed 20 September 2018).

Elliott, Brian (2016), *Natural Catastrophe: Climate Change and Neoliberal Governance*, Edinburgh: Edinburgh University Press.

Engel, Kathleen C. and Patricia A. McCoy (2011), *The Subprime Virus: Reckless Credit, Regulatory Failure and Next Steps*, Oxford: Oxford University Press.

Erdrich, Louise (1985), 'Where I Ought to Be: A Writer's Sense of Place', *New York Times*, 28 July. Available online: https://www.nytimes.com/1985/07/28/books/where-i-ought-to-be-a-writer-s-sense-of-place.html?pagewanted=all (accessed 16 August 2018).

Erdrich, Louise ([2017] 2018), *Future Home of the Living God*, London: Corsair.

Ermarth, Elizabeth Deeds (1992), *Sequel to History: Postmodernism and the Crisis of Representational Time*, Princeton: Princeton University Press.

Esposito, Elena (2011), *The Future of Futures: The Time of Money in Financing and Society*, Cheltenham: Edward Elgar.

Eve, Martin Paul (2016), '"You Have to Keep Track of Your Changes": The Version Variants and Publishing History of David Mitchell's Cloud Atlas', *Open Library of Humanities* 2 (2): e1, 1–34. DOI: http://dx.doi.org/10.16995/olh.82.

Eve, Martin Paul (2018), 'Reading Very Well for Our Age: Hyperobject, Metadata and Global Warming in Emily St. John Mandel's Station Eleven', *Open Library of Humanities* 4 (1): 8, 1–27. DOI: https://doi.org/10.16995/olh.155.

Fassler, Joe (2011), 'Colson Whitehead on Zombies, Zone One, and His Love of the VCR', *Atlantic*, 18 October. Available online: https://www.theatlantic.com/entertainment/archive/2011/10/colson-whitehead-on-zombies-zone-one-and-his-love-of-the-vcr/246855/ (accessed 31 March 2018).

Finigan, Theo (2011), '"Into the Memory Hole": Totalitarianism and Mal d'Archive in *Nineteen Eighty-Four* and *The Handmaid's Tale*', *Science Fiction Studies* 38 (3): 435–59.

Fisher, Mark (2009), *Capitalist Realism: Is There No Alternative?* Winchester: Zero Books.

Fisher, Mark (2013), 'How to Kill a Zombie: Strategizing the End of Neoliberalism', *Open Democracy*, 18 July. Available online: https://www.opendemocracy.net/mark-fisher/how-to-kill-zombie-strategizing-end-of-neoliberalism (accessed 24 September 2018).

Fitzmaurice, Andrew (2014), *Sovereignty, Poverty and Empire: 1500–2000*, Cambridge: Cambridge University Press.

Franzen, Jonathan et al. (2001), 'Tuesday, and After', *New Yorker*, 24 September.

Focillon, Henri (1969), *The Year 1000*, New York: Ungar.

Foucault, Michel (1977), 'Nietzsche, Genealogy, History', in Donald F. Bouchard (ed), *Language, Counter-Memory, Practice: Selected Essays and Interviews*, 139–64, Ithaca: Cornell University Press.

Foucault, Michel ([2008] 2010), *The Birth of Biopolitics: Lectures at the Collège de France, 1978–1979*, Basingstoke: Palgrave Macmillan.

Franklin, Benjamin (1783), 'To the Earl of Buchan'. Available online: https://founders.archives.gov/documents/Franklin/01-39-02-0200 (accessed 16 August 2018).

Freese, Peter (1997), *From Apocalypse to Entropy and Beyond: The Second Law of Thermodynamics in Post-War American Fiction*, Essen: Verlag Die Blaue Eule.

Frykholm, Amy Johnson (2004), *Rapture Culture: Left Behind in Evangelical America*, Oxford: Oxford University Press.

Fukuyama, Francis (1992), *The End of History and the Last Man*, London: Penguin.

Gee, Maggie ([2004] 2005), *The Flood*, London: Saqui.

Giddens, Anthony (1990), *Consequences of Modernity*, Cambridge: Polity.
Giggs, Rebecca (2011), 'The Green Afterword: Cormac McCarthy's *The Road* and the Ecological Uncanny', in Paul Crosthwaite (ed), *Criticism, Crisis, and Contemporary Narrative: Textual Horizons in an Age of Global Risk*, 201–17, New York: Routledge.
Giggs, Rebecca (2018), 'Imagining the Jellyfish Apocalypse', *Atlantic*, January/February issue. Available online: https://www.theatlantic.com/magazine/archive/2018/01/listening-to-jellyfish/546542/ (accessed 4 May 2019).
Golub, Adam and Carrie Lane (2015), 'Zombie Companies and Corporate Survivors', *Anthropology Now* 7 (2): 47–54. DOI: https://doi.org/10.1080/19428200.2015.1058124.
Gomel, Elana (2000), 'The Plague of Utopias: Pestilence and the Apocalyptic Body', *Twentieth-Century Literature* 46 (4): 405–33.
Gomel, Elana (2010), *Postmodern Science Fiction and Temporal Imagination*, London: Continuum.
Gray, John (2007), *Black Mass: Apocalyptic Religion and the Death of Utopia*, London: Allen Lane.
Gray, Richard J. (2011), *After the Fall: American Literature Since 9/11*, Oxford: Blackwell.
Gribben, Crawford (2009), *Writing the Rapture: Prophecy Fiction in Evangelical America*, Oxford: Oxford University Press.
Greenberg, Louis (2010), 'Rewriting the End: Douglas Coupland's Treatment of Apocalypse in *Hey Nostradamus!* and *Girlfriend in a Coma*', *English Studies in Africa* 53 (2): 21–33.
Hall, John R. (2009), *Apocalypse: From Antiquity to the Empire of Modernity*, Cambridge: Polity.
Hamerton-Kelly, Robert (2007), 'An Introductory Essay', in Robert Hamerton-Kelly (ed), *Politics and Apocalypse*, 1–28, East Lansing: Michigan State University Press.
Haraway, Donna (2016), *Staying with the Trouble: Making Kin in the Chthulucene*, Durham: Duke University Press.
Hartley, David (2015), 'Against the Anthropocene', *Salvage*, 31 August. Available online: http://salvage.zone/in-print/against-the-anthropocene/ (accessed 23 July 2018).
Harvey, David (1989), *The Condition of Postmodernity: An Enquiry into the Origins of Cultural Change*, Oxford: Blackwell.
Harvey, David (2005), *A Brief History of Neoliberalism*, Oxford: Oxford University Press.
Harvie, David and Keir Milburn (2011), 'The Zombie of Neoliberalism Can Be Beaten – through Mass Direct Action', *Guardian*, 4 August. Available online: https://www.theguardian.com/commentisfree/2011/aug/04/neoliberalism-zombie-action-phone-hacking (accessed 24 September 2018).
Hayes, Hunter M. (2007), *Understanding Will Self*, Columbia: University of South Carolina Press.
Heffernan, Teresa (2008), *Post-Apocalyptic Culture. Modernism, Postmodernism, and the Twentieth-Century Novel*, Toronto: University of Toronto Press.
Hicks, Heather J. (2016), *The Post-Apocalyptic Novel in the Twenty-First Century: Modernity beyond Salvage*, Basingstoke: Palgrave Macmillan.
Hoban, Russell ([1980] 2002), *Riddley Walker*, London: Bloomsbury.

Hoberek, Andrew (2015), 'The Post-Apocalyptic Present', *Public Books*, 15 June. Available online: http://www.publicbooks.org/the-post-apocalyptic-present/ (accessed 24 September 2018).

Hollinger, Veronica (2000), 'Future/Present: The End of Science Fiction', in David Seed (ed), *Imagining Apocalypse: Studies in Cultural Crisis*, 215–19, Basingstoke: Macmillan Press.

Hollinger, Veronica (2002), 'Apocalypse Coma', in Veronica Hollinger and Joan Gordon (eds), *Edging into the Future: Science Fiction and Contemporary Cultural Transformation*, 160–73, Philadelphia: University of Pennsylvania Press.

Hollinger, Veronica (2006), 'Stories about the Future: From Patterns of Expectation to Pattern Recognition', *Science Fiction Studies* 33 (3): 452–72.

Hollinger, Veronica (2013), 'Science Fiction as Archive Fever', in Brian Attebery and Veronica Hollinger (eds), *Parabolas of Science Fiction*, 242–60, Middletown: Wesleyan University Press.

Hopf, Courtney (2011), 'The Stories We Tell: Discursive Identity through Narrative Form in *Cloud Atlas*', in Sarah Dillon (ed), *David Mitchell: Critical Essays*, 106–26, Canterbury: Gylphi.

Huggan, Graham (1989), 'Decolonizing the Map: Post-Colonialism, Post-Structuralism and the Cartographic Connection', *Ariel* 20 (4): 115–31.

Hurley, Jessica (2013), 'Still Writing Backwards. Literature after the End of the World', *Frame* 26 (1): 61–76.

Hurley, Jessica (2015), 'History Is What Bites: Zombies, Race, and the Limits of Biopower in Colson Whitehead's *Zone One*', *Extrapolation* 56 (3): 311–33.

Hutcheon, Linda (1988), *A Poetics of Postmodernism: History, Theory, Fiction*, New York: Routledge.

Jameson, Fredric (1991), *Postmodernism, or, the Cultural Logic of Late Capitalism*, Durham: Duke University Press.

Jameson, Fredric (1994), *The Seeds of Time*, New York: Columbia University Press.

Jameson, Fredric (2003), 'Future City', *New Left Review* 21: 65–79.

Jameson, Fredric (2005), *Archaeologies of the Future: The Desire Called Utopia and Other Science Fictions*, London: Verso.

Jameson, Fredric (2015), 'The Aesthetics of Singularity', *New Left Review* 92: 101–32.

Jenkins, Keith ([1991] 2003), *Re-Thinking History*, London: Routledge.

Jenkins, Keith (2003), *Refiguring History: New Thoughts on an Old Discipline*, London: Routledge.

Jennings, Hope (2010), '"A Repeating World": Redeeming the Past and Future in the Utopian Dystopia of Jeanette Winterson's *The Stone Gods*', *Interdisciplinary Humanities* 27 (2): 132–46.

Jenzen, Olu (2009), 'Reworking Linear Time: Queer Temporalities in Jeanette Winterson's *Sexing the Cherry* and *Art & Lies*', in Margaret J-M Sönmez and Mine Özyurt Kiliç (eds), *Winterson Narrating Time and Space*, 31–48, Newcastle: Cambridge Scholars.

Kearney, Kevin (2012), 'Cormac McCarthy's *The Road* and the Frontier of the Human', *Lit: Literature Interpretation Theory* 23 (2): 160–78.

Keeble, Arin (2014), *The 9/11 Novel: Trauma, Politics and Identity*, Jefferson: McFarland.

Keller, Catherine (1994), 'The Breast, the Apocalypse, and the Colonial Journey', *Journal of Feminist Studies in Religion* 10 (1): 53–72.

Keller, Catherine ([1996] 2005), *Apocalypse Now and Then: A Feminist Guide to the End of the World*, Boston: Beacon.

Keller, Catherine (2005), *God and Power: Counter-Apocalyptic Journeys*, Minneapolis: Fortress.

Kermode, Frank ([1966] 2000), *The Sense of an Ending: Studies in the Theory of Fiction*, Oxford: Oxford University Press.

Kerslake, Patricia ([2007] 2010), *Science Fiction and Empire*, Liverpool: Liverpool University Press.

Ketterer, David (1974), *New Worlds for Old: The Apocalyptic Imagination, Science Fiction, and American Literature*, Bloomington: Indiana University Press.

Klein, Naomi (2008), *The Shock Doctrine: Rise of Disaster Capitalism*, London: Penguin.

Kollin, Susan (2011), '"Barren, Silent, Godless": Ecodisaster and the Post-Abundant Landscape in *The Road*', in Sara L. Spurgeon (ed), *Cormac McCarthy: All the Pretty Horses, No Country for Old Men, The Road*, 157–71, London: Continuum.

Konstantinou, Lee (2009), *Pop Apocalypse: A Possible Satire*, New York: Harper.

Kupperman, Karen Ordahl (2008), *The Jamestown Project*, Cambridge: Harvard University Press.

Laderman, David (2002), *Driving Visions: Exploring the Road Movie*, Austin: University of Texas Press.

LaHaye, Tim (1976), *The Bible's Influence on American History*, San Diego: Christian Heritage College, MasterBooks.

LaHaye, Tim and Jerry B. Jenkins (1995), *Left Behind: A Novel of the Earth's Last Days*, Wheaton: Tyndale House.

Latour, Bruno, Isabelle Stengers, Anna Tsing and Nils Bubandt (2018), 'Anthropologists Are Talking – About Capitalism, Ecology, and Apocalypse', *Ethnos* 83 (3): 587–606.

Lawless, Andrew (2005), 'The Poet of Prose – Jim Crace in Interview,' *Three Monkeys Online*, 1 February. Available online: https://www.threemonkeysonline.com/the-poet-of-prose-jim-crace-in-interview/ (accessed 2 May 2012).

Lawrence, D. H. ([1980] 2002), *Apocalypse and the Writings on Revelation*, Cambridge: Cambridge University Press.

Lazzarato, Maurizio (2012), *The Making of the Indebted Man: An Essay on the Neoliberal Condition*, Los Angeles: Semiotext(e).

Leggatt, Matthew (2018), '"Another World Just Out of Sight'": Remembering or Imagining Utopia in Emily St. John Mandel's *Station Eleven*', *Open Library of Humanities* 4 (2): 8, 1–23. DOI: https://doi.org/10.16995/olh.256.

Le Guin, Ursula (2009), '*The Year of the Flood* by Margaret Atwood', *Guardian*, 29 August. Available online: https://www.theguardian.com/books/2009/aug/29/margaret-atwood-year-of-flood (accessed 4 May 2019).

LeMenager, Stephanie (2012), 'The Aesthetics of Petroleum, after *Oil!*', *American Literary History* 24 (1): 59–86. DOI: https://doi.org/10.1093/alh/ajr057.
Lewis, Simon L. and Mark A. Maslin (2015), 'Defining the Anthropocene', *Nature* 519: 171–80.
Lilley, Deborah (2018), 'Pastoral Concerns in the Fictions of Jim Crace', in Katy Shaw and Kate Aughterson (eds), *Jim Crace: Into the Wilderness*, 33–48. Cham: Palgrave Macmillan.
Lincoln, Bruce (2006), *Holy Terrors: Thinking about Religion after 9/11*, Chicago: Chicago University Press.
Loewenstein, Anthony (2015), *Disaster Capitalism: Making a Killing out of Catastrophe*, London: Verso.
Löwith, Karl (1949), *Meaning in History*, Chicago: University of Chicago Press.
Luckhurst, Roger (2015), *Zombies: A Cultural History*, London: Reaktion.
Luttrull, Daniel (2010), 'Prometheus Hits *The Road*: Revising the Myth', *Cormac McCarthy Journal* 8 (1): 17–28.
Lyotard, Jean-François (1984), *The Postmodern Condition: A Report on Knowledge*, Manchester: Manchester University Press.
Machinal, Hélène (2011), 'Cloud Atlas: From Postmodernity to the Posthuman', in Sarah Dillon (ed), *David Mitchell: Critical Essays*, 127–54, Canterbury: Gylphi.
Mahoney, Dhira B. (2000), 'Introduction', in Dhira B. Mahoney (ed), *The Grail: A Casebook*, 1–115, New York: Garland.
Mandel, Emily St. John ([2014] 2015), *Station Eleven*, London: Picador.
Martin, Randy (2007), *The Empire of Indifference: American War and the Financial Logic of Risk Management*, Durham and London: Duke University Press.
Mason, Paul (2015), 'Apocalypse Now: Has the Next Giant Financial Crash Already Begun?' *Guardian*, 1 November. Available online: https://www.theguardian.com/commentisfree/2015/nov/01/financial-armageddon-crash-warning-signs (accessed 3 August 2017).
May, John R (1972), *Toward a New Earth: Apocalypse in the American Novel*, Notre Dame: University of Notre Dame Press.
McAlister, Melani (2003), 'Prophecy, Politics, and the Popular: The *Left Behind* Series and Christian Fundamentalism's New World Order', *The South Atlantic Quarterly* 102 (4): 773–98.
McBrien, Justin (2016), 'Accumulating Extinction: Planetary Catastrophism in the Necrocene', in Jason W. Moore (ed), *Anthropocene or Capitalocene: Nature, History, and the Crisis of Capitalism*, 116–37, Oakland: PM Press.
McCarry, Sarah (2014), '"I Want It All": A Conversation with Emily St. John Mandel', *Tor*, 12 September. Available online: https://www.tor.com/2014/09/12/a-conversation-with-emily-st-john-mandel/ (accessed 4 May 2019).
McCarthy, Cormac ([2005] 2006), *No Country for Old Men*, London: Picador.
McCarthy, Cormac ([2006] 2007), *The Road*, New York: Vintage.
McClure, John A. (1995), 'Postmodern/Post-Secular: Contemporary Fiction and Spirituality', *Modern Fiction Studies* 41 (1): 141–63.

McCulloch, Fiona (2012), *Cosmopolitanism in Contemporary British Fiction: Imagined Identities*, Basingstoke: Palgrave Macmillan.

McGill, Robert (2000), 'The Sublime Simulacrum: Vancouver in Douglas Coupland's Geography of Apocalypse', *Essays on Canadian Writing* 70: 252–77.

McMorran, Will (2011), '*Cloud Atlas* and *If on a Winter's Night a Traveller*: Fragmentation and Integrity in the Postmodern Novel', in Sarah Dillon (ed), *David Mitchell: Critical Essays*, 155–75, Canterbury: Gylphi.

McMurry, Andrew (1996), 'The Slow Apocalypse: A Gradualistic Theory of the World's Demise', *Postmodern Culture* 6 (3). DOI: https://doi.org/10.1353/pmc.1996.0018.

Metz, Joseph (2017), 'Genre Beside Itself: David Mitchell's *The Bone Clocks*, Pulp Intrusions, and the Cosmic Historians' War', *Critique: Studies in Contemporary Fiction* 58 (2): 121–28.

Mezey, Howard Jason (2011), '"A Multitude of Drops": Recursion and Globalization in David Mitchell's *Cloud Atlas*', *Modern Language Studies* 40 (2): 10–37.

Miller, D. A. (1981), *Narrative and Its Discontents: Problems of Closure in the Traditional Novel*, Princeton: Princeton University Press.

Mitchell, David (2004), *Cloud Atlas*, London: Sceptre.

Mitchell, David (2005a), 'The Book of Revelations', *Guardian*, 5 February. Available online: https://www.theguardian.com/books/2005/feb/05/featuresreviews.guardianreview27 (accessed 28 July 2018).

Mitchell, David (2005b), 'Genesis', *Guardian*, 16 April. Available online: https://www.theguardian.com/books/2005/apr/16/featuresreviews.guardianreview23 (accessed 28 July 2018).

Mitchell, David (2014), *The Bone Clocks*, London: Sceptre.

Mizruchi, Susan (2010), 'Risk Theory and the Contemporary American Novel', *American Literary History* 22 (1): 109–35.

Montagu, Jeremy (2002), 'Concertina', in Alison Latham (ed), *The Oxford Companion to Music*, Oxford: Oxford University Press.

Moore, Jason W. (2014), 'The End of Cheap Nature, or, How I Learned to Stop Worrying about "the" Environment and Love the Crisis of Capitalism', in Christian Suter and Christopher Chase-Dunn (eds), *Structures of the World Political Economy and the Future of Global Conflict and Cooperation*, 285–314, Berlin: LIT.

Moore, Jason W. (2017), 'The Capitalocene, Part I: On the Nature and Origins of Our Ecological Crisis', *The Journal of Peasant Studies* 44 (3): 594–630.

Moore, Jason W. (2018), 'The Capitalocene, Part II: Accumulation by Appropriation and the Centrality of Unpaid Work/Energy', *The Journal of Peasant Studies* 45 (2): 237–79.

Morgan, Wesley G. (2008), 'The Route and Roots of *The Road*', *Cormac McCarthy Journal* 6: 39–47.

Morson, Gary Saul (1994), *Narrative and Freedom: The Shadows of Time*, New Haven: Yale University Press.

Morson, Gary Saul (1998), 'Sideshadowing and Tempics', *New Literary History* 29 (4): 599–624.

Morton, Timothy (2013), *Hyperobjects: Philosophy and Ecology after the End of the World*, Minneapolis: University of Minnesota Press.

Mousoutzanis, Aris (2014), *Fin-de-Siècle Fictions, 1890s–1990s: Apocalypse, Technoscience, Empire*, Basingstoke: Palgrave Macmillan.

Mullen, Lisa (2007), 'Jeanette Winterson: Interview', *TimeOut*, 24 September. Available online: https://www.timeout.com/london/books/jeanette-winterson-interview (accessed 8 November 2018).

Mullen, Thomas ([2011] 2012), *The Revisionists*, New York: Mulholland.

Nayar, Pramod K. (2010), *Postcolonialism: A Guide for the Perplexed*, London: Continuum.

Newitz, Annalee (2006), *Pretend We're Dead: Capitalist Monsters in American Pop Culture*, Durham and London: Duke University Press.

Nilges, Mathias (2015), 'Neoliberalism and the Time of the Novel', *Textual Practice* 29 (2): 357–77. DOI: https://doi.org/10.1080/0950236X.2014.993524.

Nixon, Rob (2011), *Slow Violence and the Environmentalism of the Poor*, Cambridge: Harvard University Press.

O'Donnell, Patrick (2015), *A Temporary Future: The Fiction of David Mitchell*, New York: Bloomsbury.

Onega, Susana (2011), 'The Trauma Paradigm and the Ethics of Affect in Jeanette Winterson's *The Stone Gods*', in Susana Onega and Jean-Michel Ganteau (eds), *Ethics and Trauma in Contemporary British Fiction*, 265–98, Amsterdam: Rodopi.

Orwell, George ([1949]2008), *Nineteen Eighty-Four*, London: Penguin.

Parenti, Christian (2011), *Tropics of Chaos: Climate Change and the New Geography of Violence*, New York: Nation.

Parker, Jo Alyson (2010), 'David Mitchell's *Cloud Atlas* of Narrative Constraints and Environmental Limits', in Jo Alyson Parker, Paul A. Harris and Christian Steineck (eds), *Time: Limits and Constraints*, 201–17. Boston: Brill.

Parry, Simon (2009), 'Revealed: The Ghost Fleet of the Recession Anchored Just East of Singapore', *Daily Mail*, 8 September. Available online: https://www.dailymail.co.uk/home/moslive/article-1212013/Revealed-The-ghost-fleet-recession-anchored-just-east-Singapore.html (accessed 8 November 2018).

Perrotta, Tom. *The Leftovers*. 2011. London: Fourth Estate, 2012. Print.

Phillips, Dana (2011), '"He Ought Not Have Done It": McCarthy and Apocalypse', in Sara L. Spurgeon (ed), *Cormac McCarthy: All the Pretty Horses, No Country for Old Men, The Road*, 172–88, London: Continuum.

Pippin, Tina (1992), 'Eros and the End: Reading for Gender in the Apocalypse of John', *Semeia* 59: 193–210.

Pippin, Tina (1999), *Apocalyptic Bodies: The Biblical End of the World in Text and Image*, London: Routledge. Print.

Plumwood, Val (2003), 'Decolonizing Relationships with Nature', in William M. Adams and Martin Mulligan (eds), *Decolonizing Nature: Strategies of Conservation in a Postcolonial Era*, 51–78, London: Earthscan.

Quiggin, John (2010), *Zombie Economics: How Dead Ideas Still Walk among Us*, Princeton: Princeton University Press.

Quinby, Lee (1994), *Anti-Apocalypse: Exercises in Genealogical Criticism*, Minneapolis: University of Minnesota Press.
Rambo, Shelly L. (2008), 'Beyond Redemption?: Reading Cormac McCarthy's *The Road* after the End of the World', *Studies in the Literary Imagination* 41 (2): 99–120.
Redfield, Marc (2007), 'Virtual Trauma: The Idiom of 9/11', *diacritics* 37 (1): 55–80.
Rich, Nathaniel (2006), 'Cabbie Road', *New York Times*, 12 November. Available online: https://www.nytimes.com/2006/11/12/books/review/Rich.t.html (accessed 17 December 2017).
Rich, Nathaniel (2013), *Odds Against Tomorrow*, New York: Farrar, Straus and Giroux.
Ricoeur, Paul (1984), *Time and Narrative*, volume 1, Chicago: University of Chicago Press.
Rieder, John (2008), *Colonialism and the Emergence of Science Fiction*, Middletown: Wesleyan University Press.
Rine, Abigail (2011), 'Jeanette Winterson's Love Intervention: Rethinking the Future', in Ben Davies and Jana Funke (eds), *Sex, Gender and Time in Fiction and Culture*, 70–85, Basingstoke: Palgrave Macmillan.
Roberts, Adam (2006), *Science Fiction*, Abingdon: Routledge.
Robinson, Douglas (1985), *American Apocalypses: The Image of the End of the World in American Literature*, Baltimore: John Hopkins University Press.
Robinson, Iain (2013), 'The Curse of Ham: Apocalypse and Utopia in Will Self's *The Book of Dave*', *C21 Literature: Journal of 21st-Century Writings* 2 (1): 89–104.
Rosen, Elizabeth K. (2008), *Apocalyptic Transformation: Apocalypse and the Postmodern Imagination*, Plymouth: Lexington.
Sanders, William ([2001] 2015), 'When This World Is All on Fire', in Grace L. Dillon (ed), *Walking the Clouds: An Anthology of Indigenous Science Fiction*, 185–210, Tucson: The University of Arizona Press.
Schulman, Martha (2011), 'My Horrible '70s Apocalypse: *PW* Talks with Colson Whitehead', *Publishers Weekly*, 15 July. Available online: https://www.publishersweekly.com/pw/by-topic/authors/interviews/article/48015-my-horrible-70s-apocalypse-pw-talks-with-colson-whitehead.html (accessed 7 July 2018).
Schwartz, Hillel (1990), *Century's End: A Cultural History of the Fin de Siècle from the 990s to the 1990s*, New York: Doubleday.
Seed, David (2007), 'Constructing America's Enemies: The Invasions of the USA', *The Yearbook of English Studies* 37 (2): 64–84.
Self, Will (1998), 'Introduction', in *Revelation*, vii–xiv, Edinburgh: Canongate.
Self, Will (2002), 'Introduction', in Russell Hoban, *Riddley Walker*, v–x, London: Bloomsbury.
Self, Will ([2006] 2007), *The Book of Dave: A Revelation of the Recent Past and the Distant Future*, London: Penguin.
Self, Will (2007), 'In the Beginning: Will Self on the Genesis of *The Book of Dave*', *Guardian*, 16 June. Available online: https://www.theguardian.com/books/2007/jun/16/willself (accessed 4 October 2012).
Sharpe, Matthew ([2007] 2008), *Jamestown*, Orlando: Harcourt.

Shriver, Lionel ([2017] 2016), *The Mandibles: A Family, 2029–2047*, London: Borough Press.
Shuck, Glenn W. (2004), *Marks of the Beast: The Left Behind Novels and the Struggle for Evangelical Identity*, New York: New York University Press.
Skrimshire, Stefan ed (2010), *Future Ethics: Climate Change and Apocalyptic Imagination*, London: Continuum.
Smith, Philip (2016), 'Shakespeare, Survival, and the Seeds of Civilization in Emily St. John Mandel's *Station Eleven*', *Extrapolation* 57 (3): 289–303. DOI: https://doi.org/10.3828/extr.2016.16.
Sollazzo, Erica (2017), '"The Dead City": Corporate Anxiety and the Post-Apocalyptic Vision in Colson Whitehead's *Zone One*', *Law & Literature* 29 (3): 457–83.
Sorensen, Leif (2014), 'Against the Post-Apocalyptic: Narrative Closure in Colson Whitehead's *Zone One*', *Contemporary Literature* 55 (3): 559–92.
Sorlin, Sandrine (2006), 'Time, Distance and Language: The Three Dimensions of Will Self's *The Book of Dave*', *In-Between: Essays & Studies in Literary Criticism* 15 (2): 99–113.
Stengers, Isabelle (2015), *In Catastrophic Times: Resisting the Coming Barbarism*, London: Open Humanities Press.
Stiegler, Bernard (2010), *For a New Critique of Political Economy*, Cambridge: Polity.
Stiegler, Bernard (2011), *Techniques and Time, 3: Cinematic Time and the Question of Malaise*, Stanford: Stanford University Press.
Stout, Janis P. (1983), *The Journey Narrative in American Literature: Patterns and Departures*, Westport: Greenwood.
Stowers, Cath (1995), 'Journeying with Jeanette: Transgressive Travels in Winterson's Fiction', in Mary Maynard and June Purvis (eds), *(Hetero)sexual Politics*, 139–58, London: Taylor & Francis.
Sutton, Matthew Avery (2014), *American Apocalypse: A History of Modern Evangelicalism*, Cambridge: Harvard University Press.
Swirski, Peter (2014), '"To Sacrifice One's Intellect Is More Demonic than Divine": American Literature and Politics in *Left Behind: A Novel of the Earth's Last Days*', *European Journal of American Studies* 9 (2): 1–18.
Sykes, Rachel (2018), *The Quiet Contemporary American Novel*, Manchester: Manchester University Press.
Taibbi, Matt (2013), 'Apocalypse, New Jersey: A Dispatch from America's Most Desperate Town', *RollingStone*, 11 December. Available online: https://www.rollingstone.com/culture/culture-news/apocalypse-new-jersey-a-dispatch-from-americas-most-desperate-town-56174/ (accessed 7 October 2018).
Tate, Andrew (2007), *Douglas Coupland*, Manchester: Manchester University Press.
Tate, Andrew (2017), *Apocalyptic Fiction*, London: Bloomsbury.
Taylor, Sam (2008), 'Sam Taylor Interview Part 2', *Three Guys One Book*, 6 December. Available online: http://threeguysonebook.com/sam-taylor-interview-part-2/ (accessed 9 July 2018).

Taylor, Sam ([2009] 2010), *The Island at the End of the World*, London: Faber.
Tew, Philip (2006), *Jim Crace*, Manchester: Manchester University Press.
Theroux, Marcel (2009), *Far North*, London: Faber.
Thompson, Derek (2017), 'What in the World Is Causing the Great Retail Meltdown of 2017?' *Atlantic*, 10 April. Available online: https://www.theatlantic.com/business/archive/2017/04/retail-meltdown-of-2017/522384/ (accessed 3 August 2017).
Thoreau, Henry David (1862), 'Walking', *Atlantic*, June 1862. Available online: https://www.theatlantic.com/magazine/archive/1862/06/walking/304674/ (accessed 22 June 2018).
Trexler, Adam (2015), *Anthropocene Fictions: The Novel in a Time of Climate Change*, Charlottesville: University of Virginia Press.
University of Leicester Press Officer (2016), 'Media Note: Anthropocene Working Group (AWG)'. Available online: https://www2.le.ac.uk/offices/press/press-releases/2016/august/media-note-anthropocene-working-group-awg (accessed 17 July 2018).
Vergès, Françoise (2017), 'Racial Capitalocene'. Available online: https://www.versobooks.com/blogs/3376-racial-capitalocene (accessed 17 July 2018).
Versluys, Kristiaan (2009), *Out of the Blue: September 11 and the Novel*, New York: Columbia University Press.
Vials, Chris (2015), 'Margaret Atwood's Dystopic Fiction and the Contradictions of Neoliberal Freedom', *Textual Practice* 29 (2): 235–54.
Virilio, Paul (2010), *The Futurism of the Instant: Stop-Eject*, Cambridge: Polity.
Wagar, Warren W. (1982), *Terminal Visions: The Literature of Last Things*, Bloomington: Indiana University Press.
Walker, Karen Thompson (2012), *The Age of Miracles*, New York: Random House.
Watson, David (2016), 'Vanishing Points; or, the Timescapes of the Contemporary American Novel', *Studia Neophilologica* 88 (1): 57–67.
Welsh, Louise (2018), '*Future Home of the Living God* by Louise Erdrich Review: A Fable for Our Times', *Guardian*, 6 January. Available online: https://www.theguardian.com/books/2018/jan/06/future-home-of-the-living-god-by-louise-erdrich-review (accessed 22 June 2018).
West, Mark (2018), 'Apocalypse without Revelation? Shakespeare, Salvage Punk and *Station Eleven*', *Open Library of Humanities* 4 (1): 7, 1–26. DOI: https://doi.org/10.16995/olh.235.
White, Hayden (1987), *Content of the Form: Narrative Discourse and Historical Representation*, Baltimore: John Hopkins University Press.
Whitehead, Colson ([2011] 2012), *Zone One*, London: Vintage.
Whyte, Kyle Powys (2016), 'Is It Colonial Déjà-Vu? Indigenous People and Climate Injustice', in Joni Adamson, Michael Davis and Hsinya Huang (eds), *Humanities for the Environment: Integrating Knowledges, Forging New Constellations of Practice*, 88–104, London: Earthscan.

Williams, Evan Calder (2011), *Combined and Uneven Apocalypse*, Winchester: Zero Books.
Williams, Paul (2011), *Race, Ethnicity and Nuclear War: Representations of Nuclear Weapons and Post-Apocalyptic Worlds*, Liverpool: Liverpool University Press.
Winterson, Jeanette ([1985] 1991), *Oranges Are Not the Only Fruit*, London: Vintage.
Winterson, Jeanette (2004), *Lighthousekeeping*, Boston: Harcourt.
Winterson, Jeanette ([2007] 2008), *The Stone Gods*, London: Penguin.
Wojcik, Daniel (1997), *The End of the World As We Know It: Faith, Fatalism and Apocalypse in America*, New York: New York University Press.
Yuknavitch, Lidia ([2017]2018), *The Book of Joan*, Edinburgh: Canongate.
Zakai, Avihu ([1992] 2002), *Exile and Kingdom: History and Apocalypse in the Puritan Migration to America*, Cambridge: Cambridge University Press.
Zamora, Lois Parkinson (1989), *Writing the Apocalypse: Historical Vision in Contemporary U.S. and Latin American Fiction*, Cambridge: Cambridge University Press.
Žižek, Slavoj (2002), *Welcome to the Desert of the Real: Five Essays on September 11 and Related Dates*, London: Verso.
Žižek, Slavoj (2014), *Event: Philosophy in Transit*, London: Penguin.

Index

absent apocalypse 50, 89–91, 109
agency 2. *See also* contingency; possibility
    apocalyptic determinism 13, 101, 137, 163, 168
    Cloud Atlas 23, 110, 113, 116, 117–19, 130
    contemporary post-apocalyptic novel 15, 19, 21, 56
    future 10
    Player One 155, 160–1
    The Book of Joan 24, 169
    The Revisionists 19
    The Stone Gods 130
    Zone One 144
alternate history
    Player One 24, 137, 144, 153, 162
    Station Eleven 24, 137, 144, 145–7, 151, 162
American exceptionalism 10, 22, 57, 58, 61, 63, 68, 163
    American War 64
    Future Home of the Living God 65
    The Pesthouse 84, 86
    The Road 70, 74, 81
    Zone One 67
Anthropocene 14, 21, 94, 95–130, 134, 169. *See also* climate change; environmental *under* risk
    American War 7, 64
    Cloud Atlas 7, 23, 97, 102, 106, 108, 113, 115, 116, 118, 119
    colonialism 23, 51 n.27, 97–102, 112, 116, 124
    definitions and problems 7, 99–101
    Far North 23, 96
    hyperobject 23, 106, 110, 148, 152
    Jamestown 23, 97, 103
    MaddAddam trilogy 7
    Player One 154
    Station Eleven 148
    The Age of Miracles 140
    The Bone Clocks 7, 108

    The Book of Dave 7
    The Book of Joan 23, 97, 105, 169
    The Stone Gods 23, 97, 102, 106, 123, 124, 130
anticipation of retrospection 17, 20, 110. *See also* epistemic primacy of the end; sense of an ending
Apocalypse America 22, 56, 58, 63, 94
    The Pesthouse 69, 84, 86, 92
    The Road 69, 78
apocalyptic model of history 10, 13, 21, 56, 101, 163, 171. *See also* teleology
    Cloud Atlas 102, 106, 112, 117, 130
    constructedness 19–20, 22, 28
    determinism 32, 168
    neoliberalism 61, 137
    Player One 153, 161
    sense of an ending 17
    The Book of Dave 46, 167
    The Book of Joan 170
    The Flood 30
    The Island at the End of the World 50, 54, 167
    The Pesthouse 90–1, 93
    The Revisionists 19, 167
    The Road 22, 71, 73, 75, 79, 83
    The Stone Gods 102, 120, 127, 130
apocalyptic model of narrative 10, 20, 83, 112, 153. *See also* sense of an ending; teleology
apocalyptic temporality 6, 8, 10, 18, 49, 69, 148. *See also* apocalyptic model of history
aporia 17, 49, 89, 90, 160
archive 163–71
    anti-apocalyptic archive fever 25, 163, 167
    Cloud Atlas 168
    The Book of Joan 106, 168–71
    The Island at the End of the World 167
    The Stone Gods 128
archive fever (*see* Derrida, Jacques)

post-apocalyptic archive 24, 25, 33 n.10, 163–71
   Cloud Atlas 24, 117, 166, 167
   Future Home of the Living God 165–6
   Jamestown 165–6
   Station Eleven 148 n.16, 164
   The Book of Dave 39, 167
   The Book of Joan 24, 168–71
   The Island at the End of the World 48
   The Pesthouse 88
   The Revisionists 24, 167
   The Road 24, 165
   The Stone Gods 24, 127, 165
   Zone One 165
Atwood, Margaret
   MaddAddam trilogy (*Oryx and Crake*, *The Year of the Flood*, *MaddAddam*) 5, 7, 20, 22, 28, 34–5, 140 n.8
   The Handmaid's Tale 4 n.8, 65, 166–7

backshadowing 50, 52, 114
Baudrillard, Jean
   illusion of the end 17, 49
   9/11 60–1
   simulacra 38, 113, 114, 116
Berardi, Franco 'Bifo' 133, 136, 137, 139, 158
Bible 9, 29, 30, 33 n.10, 48, 81. *See also* Genesis; Revelation (book of)
   Station Eleven 148 n.16
   The Book of Dave 42
   The Flood 34
   The Island at the End of the World 47, 49, 167
Brooks, Peter 17–18, 110

Capitalism. *See also* capitalist realism; neoliberalism
   Anthropocene 23, 94, 96–7, 130
   apocalyptic logic 10, 163
   Cloud Atlas 106, 108–9, 114–17
   colonialism 23, 98–101
   disaster capitalism 14, 134, 137–9, 143
   fast capitalism 141
   financial capitalism 132, 137
   global capitalism 13
      Cloud Atlas 113, 115

   end of history 133–5
   Player One 24, 137, 144, 152, 156
   slow apocalypse 140
   Station Eleven 24, 137, 144–5, 147–51
   The Pesthouse 90
   Jamestown 103–4
   late capitalism 13
      Anthropocene 97
      Player One 24, 144, 155–6
      Station Eleven 24, 148
      The Age of Miracles 139
      The Road 79
      The Stone Gods 120, 127
      The Book of Dave 44–5
      The Book of Joan 105
      The Island at the End of the World 51
      The Road 78
      The Stone Gods 106, 120–5
      Zone One 132
capitalist realism 132, 134–7. *See also* capitalism; neoliberalism
   Player One 152, 160
   Station Eleven 144, 147–8, 150–1
   The Age of Miracles 139
Capitalocene 99–100. *See* Anthropocene
Cheap Nature 98, 122, 123, 124, 130. *See also* Anthropocene; Capitalocene
   Cloud Atlas 115–16
   Jamestown 103
   The Book of Joan 105
   The Stone Gods 120–1, 124
Christian fundamentalism 27, 28 n.2, 30, 31, 56. *See also* dispensationalism; evangelicalism; postmillennialism; premillennialism; Rapture
   The Island at the End of the World 47–9
chronotope
   American 75
   apocalyptic 71, 75
   Bakhtin 70, 75, 76
   The Road 70, 72, 74, 75, 76–9, 82, 83
climate breakdown. *See* climate change
climate change 1, 7, 95–130, 161. *See also* Anthropocene; environmental *under* risk
   American War 7

capitalism 14, 132
Cloud Atlas 7
colonialism 5, 101–2
Far North 96
MaddAddam trilogy 7
Odds Against Tomorrow 138
Player One 154
Station Eleven 147–8
The Age of Miracles 139–40
The Bone Clocks 7
The Book of Dave 7
The Pesthouse 88
The Stone Gods 123
Zone One 142
colonialism
   Anthropocene 23, 95–130, 163
   apocalyptic logic 12, 14, 19, 21, 95–130, 163
   capitalism 23, 95–130, 163
   civilizing mission 96, 102, 103, 114, 115, 124
   climate change 5
   Cloud Atlas 23, 95, 102, 106–8, 112–17, 130
   Columbus 97–8
   Far North 23, 96, 130
   Jamestown 23, 95, 102–4, 130
   modernity 10, 152
   (neo-)colonialism 14, 19, 21, 23, 95–130
   New World 12, 22, 58, 95–130
   science fiction 95–6
   Station Eleven 152
   The Book of Joan 23, 102, 105, 130
   The Stone Gods 23, 95, 102, 106, 119–27, 130
contemporary apocalyptic discourse. *See* contemporary apocalyptic imagination
contemporary apocalyptic imagination 1, 2, 9, 10, 21
contemporary apocalyptic paradigm. *See* contemporary apocalyptic imagination
contingency. *See also* agency; possibility
   chaos of 30, 33, 66, 88
   Cloud Atlas 110, 119
   end of history 24, 132–3, 135
   Future Home of the Living God 66
   Odds Against Tomorrow 138

   Station Eleven 145
   The Age of Miracles 132
   The Pesthouse 88
   The Revisionists 19
   The Stone Gods 129
   Zone One 144
Coupland, Douglas 140, 147, 169
   Generation X 141, 152 n.21, 153–4
   Girlfriend in a Coma 24, 152, 158–61
   Player One 20, 22, 24, 27, 28, 30, 36, 51, 56, 132, 137, 152–62
Crace, Jim
   'Love, Hate & Kicking Ass' 85, 93
   The Pesthouse 5, 9, 20, 22, 23, 50, 57, 58, 59, 63, 65, 67, 69, 78, 83–94, 160, 161, 165
   Useless America 84 n.26, 94 n.41
critical temporalities
   Anthropocene 97, 100, 104, 116, 122
   Apocalypse America 22, 57–8, 63, 86, 94
   apocalyptic model of narrative 18–19, 108–9, 129–30, 146
   aporia 89, 94
   archive 118, 164, 170
   chronotope 70, 82, 83
   concertina 107
   contemporary apocalyptic imagination 4, 6, 9, 31, 163
   cyclical 23, 120, 123, 128
   definition 1, 10
   denarration 152, 156
   determinism 56
   dystopian teleology 44, 116, 132
   extended present 15, 24, 132, 142, 161
   modernity 14
   no future 137, 139
   ongoing apocalypse 139, 146
   paratactic 90–1, 161
   parody 28, 32
   patterns of repetition 23, 79, 101, 102, 130
   postmodern theories of history 10, 15–16
   self-referentiality 22, 36
      The Book of Dave 37, 41–2, 46
      The Island at the End of the World 50, 52, 54
   static

The Road 70, 72, 76, 82, 83
Zone One 68
temporal inversion 95
  Cloud Atlas 109–10
  definition 9, 22
  Future Home of the Living God 65–7
  Jamestown 95
  The Book of Dave 42, 44–5
  The Pesthouse 63, 69, 84–8
  The Road 63, 75, 79

DeLillo, Don
  Falling Man 60
  Zero K 2, 17
denarration 24, 144, 147, 152–61
Derrida, Jacques
  aporia 49–50, 89
  archive fever 24–5, 163–70
  critique of apocalyptic logic 16–17
determinism. *See also* sense of an ending
  of apocalyptic history 10, 32, 52, 97, 101, 163, 168
    Cloud Atlas 23, 106, 107, 110, 112, 113, 116–19
    MaddAddam trilogy 35
    neoliberalism 24, 132–5, 137
    Odds Against Tomorrow 138
    Player One 144, 160–2
    predetermined end 13
    predetermined pattern 91
    Station Eleven 33, 144–7, 150, 162
    The Age of Miracles 139
    The Flood 30
    The Island at the End of the World 50, 54, 55, 56
    The Revisionists 19
    The Stone Gods 106, 120, 125–7, 130
  of narratives 10, 19
    Cloud Atlas 106, 107, 109, 113, 119, 130
    Player One 160–1
    Station Eleven 145, 151
    The Stone Gods 106, 127, 129
dispensationalism 10, 28–31, 50, 62. *See also* Christian fundamentalism; evangelicalism; postmillennialism; premillennialism; Rapture

El Akkad, Omar
  American War 7, 22, 58, 63–5, 94
end of history. *See also* extended present; neoliberalism; no future
  Fukuyama 13, 71, 88, 133
  neoliberalism 15, 24, 132
  Odds Against Tomorrow 132, 137–9, 161
  Player One 132, 137, 144, 152–9, 161–2
  Station Eleven 132, 137, 144–7, 161
  The Age of Miracles 132, 137, 139–40, 161
  The Pesthouse 88
  The Road 71
  Zone One 132, 137, 141–4
epistemic primacy of the end 10, 17, 18, 21, 73, 109. *See also* sense of an ending
  Cloud Atlas 109
  The Road 73
Erdrich, Louise 103
  Future Home of the Living God 22, 58, 63, 65–7, 104, 165
Ermarth, Elizabeth Deeds 16, 20, 91, 161
evangelicalism 13, 21, 29, 30, 33. *See also* Christian fundamentalism; dispensationalism; postmillennialism; premillennialism; Rapture
extended present 3, 24, 132, 155, 157, 159, 161. *See also* end of history; neoliberalism; no future

financial crisis 7, 132, 134, 135
  Odds Against Tomorrow 137
  Station Eleven 24, 145–9
  Zone One 142
Fisher, Mark 44, 132, 134
foreshadowing 20, 50, 52–3, 109–10, 112, 145
Foucault, Michel 17, 133
Fukuyama, Francis 13, 61, 71, 88, 133

Gee, Maggie
  The Flood 22, 28, 30, 34, 41, 56
Genesis 41 n.19, 72
  Fall 35, 46, 47, 48, 54, 55
  Flood 47, 48, 51, 52
  The Island at the End of the World 22, 28, 36, 46–8, 51, 54, 55

Gray, John
  Apocalypse America 63, 86
  apocalyptic logic and modernity 12
  apocalyptic logic and neoliberalism 13, 133
  9/11 13, 30, 61, 62

Harvey, David 62, 124, 133, 134, 136 n.4, 141 n.10, 155
Hoban, Russell
  Riddley Walker 5, 39 n.18, 43 n.20, 109 n.11
Hollinger, Veronica
  future-present 141, 142 n.12
  Girlfriend in a Coma 158–9
  postmodern theory and critique of apocalyptic logic 15
  science fiction 3–4, 164
Hutcheon, Linda
  historiographic metafiction 20–1, 113
  parody 28, 32
Hyperobject. *See under* Anthropocene

Jameson, Fredric
  end of history 132, 135, 136, 141, 161
  postmodernism 14
  science fiction 166

Keller, Catherine
  apocalypse pattern 30, 32, 52
  apocalyptic history 11 n.16, 49, 53
  apocalyptic logic and colonialism 12, 97–9
  apocalyptic logic and modernity 12
  Revelation 40, 41, 51, 53
  United States of Apocalypse 62, 75
Kermode, Frank 8, 10, 17, 18, 66, 123, 157. *See also* sense of an ending

LaHaye, Tim and Jerry B. Jenkins
  Left Behind 10 n.15, 21, 27–31, 32, 33, 50, 56
Lazzarato, Maurizio 115, 133, 135, 136

Mandel, Emily St. John
  Station Eleven 3–4, 8, 9, 15, 20, 22, 24, 28, 30, 33–4, 56, 132, 134, 136, 137, 140, 144–52, 153, 155, 161, 164

Manifest Destiny 22, 58, 63, 74, 163
  Girlfriend in a Coma 159
  The Pesthouse 23, 63, 69, 84–6, 92–4
  The Road 22, 63, 69, 78
McCarthy, Cormac
  Blood Meridian 21 n.22, 70
  No Country for Old Men 80–1
  The Road 4, 5, 8, 9, 21, 22, 24, 50, 57, 58, 59, 63, 67, 68, 69–83, 84, 86, 87, 88, 89, 91, 94, 104, 165
Mitchell, David
  Cloud Atlas 5, 7, 8, 15, 20, 21, 23, 38, 39 n.18, 57 n.2, 79 n.25, 95, 97, 102, 106–19, 120, 121, 125, 127, 140, 145, 166–8
  The Bone Clocks 5, 7, 20, 95, 108
Moore, Jason W. 23, 97, 98–100, 103, 116. *See also* Cheap Nature
Mullen, Thomas
  The Revisionists 18–19, 24, 167

narrative turn. *See* postmodern history
neoliberalism 131–62. *See also* capitalism; end of history; extended present; no future
  apocalyptic logic 13, 14, 15, 19, 21, 24, 51 n.27, 63, 130, 163
  Cloud Atlas 115–17
  extended present 3, 15, 23, 24, 71
  Odds Against Tomorrow 24, 138
  Player One 24, 144, 152–62
  post-apocalyptic genre 7, 14
  Station Eleven 24, 144–52
  The Age of Miracles 24, 131, 139
  The Road 71, 79
  The Stone Gods 123–5
  War on Terror 61–2
  Zone One 24, 69, 132, 137, 141–4
New Jerusalem 61
  and colonialism 96–8, 122
  and gender 40, 41, 98, 122
  Book of Revelation 8, 11, 37, 40
  Cloud Atlas 114, 115
  Far North 96
  The Book of Dave 41–5
  The Island at the End of the World 48, 49, 51, 52
  The Road 70, 71, 73
  The Stone Gods 120, 121

Index

9/11 7, 22, 89, 94, 163. *See also* War on Terror
   America's messianic innocence 22, 63, 64, 65, 81, 94
   American War 64
   apocalyptic moral dualism 13, 61, 69
   as apocalypse 2 n.3, 58, 60
   Christian fundamentalism 30, 62
   exceptionalism 60–1, 63, 64, 70, 73
   event 60–1
   Future Home of the Living God 65–6
   trauma 59
   The Pesthouse 85–6, 89, 94 n.41
   The Road 73, 81
   Zone One 59 n.5, 68–9
no future. *See also* end of history; extended present; neoliberalism
   neoliberalism 23–4, 132, 136–7
   Odds Against Tomorrow 137, 139
   Player One 144, 154, 156, 159
   Station Eleven 146
   The Age of Miracles 139
   The Book of Joan 104
   The Road 68, 71
   Zone One 132, 143

parody
   definition 27–8
   Jamestown 102–3
   of American myths 22, 67, 102–3
   of Bible 21, 27
   of Genesis 22, 28, 36, 46–56
   of prophets 21, 32–8
   of Rapture 31–2
   of Revelation 22, 28, 33, 36–46, 48, 50–1, 53, 55
   of traditional apocalyptic logic 24, 50, 121
   Player One 24, 36, 152, 158, 159–60
   The Book of Dave 22, 27, 28, 36–7
   The Island at the End of the World 22, 27, 28, 36, 46–52
   The Leftovers 21, 31–2
   The Stone Gods 121
   Zone One 22, 67, 141
Perrotta, Tom
   The Leftovers 21, 28, 30, 31–2, 33, 34, 56
possibility. *See also* agency; contingency
   apocalyptic determinism 13, 31

Cloud Atlas 110, 118, 130
end of history 135, 137
loss of the archive 163–4, 167
sense of 151
The Age of Miracles 139
The Island at the End of the World 47, 54
The Road 70–4, 79–80, 82, 94
The Stone Gods 120, 125, 128–30
unrealized 145
Zone One 67–9, 143, 144
postmodernism 20, 21, 28
   critique of metanarratives 14–16, 20
   postmodern condition 14–16, 31
   postmodern theories of history 10, 15–17, 113, 128
postmillennialism 29, 62. *See also* Christian fundamentalism; evangelicalism; dispensationalism; premillennialism; Rapture
power of narrative 15, 24, 106, 162–3
   Cloud Atlas 117–18
   The Book of Joan 120
   The Island at the End of the World 46–7
   The Stone Gods 128, 130
premillennialism 10, 28–31. *See also* Christian fundamentalism; evangelicalism; dispensationalism; postmillennialism; Rapture
progress
   apocalyptic logic 10–12, 23, 63, 95, 130
   Cloud Atlas 108–10, 113–17
   colonialism 96, 98, 99
   Future Home of the Living God 65–6
   Girlfriend in a Coma 159
   Jamestown 102, 104
   The Age of Miracles 131–2
   The Book of Dave 45
   The Book of Joan 104–5, 169
   The Pesthouse 87, 88
   The Road 78, 79

Quinby, Lee 13, 63, 89

Rapture 21, 27–32, 62. *See also* Christian fundamentalism; dispensationalism; postmillennialism; premillennialism
Revelation (book of)11, 12, 81, 157

Babylon 33, 40, 48, 51
crisis 10 n.6, 10 n.8, 33
gender politics 33, 40, 41, 122
Last Judgment 8, 33, 41, 42, 48
New Jerusalem 8, 41, 42, 55, 73, 97, 98, 121, 122
Odds Against Tomorrow 138
prophecy 32, 37, 72
The Book of Dave 22, 28, 36–42
The Island at the End of the World 22, 28, 36, 47–8, 50–1, 55
Rich, Nathaniel 39
Odds Against Tomorrow 24, 132, 134, 137–9, 161
Ricoeur, Paul 17, 155
risk 10
American War 64
apocalyptic logic 5, 132, 137, 166, 170
capitalism 44–5, 97, 145, 147
Cloud Atlas 115
environmental 97, 99, 101, 130, 134
risk society 6–7, 135, 137–8
Station Eleven 149, 152
The Book of Dave 44–5
The Book of Joan 105, 170
The Pesthouse 87
The Stone Gods 124, 163

science fiction 1, 5, 8, 9
as future-oriented genre 3, 164, 166
colonialism 95–6
contemporary post-apocalyptic novel 3–5, 21
Self, Will 58
The Book of Dave 5, 7, 20, 21, 22, 27, 28, 31, 36–46, 48, 53, 54, 55, 56, 73, 167
sense-making function of apocalyptic logic 3, 20, 29, 32
Future Home of the Living God 65, 67
Player One 156–7
Station Eleven 146
The Book of Dave 41–2
The Pesthouse 69, 89–91
The Road 69, 71, 73–5, 81–3
Zone One 68
sense of an ending 10, 17–20, 135, 163. *See also* apocalyptic model of narrative; Kermode; anticipation of retrospection; epistemic primacy of the end; teleology
Cloud Atlas 106–10, 112, 117
Future Home of the Living God 66
Player One 157, 160–1
Station Eleven 145–6, 151
The Book of Dave 44–5
The Island at the End of the World 50, 54
The Pesthouse 90–1, 94
The Road 76, 81, 83
The Stone Gods 106, 120, 123, 127, 129–30, 164
Zone One 69
Sharpe, Matthew
Jamestown 23, 57 n.1, 95, 102–4, 130, 165
Shriver, Lionel
The Mandibles 74 n.22, 86 n.29
sideshadowing 119, 145
simulacra 38, 42, 43, 47, 49, 52, 113–18, 121. *See also* Baudrillard, Jean
slow apocalypse 24, 140, 161
Player One 154
Station Eleven 146–8
The Age of Miracles 137, 140
Zone One 142–3
speculative fiction. *See* science fiction

Tate, Andrew
apocalyptic fiction 2 n.2, 9, 32, 34 n.11, 35, 79 n.24, 147, 164
Douglas Coupland 153, 155 n.22, 158 n.23
Taylor, Sam
The Island at the End of the World 20, 22, 27, 28, 36, 46–56, 73, 89, 114, 160, 167
teleology. *See also* apocalyptic model of narrative; sense of an ending
apocalyptic 12, 23, 41, 54, 56, 94, 163
Cloud Atlas 108–10, 112–17, 130
dystopian 6, 10
Future Home of the Living God 66
historical 2, 9, 10–12, 18–19, 49
Jamestown 102
narrative 9, 18–21
neoliberalism 134, 136
Player One 144, 153, 156
Station Eleven 144–6, 149–51
The Book of Dave 42, 44

The Book of Joan 104
The Island at the End of the World 52
The Pesthouse 84, 87, 89–91, 93
The Road 70–1, 74, 76–7, 82–3
The Stone Gods 120, 130
utopian 3, 9, 13, 32
    Apocalypse America 58, 61, 63
Zone One 69, 132
temporal inversion. *See under* critical temporalities
Theroux, Marcel
    Far North 23, 96, 130
traditional apocalyptic discourse 61, 130, 133, 163
    American War 63
    biblical 21, 27–8, 56
    Cloud Atlas 106–7, 113, 116
    Future Home of the Living God 65
    gender politics 33–4, 40–1, 98, 170
    history of 7, 10
    Odds Against Tomorrow 138
    Player One 36
    Station Eleven 33
    The Book of Dave 39–41, 44
    The Book of Joan 105, 170
    The Island at the End of the World 52
    The Leftovers 31
    The Stone Gods 106, 124, 125
    time 1, 8, 32
    Zone One 67
traditional apocalyptic paradigm 1, 3, 5, 6, 8, 9, 60
    Cloud Atlas 117–18, 130
    Girlfriend in a Coma 159

Player One 157
The Book of Dave 36, 41
The Island at the End of the World 36, 46, 52–3
The Leftovers 32
The Road 71, 75

Walker, Karen Thompson
    The Age of Miracles 1, 24, 131–2, 137, 139–40, 142, 144, 153, 161
War on Terror 13, 62, 63 n.10, 64, 94. *See also* 9/11
    apocalyptic moral dualism 22, 58, 62, 69, 81
Whitehead, Colson
    Zone One 8, 9, 22, 24, 58, 59, 63, 67–9, 72, 77 n.23, 81, 94, 121, 131–2, 134, 137, 139, 140–4, 146, 147, 151, 153, 155, 161, 165
Williams, Evan Calder 14, 134, 139, 140
Winterson, Jeanette
    Lighthousekeeping 129
    Oranges Are Not the Only Fruit 128 n.18
    The Stone Gods 20, 23, 24, 79 n.25, 95, 97, 102, 106, 108, 116, 119–30, 134, 163, 164

Yuknavitch, Lidia
    The Book of Joan 15, 21, 23, 24, 65 n.14, 97, 104–6, 117, 120, 121, 130, 163–4, 168–71

Žižek, Slavoj 59, 61, 73

www.ingramcontent.com/pod-product-compliance
Lightning Source LLC
Chambersburg PA
CBHW052044300426
44117CB00012B/1970